The Circassian Genocide

THE CENTER FOR THE STUDY OF
GENOCIDE, CONFLICT RESOLUTION
& HUMAN RIGHTS

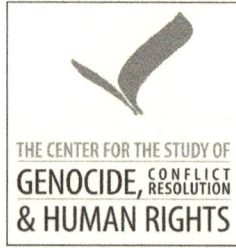

Genocide, Political Violence, Human Rights Series

Edited by Alexander Laban Hinton, Stephen Eric Bronner, and Nela Navarro

Alan W. Clarke, *Rendition to Torture*

Lawrence Davidson, *Cultural Genocide*

Alexander Laban Hinton, ed., *Transitional Justice: Global Mechanisms and Local Realities after Genocide and Mass Violence*

Irina Silber, *Everyday Revolutionaries: Gender, Violence, and Disillusionment in Postwar El Salvador*

Samuel Totten and Rafiki Ubaldo, eds., *We Cannot Forget: Interviews with Survivors of the 1994 Genocide in Rwanda*

Ronnie Yimsut, *Facing the Khmer Rouge: A Cambodian Journey*

The Circassian Genocide

WALTER RICHMOND

RUTGERS UNIVERSITY PRESS

NEW BRUNSWICK, NEW JERSEY, AND LONDON

Library of Congress Cataloging-in-Publication Data

Richmond, Walter.
   The Circassian genocide / Walter Richmond.
      pages cm. — (Genocide, political violence, human rights series)
   Includes bibliographical references and index.
   ISBN 978–0–8135–6068–7 (hardcover : alkaline paper) — ISBN
   978–0–8135–6067–0 (paperback : alkaline paper) — ISBN 978–0–8135–6069–4
   (e-book)
      1. Circassians—Russia (Federation)—Caucasus, Northern—History. 2. Russia—
   Relations—Russia (Federation)—Caucasus, Northern. 3. Caucasus, Northern
   (Russia)—Relations—Russia. 4. Genocide—Russia (Federation)—Caucasus,
   Northern—History. I. Title. II. Series: Genocide, political violence, human
   rights series.
      DK34.C57R53 2013
      947.08'1—dc23   2012023501

A British Cataloging-in-Publication record for
this book is available from the British Library.

Visit our website: http://rutgerspress.rutgers.edu

Manufactured in the United States of America

For my mother

CONTENTS

ACKNOWLEDGMENTS

M y heartfelt gratitude goes out to John Colarusso for his enthusiastic support of my work on the Circassians and for his expertise on the Circassian language. I'm deeply indebted to Ali Berzek, who compiled the archival materials used in this study, and Zack Barsik, who provided me not only with those materials but countless other valuable sources. In addition, I would like to thank Moshe Gammer, Iyad Youghar, Metin Sönmez, and Cicek Chek for the material and moral support they have given me. I'm also grateful to the Circassians around the world who graciously answered my many questions. Finally, a special thanks to Lee Croft, who gave me my love for the Russian language, without which I could never have completed this book.

The Circassian Genocide

Introduction

On May 20, 2011, the Parliament of Georgia passed a resolution that labeled as genocide the "preplanned" mass killing of Circassians by the Russian Imperial Army in the 1860s. The resolution also stated that those who survived but were driven from their homeland and their descendants should be recognized as refugees. The move was stunning, since the Circassian genocide as well as Circassians themselves had been forgotten by the world within decades of the destruction of their nation in 1864.

The Circassians went from being an almost legendary people of the northwestern Caucasus Mountains, a subject of travelogues about exotic warriors and beautiful maidens, to a central concern of the European powers, and then to a forgotten nation in a span of only a century. The erasure of Circassia from the cultural memory of Europe was abrupt and total: whereas between the 1830s and the 1860s it was nearly impossible to pick up a European newspaper without finding an article discussing the Circassians' plight, by 1900 the only reference to "Circassia" in the European press concerned a luxury liner bearing that name. However, the tragedy didn't end for those who survived Russia's campaign in the Caucasus Mountains. After their deportation, nearly half were driven from their new homes in the Balkans by Russian troops in the 1870s. They were forced to migrate further, to the Middle East and beyond. They fought against all odds to preserve their identity, always with the hope of one day returning to their homeland, but the bloody twentieth century diverted the world's attention from their struggle, and they really did face the possibility that they would be forgotten forever.

How, then, were the Circassians able to bring the attention of the world back to their tragedy nearly 150 years after the nations of Europe abandoned them? Why is their story once again appearing on the pages of Reuters, *Time*, and other international publications? And why is the Russian government pushing back so hard against the effort to explore fully the events that caused the Circassians' dilemma, even going so far as to create a presidential commission "to counter the attempts to falsify history to the detriment of Russia"?[1]

One answer lies about twenty-five miles from the northeastern Black Sea coastal city of Sochi, tucked away at an elevation of about 1,800 feet. It is a small canyon once known as Qbaada ("fortified ravine").[2] It was here that the Circassians and their Abkhaz allies made their last stand against the Russians in May 1864. After the Circassians' surrender on May 21 (according to the Old Russian calendar[3]) the Russians held a victory parade and banquet in Qbaada at which medals were presented to the officers responsible for the final victory. The Circassians were driven to Sochi, where they died by the thousands as they waited for ships to take them to the Ottoman Empire. Russian officer Ivan Drozdov described the scene around Sochi while the Russians were celebrating: "On the road our eyes were met with a staggering image: corpses of women, children, elderly persons, torn to pieces and half-eaten by dogs; deportees emaciated by hunger and disease, almost too weak to move their legs, collapsing from exhaustion and becoming prey to dogs while still alive."[4] In 1869 Qbaada was settled by Russian immigrants and renamed Krasnaya Polyana (Red Meadow), a reference to all the blood spilled on the field during the final battle. It, too, might have been forgotten entirely if the International Olympic Committee (IOC) had not awarded the 2014 Winter Games to Sochi, to be held on the 150th anniversary of Circassians' defeat on that very Red Meadow where the Russians celebrated and handed out medals while the Circassians died on the coast. The IOC pointed the spotlight directly on the nearly-forgotten genocide and brought the Circassians' plight back into the international arena.

HOW THE CIRCASSIANS, who call themselves Adyge, originally came to occupy the northeastern shores of the Black Sea is yet another story of exile. They are most likely the descendants of the Hattians, who developed an advanced society in central Anatolia as early as the third millennium BCE. When the Hittites invaded ca. 2000 BCE, many migrated to the northeast and occupied the land between the modern cities of Sukhumi and Anapa along the coast of the Black Sea.[5] They eventually separated into the Abkhaz, Abaza, Circassian, and Ubykh peoples (although most Circassians consider the Ubykhs a Circassian tribe).[6] Known as the Zigei (a corruption of Adyge?) to the Greeks and Romans, the Circassians had commercial and political ties with both peoples and had built a set of fortified cities by the early Middle Ages.[7] The Mongols, who destroyed their civilization in the thirteenth century, referred to them as the Jerkes, literally "one who blocks a path."[8] Originally a term used to describe all the peoples of the North Caucasus, the Russian variant of the term, Cherkes, became attached exclusively to the Adyge people by the nineteenth century and was translated into "Circassian" in Western Europe.

There were at least one million Circassians in the seventeenth century, and possibly as many as 1.7 million.[9] Several legends refer to a *pshi* (prince) named Inal who reunited the Circassian tribes after the Mongols drove them into the high mountains.[10] While the claim that he managed to unite the freedom-loving Circassians into a single political entity is probably a romantic myth, Inal does appear to have led the Qabartay tribe, known to the world as the Kabardians, to the secure central valleys of the North Caucasus. Not only were they more insulated from raids by their nomadic neighbors, they also controlled the critical Daryal Pass, the only route through the Caucasus Mountains. As a result, the Kabardians were able to develop a relatively advanced feudal structure and exercise authority over their neighbors, and to become a major player in the politics of the region. However, although there was in theory a single ruler called the *pshi tkhamade*, no one but Inal ever exercised anything resembling complete authority. Far more often, the aristocratic families fought vehemently over the rank of pshi tkhamade and plotted to undermine the authority of whoever held the title. Outside powers frequently played one clan off another, and Russian interference even caused the tribe to fracture into Greater and Lesser Kabardia by the sixteenth century.[11] Until Russian colonization pushed the Kabardians back into the mountains, Kabardia stretched two hundred miles from present-day Karachaevo-Cherkessia in the west to the border of Chechnya in the east. The Besleney tribe, created when a clan broke off from the Kabardians, lived to the west. In similar fashion, the Temirgoys broke from the Besleneys to become a separate tribe, and the Hatukays broke from the Temirgoys.[12] Other tribes, such as the Mahosh, Hamysh, Bjedukh, and Cherchenay, developed independently from the Kabardians and possessed similar, albeit weaker, aristocratic hierarchies.

Four tribes were little known to anyone. On most Russian maps of the nineteenth century, three of them are simply referred to as the "free tribes." Their aristocratic families never exercised much authority, and in 1803 they were stripped of what little power they had at the Pechetniko Zafes (Congress).[13] The most settled of the three were the Natuhays, who lived along the Black Sea coast from the Sea of Azov south, halfway to Sochi. In addition to taking full advantage of the fertile lands they occupied and raising a variety of crops and fruits, the Natuhays conducted extensive trade with the Turks. The Shapsug tribe consisted of a group that lived close to the coast south of the Natuhays and a much larger contingent that lived in the impenetrable valleys of the Caucasus Mountains. The Abzakhs, the third "free" society, lived exclusively in the high mountains, while the feudal Ubykhs occupied the southernmost region around Sochi. Both were virtually unknown to the Russians until 1840. Reclusive, wary of outsiders, and uncompromising in defense of their independence, these four tribes admitted to their ranks other Circassians fleeing attacks by the Crimeans, Ottomans, and Russians. As a result, by the nineteenth century they far outnumbered all the other Circassian tribes combined. These were the people who refused to surrender to Russian demands, and in their frustration the Russian military command decided to eliminate them at any cost.

Long before the Russians began their conquest, the Circassians had established a way of life that was destined to clash with Russian aspirations in the Caucasus. In many ways a democratic and almost communistic society, Circassian life revolved around the *aul*, which translates as "village" but more accurately means several extended families who stuck together in the harsh Caucasus climate. But, in fact, Circassians were so frequently raided by their larger neighbors that they put little care into their homes and abandoned them when attacked, only to rebuild somewhere else once the danger had passed. Each aul was theoretically under the rule of its own pshi, but problems were resolved by a village council. The village elders' opinions were considered sacred, and no one under the age of forty would dare contradict them or even speak at a council unless specifically asked to. Consensus was the rule of Circassian day-to-day life as well, and life was communal in many ways. If you needed a horse, you could borrow your neighbor's without asking as long as you returned it when you were done. A misbehaving child saw the negative side of this way of life: any adult in the aul had the right punish the child as if he or she were the child's own parent. One aspect of this communal approach that ran afoul of the Russian notion of order was the Circassian concept of hospitality: anyone who turned up on a Circassian's doorstep was treated like one of the family. This was most likely a result of necessity: the traveler, hungry and exhausted from the trials of mountain travel, could count on safe harbor at any household he came across. Not only was the host obliged to defend the guest even at the cost of his own life, he was forbidden to inquire about the guest's background.[14] Upholding this custom was not simply a matter of pride but of survival: Circassian ethnographer Khan-Girey explains that if a person violated this rule, "honest people would lose respect for them and society would shun them; their every step would be met with insulting reproaches."[15] This made it quite easy for fugitives and Russian deserters to find a safe refuge, and the Russians were repeatedly frustrated to find that the Circassians would rather die than turn over their guests. Likewise, the difficult-to-translate concept of *tkheriwage* caused Russian conquerors a great deal of grief. Tkheriwage is similar to the concept of blood brothers, that is, unrelated men who have taken an oath of personal alliance. To turn one's *zetkheriwegu* (blood brother) over to the authorities even if he committed a crime was an unimaginable act. The Russians also saw the practice of *pur* as a threat to their plans. In this tradition, which was widespread throughout the North Caucasus, a child would be sent to grow up with a family in another aul, or even another nation. While it weakened the bonds of parent–child in a way we would find completely alien, it strengthened intertribal loyalties. Since one of the Russians' main strategies to control the North Caucasus peoples was divide and conquer, they found this tradition intolerable.

The Circassians' approach to religion was also unconventional. Repeated attempts by their more powerful neighbors to convert them to either Christianity or Islam met with only superficial success. In 1818 Édouard Taitbout de Marigny wrote that Circassian Christianity consisted of "the mechanical exercise of a number of pagan and Christian ceremonies," and that while he saw crosses, the Circassians "know not what it represents."[16] As for Islam, Taitbout de Marigny reported that "the Circassian Mahometans are very indifferent to their religion."[17] The true "religion" of the Circassians was (and still is to some degree) Adygage, which translates as "to be Adyge." The main principles of Adygage are memory of ancestors, consciousness of Circassia as the home of those ancestors, and tolerance of other ways of life and religious beliefs.[18] The practical manifestation of Adygage was the Circassians' legal–ethical code by which they regulated their society, adyge habze. This little-understood code of behavior has been compared to the Bushido Samurai code of honor and Spartan society.[19] Adyge habze can at times appear to be brutal and unforgiving, but it possessed its own internal logic. For example, what might appear to be a minor offense such as imped-ing someone's flocks could result in the death not only of the victim's family but of his entire aul. The victim was therefore permitted to use extreme measures against the offending party. For crimes committed within the aul, on the other hand, councils of elders focused on compensation, not retri-bution. In fact, after receiving such compensation, the injured party would often apologize to the offender's family for having to ask for payment. In both cases the underlying principles of Circassian justice were diametrically opposed to the notion of a central authority with power to mete out justice. When the Russians tried to impose such an authority, they saw their sacred way of life under attack and fought to the bitter end.

If a major threat arose, one or more of the leading tribes would call a *hase* ("hah-say"), a rudimentary form of congress at which hundreds of "delegates" would assemble. A second assembly, the *zafes*, was called less frequently and dealt with more critical issues. Both the hase and zafes suf-fered from several shortcomings that turned out to be fatal in the war with Russia. First, there was no protocol for the meeting; theoretically, anyone who wished to speak could come forward. Often the person who was most eloquent carried the day, regardless of the wisdom of his ideas (a phenom-enon not unknown in modern politics). Even the dialect was important; the Kabardians and Besleneys were considered the most prestigious, so dele-gates from those tribes held particular sway over the hase. Second, a unani-mous vote was required for any measure to be adopted. As a result, hases often ran for weeks without any decisions being made. In a time of war, particularly the war for national survival that they faced in the nineteenth century, this indecision kept the Circassians from taking decisive action. Third, there was no enforcement mechanism, so individual tribes frequently ignored the decisions of the hase. In the 1850s leaders among the Circassians tried to create a more effective system, but it was already too late.

It wasn't only the lack of a central authority that kept the Circassians from developing a stable, unified state. On the one hand, the rugged Caucasus Mountains allowed for little agriculture, so the Circassians lived a semi-migratory life, tending huge herds of sheep and, in lesser numbers, cattle. Where agriculture was possible, the growing season was very short; a late spring or early fall meant widespread famine. In addition, plagues frequently annihilated large segments of the population, and because of their strategic location along the Black Sea coast, the Circassians suffered from countless raids by their neighbors that often decimated their population. Humans were the main capital sought in these raids, taken for sale at the slave markets throughout the Middle East and Europe. Established by Genoan colonists in the 1300s, the slave trade was institutionalized by the Mongols and remained a thriving business well into the nineteenth century. The Crimeans and Ottomans also demanded tribute on a regular basis, particularly from the western tribes, and this further crippled their ability to establish a stable way of life. Some tribes, such as the once powerful Jane, disappeared altogether. The Circassians participated in the slave trade themselves, a fact that has been regularly used by the Russians to justify their actions, although the accusation rings somewhat hollow when one considers that the Russians practiced institutionalized slavery on a far more massive scale all the way until 1861. Also, despite Russian claims that slaves were the only goods the Circassians traded in, the truth is that the Circassians also sold furs, leather, wax, honey, copper, hard woods, jewelry, and other goods to the Turks.[20]

THE RUSSIAN MINDSET that led to the fateful decision to destroy this reclusive nation in the 1860s had its beginnings in the military command of previous generations. These officers ruled the Caucasus as their own personal fiefdom, and the tsar and his ministers were not sufficiently knowledgeable about the region to challenge their judgment. As Muriel Atkin has pointed out, this weakness in the system of governance created problems for Russia throughout the Caucasus and beyond:

Although both [emperors] Paul and Alexander, and not their advisors, made their foreign policies, the options that each entertained were effectively limited by the kinds of information they received. This was especially true in dealing with such areas as the Caucasus and Iran, which were remote from the traditional interests of most of the Russian elite. Few people understood, or even claimed to understand, those areas, so Paul and Alexander had little choice but to rely on many of the same ignorant or biased people that Catherine had.[21]

These advisors went beyond simply providing biased information. Commanders from Alexei Ermolov in the 1820s to Nikolai Evdokimov in the 1860s regularly misled St. Petersburg and deliberately sabotaged policies that might have led to a peaceful conclusion to the war.

The destruction of the Circassian nation began in a very physical sense decades before the final blow in the 1860s and continued well after the genocide of 1864. Once Catherine the Great decided in the 1760s that the northeastern shores of the Black Sea should be Russia's, the Russian military worked to hem in the Circassians bit by bit until they were surrounded in the high mountains. By the 1820s the vast majority of the Kabardians had either been killed or expelled into western Circassia, where they continued to fight until 1864. After the Circassians' expulsion, nearly half the survivors were subjected to a second ethnic cleansing in 1878 when the Russians chased them from their new homes in the Balkans. Both those who remained in Russia and those in diaspora struggled for the next five generations to preserve their culture. Unfortunately, the states in which they lived were more interested in assimilating them.

With this book, then, I will acquaint the reader with the entire story of the Circassians: why the Russians chose to destroy their nation, how they briefly entered the international consciousness, the horrifying details of their final days in their homeland, their life in exile, and finally how Russia's opposition to their efforts at gaining recognition for the genocide and repatriation have not only failed to dampen their spirits but have actually energized the Circassians and propelled a nearly forgotten chapter in history into the international arena once again. I will also introduce the reader to the Circassian people, whose way of life before their deportation was quite alien to ours but it possessed a logic and dignity all its own.

1

"The Plague Was Our Ally"

"We have never known the Russians," they say, "but with weapons in their hands."

—Édouard Taitbout de Marigny

A Caucasus Vendetta

In June 1808 Izmail-Bey Atazhukin, a Kabardian nobleman and colonel in the Russian Imperial Army, asked for permission to cross a quarantine line from Fort Konstantinovskaya into Kabardia with a shipment of desperately needed salt. Technically, anyone who wanted to cross the line was supposed to undergo a twenty-day "quarantine," but Atazhukin had already been in the fortress since March. Under the circumstances, fort commander Major-General Veryovkin saw no reason to detain him. So when he crossed the quarantine line into Kabardia, Atazhukin couldn't possibly have conceived of the reign of terror that would strike his people as a result of his trip.[1]

Atazhukin and his family were in many ways a microcosm of Kabardia's troubled relationship with Russia. As the son of a powerful pshi, he was sent as a boy to St. Petersburg as an ataman, that is, a hostage, to ensure his clan's loyalty to Russia. Despite his father's strong anti-Russian sentiments, he and his brother Adil-Girey both joined the Russian army and served with distinction. Then in 1795 both Atazhukins were arrested and charged with "unreliability."[2] Izmail-Bey believed that anti-Russian forces in Kabardia conspired with Caucasus commander in chief Ivan Gudovich to undermine the brothers' efforts to establish peace between Kabardia and Russia.[3] In 1798 Adil-Girey escaped and became the leader of the anti-Russian movement, but Izmail-Bey still believed Kabardia's future lay with Russia and repeatedly petitioned for release.

When Alexander I came to power in 1801, he granted Atazhukin amnesty and in 1803 promoted him to colonel. Now Atazhukin believed he could contribute to Russo-Circassian relations, so he submitted "A Note on the Disorder on the Caucasus Line and Methods to End It" to the Russian minister of internal affairs, Viktor Kochubey. In it he argued that "we will never pacify the mountain peoples through force," and he proposed developing a working relationship with the Kabardian nobility, who were respected throughout Circassia. In turn, they would influence the other tribes, and peace would gradually be established.[4] In the summer of 1804 Alexander sent Izmail-Bey and his "Note" to the new Caucasus commander in chief, Pavel Tsitsianov, who called Atazhukin's proposal to remove Cossack *stanitsy* (fortified villages) from Kabardia "unworkable."[5] The "Note" was forgotten.

Next Izmail-Bey tried to work for peace from the Kabardian side, calling for a hase in early 1805. Threats on his life from anti-Russian forces (perhaps in his own family) compelled him to flee Kabardia for a time, but he was finally able to address his fellow citizens in May. He issued a plea for moderation and a dire warning of Russia's military potential: "The wealth, forces, and might of the Russian state are unbelievable. There are thirty-six million people, and if the government chooses it could mobilize a third of them. Living alongside a powerful neighbor, we should direct all our efforts toward self-preservation and peaceful use of our land. Believe me, my dear compatriots, if you haven't lost your senses, we must not provoke such a powerful neighbor."[6] Much of Atazhukin's speech was devoted to enumerating the advantages of a close relationship with Russia. However, the Kabardian aristocracy rejected his proposal and he returned to the Russian command empty-handed. Next he tried to persuade individual clans that were leaning toward Russia to promote peace, an activity that Tsitsianov called "more dangerous to us than helpful."[7] Undaunted, he renewed his efforts after Tsitsianov's death in 1806 and continued to be a voice for peace and cooperation up until June 1808, when he crossed the quarantine line.

By the time of Atazhukin's trip the military command in the North Caucasus was in a rather pathetic state. Shortly after Napoleon destroyed the Russian army at Austerlitz in 1805, Emperor Alexander found himself at war with both Iran and the Ottoman Empire, and another war with France seemed inevitable. Running short of qualified officers, the tsar appointed aging general Sergei Bulgakov as field commander of the Caucasus Line.

Bulgakov apparently took personal offense at Atazhukin's crossing of the quarantine line and sent an angry letter to Caucasus commander in chief Ivan Gudovich, who considered the crossing a nonissue: Atazhukin was a Russian officer and had been granted permission. Bulgakov pleaded his case to Defense Minister Alexei Arakcheev, but again Gudovich stepped in to defend Atazhukin. Bulgakov became Atazhukin's mortal enemy, and because of this unjustified hatred of his fellow officer, he unleashed a catastrophic reign of terror on the Kabardian people.

The Kabardians, who had been allies with Russia since 1557, had watched their friendly relations with their powerful neighbor deteriorate for some time. Ever since Peter the Great had set his sights on conquest of Iran, Russia's rulers stopped looking at the peoples of the North Caucasus as neighbors and began treating them as subjects waiting to be conquered. The first clear sign of this new attitude came with the Treaty of Belgrade, which concluded the Russo-Turkish War of 1736–1739. During the negotiations—to which the Kabardians were not invited—Kabardia was stripped of its status as Russia's ally and declared a "neutral" buffer state between the two empires. Furthermore, while neither the Russians nor the Ottomans were permitted under the treaty to meddle in Kabardian affairs, both powers had the authority to take hostages and punish the Kabardians if they had "cause for complaint."[8] The actual effect of the treaty was to leave Kabardia completely defenseless against aggression from either side.

Accompanying Russia's new attitude toward the Kabardians was a change in administrative style. In 1719 Peter appointed Artemy Volynsky governor of the newly formed Astrakhan Province, east of Kabardia. Historian Michael Khodarkovsky describes Volynsky as "an embodiment of that arrogance of power which reflected the new confidence of an expanding and modernizing Russia."[9] Immediately after Volynsky's arrival, Russian policies became more aggressive and directed toward the eventual expansion of the empire into the Caucasus and beyond. His first project was to convince Peter of the desirability of an attack on Persia, and in 1722 Peter launched an invasion that resulted in Russia's acquisition of a small part of the western shore of the Caspian Sea.[10] Volynsky convinced Peter to construct the Kizlyar fortress on the Terek River in 1735 as a first step toward conquest of the North Caucasus, and this began the military line that would eventually stretch from the Crimean Peninsula to the Caspian

Sea. Volynsky also ignored Russia's longstanding treaty with Kabardia. Pshi Arslan Kaituke repeatedly asked for assistance in repelling Crimean attacks from 1718 to 1721, but Volynsky refused to send any troops. Realizing the Kabardians' allies had abandoned them, the Khanate launched a major invasion, resulting in the devastation of Kabardia.[11]

Volynsky was succeeded by a series of commanders who treated the North Caucasus peoples as rebellious subjects. Rather than wasting resources trying to conquer them one at a time, the Caucasus command opted for a vassal system. In exchange for monetary and material assistance, a local sheikh or chieftain would pledge allegiance to Russia. This arrangement ended with the appointment of Pavel Tsitsianov as Caucasus commander in chief in 1802. Although he only held the post for four years, he set in motion the brutality that was the hallmark of subsequent Russian efforts to conquer the North Caucasus. Russian historians have nearly unanimously praised Tsitsianov: speaking of his administration in the South Caucasus, tsarist historian Vasily Potto remarked that "with [Tsitsianov's] appointment came better times . . . and a complete transformation of domestic and foreign politics."[12] Writing at the turn of the twentieth century, British traveler John Baddeley praised Tsitsianov for "administrative ability of a high order, coupled with an aggressive, overbearing spirit, that served him admirably in his dealings with the native rulers, Christian as well as Mussulman."[13] American scholar Muriel Atkin holds quite a different position, claiming that Tsitsianov's "eloquence was marred by bluster, just as his nobility of character was marred by deceit; the energy he spent was largely other peoples'; and his determination manifested itself in slaughter," while British historian David Lang gives a more nuanced description, calling him "a renegade to his own people, but a man who, in serving Russia, dealt many a crushing blow to Georgia's traditional enemies."[14]

Oddly enough, there is truth in all of these statements, but unfortunately only Tsitsianov's negative characteristics were emulated by his successors, particularly his brutality and almost pathological hatred of "Asiatics." Potto reports that Tsitsianov's method of dealing with the Caucasus peoples was based upon the belief that "the Asiatic people demand that they be treated with exceptional scorn." And this he did. In approaching a target population, Tsitsianov "tried first of all to clarify for them in his proclamations all the immense greatness of Russia and their insignificance before her," heaping threats and insults upon the local leaders.[15] In letters to various Dagestani sheikhs, which frequently opened with the colorful salutation "untrustworthy bastards," Tsitsianov used stock phrases such as "I thirst to wash my boots with your blood" and regularly promised to burn villages and run entire populations off their land.[16] Tsitsianov had no faith in the vassal system, believing that the only effective method of ensuring the "Asiatics" would remain loyal was conquest and assimilation. Therefore, Yakov Gordin argues, his bombastic style when dealing with the Caucasus peoples was calculated to provoke them to rebellion, and he would use the rebellion as an excuse for military conquest.[17] It was a pattern that would be repeated by nearly all of Tsitsianov's successors.

Bulgakov was of the same mold as Tsitsianov, a firm believer in Russia's superiority and contemptuous of the peoples of the Caucasus. Even before the June incident, he had targeted Atazhukin for harassment, insisting that he undergo quarantine after his return from Kabardia in March. This turned out to be a house arrest, with Atazhukin being deprived of his weapon and held until his request to return to Kabardia in June.[18] This is why Veryovkin saw no problem in allowing Atazhukin to cross the quarantine line. Bulgakov saw things differently and ordered Veryovkin to hold Atazhukin for an additional twenty days, but the two of them simply ignored him.

The fact of the matter was that the Kabardians were on the verge of extinction as a result of their former ally's actions. To control the Kabardians more effectively and prepare for eventual conquest, the Russians built the Mozdok Fortress and supporting stanitsy in Kabardia beginning in 1763.[19] This disrupted and destroyed centuries-old migration routes that were essential for the survival of all the people of the region. Dozens more stanitsy and fortresses across Kabardia's northern border resulted in more than loss of territory—it created an existential threat to North Caucasus society, whose survival depended on free migration of their herds. After their petitions were repeatedly rejected, the Kabardians had little choice but to fight back, and the war that resulted devastated their society by the beginning of the nineteenth century.

Compounding the crisis was a plague, possibly malaria or typhus, that struck the North Caucasus in April 1804. It quickly spread throughout the region, and the Kabardians were hit worst of all. Tens of thousands died, including two of their most important leaders, Izmail-Bey's brother

Adil-Girey and Ishak Abuke.[20] The Russian response was predictable: a quarantine line that impeded Kabardian herds further. Disease coupled with starvation drove the entire population to the verge of annihilation. This was why Veryovkin ignored Bulgakov's order and allowed Atazhukin's party across the quarantine line—to save lives. Bulgakov seemed to view the plague differently, however. He turned the quarantine into a complete economic blockade of Kabardia that threatened the tribe with extinction. Weakened from hunger and disease, the Kabardians became victims of their Cossack neighbors, who raided their auls with impunity. "Our people," a group of Kabardian pshis wrote in an appeal to the Emperor, "naked and swollen from lack of salt, have fled into the forests like hungry wild beasts."[21] Perhaps this is why Bulgakov took such a strong dislike to Atazhukin even before he crossed the quarantine line in June. His blockade of Kabardia wasn't only to stop the spread of the plague but to physically crush the Kabardians into complete submission. This certainly seemed to be the Kabardians' opinion of Bulgakov's quarantine. Regional commander Ivan Del Pozzo sent him a report in early April 1807 relaying the Kabardians' pleas and quoting the influential aristocrat Kasbulat Kilchuke's accusation that "they want us all to die of starvation. Maybe the Emperor and the administration have decided we're no longer needed? So be it! God knows how this will end! The result of this will be that we won't have the ability to control raids in Kabardia or on the Russian frontier. We're not asking you and not troubling you to give us free passage everywhere, but at least lift the quarantine enough to allow us to acquire the things we need to survive."[22] Despite Del Pozzo's report, Bulgakov made no adjustments to the quarantine. Bulgakov had stumbled upon a strategy that would be used again and again by his successors—conquest through starvation—and Atazhukin's humanitarian efforts ran counter to this goal.

After Atazhukin crossed the quarantine line, Bulgakov filed a series of petitions demanding that charges be brought against Atazhukin and Veryovkin. Gudovich considered the entire case nonsense, but War Minister Arakcheev took it up with the Interior Ministry. Veryovkin was arrested, but the emperor pardoned Atazhukin in February 1809, citing his "praiseworthy feats and loyalty to Russia."[23] He was assigned to duty in Georgia, and that should have been the end of the matter. However, throughout 1809 Bulgakov sent reports about a conference that he had arranged with

Kabardian pshis concerning their submission, which he claimed Atazhukin sabotaged.[24] Of course, Atazhukin wasn't in Kabardia at the time, but even if he had been, he couldn't have sabotaged the conference because there was none.[25] The entire event was a fabrication Bulgakov created to trick St. Petersburg into allowing him to punish his enemy. When this failed, Bulgakov sent Atazhukin a series of letters in spring 1809, demanding pledges of unconditional loyalty from all the pshis of Kabardia. Atazhukin returned home, called a hase to discuss the issue, and told Bulgakov the conditions were unacceptable. Bulgakov submitted another report, this time to the new Caucasus commander in chief, Alexander Tormasov. Bulgakov now claimed that he called the hase himself and had summoned Atazhukin, who had been evading arrest. He reported that the Kabardian pshis had taken an oath of loyalty to the Russian tsar and promised not to engage in "theft or rapaciousness."[26] None of this was true.

Bulgakov then took his vengeance against the entire Kabardian nation. Accusing them of raiding Cossack settlements in violation of the oath that they never took, Bulgakov arrested Atazhukin and launched a series of attacks on the Kabardians. Potto approvingly reports Bulgakov's campaign:

> In order to soothe the disturbed people of the region [Cossacks] and to cheer up the settlers, in the beginning of 1810 Bulgakov himself went into the Kuban and burned villages, destroyed fortifications and penetrated into areas the mountaineers themselves thought impregnable. . . . The energetic Bulgakov, never forgetting the danger, quickly moved his troops into the Kabardian lowlands and seized 25,000 head of livestock, and immediately ordered that they be distributed for the use of the suffering villagers on the line. Deprived of nearly all their means of subsistence, the Kabardians were forced to make peace and accepted the conditions dictated by Bulgakov.[27]

Such raids were actually common. The Russian military command considered them "punitive expeditions" in retaliation for Circassian *khishchni-chestvo* (rapaciousness), that is, raids on the Cossacks. In fact, in a letter of August 1806 to Gudovich, Del Pozzo explained that the Kabardian attacks were retaliation for Cossack raids upon them, adding that when they submitted petitions to the local military authorities asking for justice, they were frequently chased off and even imprisoned.[28]

Bulgakov took his assault on Kabardia beyond the frontier auls that he accused of "rapaciousness," using as his justification a report submitted by Del Pozzo in early 1810. In it Del Pozzo claimed that the peasants of Kabardia had requested Russian protection from the aristocrats. This was true: a civil war was brewing in Kabardia independent of Russia's actions. On April 14, under the pretext of protecting the peasants, Bulgakov invaded Kabardia and burned everything in his path. He also stole an enormous amount of livestock. Although Potto mentions twenty-five thousand head were taken, the Kabardians stated in just one complaint to St. Petersburg that among the goods Bulgakov had absconded with were forty-four thousand sheep, six thousand head of cattle, and more than one hundred tons of honey. The report also claimed that Bulgakov's troops burned nearly ten thousand homes, more than one hundred mosques, and one thousand farmsteads.[29] Even if one assumes this complaint doubles the actual damages, it still represents a crippling loss. As a result of Bulgakov's raids, thousands of people died from starvation, exposure, and the plague (which was certainly exacerbated by lack of food and shelter).[30] Then Bulgakov took his campaign into western Circassia, where he destroyed all the auls he could and blockaded the survivors until they starved or succumbed to the elements.[31]

For his devastation of Kabardia, Tormasov recommended that Bulgakov be decorated. Defense Minister Barclay de Tolly rejected the request, stating that

> various rumors have reached us that cause [the Emperor] to conclude that in pacifying the rebels, General Bulgakov's use of exorbitant degrees of brutality and inhumanity went beyond the limits of his responsibility.
>
> If one believes the reports, the expeditions against the Kabardians and the Kuban mountaineers consisted of the absolute plunder and burning of their homes; these brutal actions, which have driven those people to the brink of despair, have only aroused their hatred for us, and his dealings with the neighboring peoples have served more to create loathing of us than establish peace in that region.[32]

Tormasov changed his tune, now claiming that he had always been opposed to Bulgakov's "punitive" raids.[33] For his pillaging of Kabardia, Bulgakov was charged with extortion. After an investigation Atazhukin was released from custody and Bulgakov was relieved of his command for embezzlement, bribery, abuse of authority, and numerous other charges.[34] Tormasov was replaced by Nikolai Rtishchev, who did all he could to patch over the animosity that Bulgakov had sown, endorsing a Kabardian delegation that traveled to St. Petersburg to negotiate, and facilitating the few concessions that the Russian government had authorized. He allowed the Kabardians across the quarantine line to trade in Cossack towns and reinstated their right to exploit the salt fields in the Caucasus, which had been suspended by Tormasov.[35] He worked closely with Kabardian pshi Kuchuk Janhote to establish peaceful relations between the Kabardians and their neighbors the Ossetians, who had been forced by the Russians to migrate to Kabardia (a fate that the Ossetians would suffer repeatedly throughout the nineteenth century).[36] During Rtishchev's rule hostilities slowly decreased, although by no means stopped.[37] Meanwhile Atazhukin continued to work as a mediator between the Kabardians and Russians until his death in 1812.

In this one conflict between Atazhukin and Bulgakov, we can see many of the problems that plagued Russo-Circassian relations and led directly to the genocide of 1864. Bulgakov was not the last field commander to deceive administrators in St. Petersburg in order to gain permission to carry out his own agenda. The mentality of the Caucasus military command was shaped by people who behaved as if they were in charge of their own country, which outsiders couldn't understand. Contemptuous of their superiors in St. Petersburg, they fabricated whatever story suited their needs. Furthermore, they adopted Tsitsianov's view that conquest was the only viable option for control of the region. As we'll see, when civilian administrators used peaceful methods, the military commanders undermined them both by petitioning St. Petersburg and by launching raids into Circassia to sow animosity. This continued all the way up to the 1860s, when Field Commander Nikolai Evdokimov sabotaged St. Petersburg's final attempt to reach a settlement with the Circassians. Bulgakov was also the first Russian commander to use tactics that might today be considered genocidal. His blockade was the beginning of the oft-repeated Russian strategy of starving the population into submission. Likewise, his raids of 1810 weren't intended to punish the Kabardians but to annihilate them. Rather than confine his attacks to a handful of auls close to Russian territory, he took his army into the heart of Kabardia and destroyed everything in his path, leaving thousands homeless and starving. On the other hand, Bulgakov was the last Caucasus commander to be punished for his atrocities. His successors would not only commit even more egregious acts of terror against the Circassians with impunity, but they would be regularly be decorated and promoted for them.

The troubles Atazhukin faced were also typical of Circassians who understood the magnitude of the threat posed by Russia and who sought a peaceful solution. The Russian military command disliked all such peacemakers and did all they could to thwart their efforts. Many Circassians likewise distrusted their compatriots who sought peace with Russia, and they worked to undermine their credibility in Circassia. This would be the fate of all so-called peaceful Circassians—threats from the Russian side and attacks from the Circassian side. More importantly, all proposals from figures such as Atazhukin that cut to the heart of the Circassian position— that they wanted to be good neighbors with the Russians, not subjects of the tsar—were dismissed out of hand by both the Caucasus command and St. Petersburg. In this respect, both the civil and military commands were united in the belief that the only acceptable form of peace was the Circassians' unconditional surrender or their elimination.

Ermolov, Grandfather of the Genocide

At the beginning of the twentieth century John Baddeley wrote the first comprehensive English narrative about Russia's conquest of the Caucasus. In it he spends a great deal of time discussing the tenure of Alexei Ermolov as Caucasus commander in chief. A veteran of the War of 1812 and the greatest hero of the Caucasus wars, Ermolov is eulogized in the poetry of Alexander Pushkin as well as every history written before the Bolshevik Revolution. Monuments to Ermolov can be found throughout the North Caucasus today, and he is still considered one of Russia's great military figures. Baddeley seems torn between relying upon the traditional Russian portrait of a severe yet fair leader and his own sense of human decency:

> If . . . his name and fame still linger in the memory of the mountaineers of Dagestan and Tchetchnia when those of most of his contemporaries and successors have already been forgotten, it

must be admitted that this survival is due not merely to his com-
manding personality or actual accomplishment, but in part, at
least, to the calculated cruelty of his methods—methods, unhap-
pily, too generally characteristic of Russian warfare, morally inde-
fensible, but possessed of undoubted advantages in dealing with
Oriental peoples . . . campaigns conducted on the good old plan
with fire and sword—the devastation of crops, the sacking of villages, the massacre of men and the ravaging of women—gave a lesson they thoroughly understood and fully appreciated.[38]

Just a few paragraphs later, Baddeley describes Ermolov's theory of civil
administration, considered a cornerstone of his famous "system" for paci-
fying the Caucasus: "Yermoloff was wont to insist that the word of a Russian official should be sacred, so that the natives might be led to believe
it more firmly than the Koran itself; and to the extent of his power he
enforced good faith on either side."[39] How anyone could expect a people
to believe the word of, or have good faith in, a man who led his troops
on rampages of pillage, rape, and slaughter against them is a puzzle Baddeley never solves. However, it does give us a glimpse into the incoherence
of the Ermolov "system." Such was Ermolov's mentality that he believed
that the people he killed, robbed, and kidnapped should have understood
he was doing it for their own good and been thankful. As Yakov Gordin
explains, Ermolov considered his brutality justified because of his "higher"
motivations: "Ermolov and his close associates truly believed themselves
to be paladins of 'peace, prosperity and enlightenment,' which they were
bringing to a kingdom of barbarity and cruelty. . . . Ermolov could be cruel,
but he was cruel in the name of enlightenment and prosperity, he shot and
hanged people—sometimes by their feet—in the name of progress for this
edge of the empire, for its people."[40] Baddeley ultimately finds the truth
beneath this implausible theory:

The Russian General Erckert says of Yermoloff, "he was at least as
cruel as the natives themselves." He himself said: "I desire that the
terror of my name should guard our frontiers more potently than
chains or fortresses, that my word should be for the natives a law
more inevitable than death. Condescension in the eyes of Asiatics
is a sign of weakness, and out of pure humanity I am inexorably

severe. One execution saves hundreds of Russians from destruction, and thousands of Mussulmans from treason." "In these words," says Potto, "we have his whole system. . . . In his hands the former system of bribery and subsidies gave place to one of severe punishments, of harsh, even cruel, measures, but always combined with justice and magnanimity." Politically, it is difficult to see where justice came in, but in this respect Russia was only doing what England and all other civilised States have done, and still do, wherever they come in contact with savage or semi-savage races. By force or by fraud a portion of the country is taken, and, sooner or later, on one excuse or another, the rest is bound to follow.[41]

Somewhat resigned to the reality of the situation, Baddeley sees Russia's invasion and conquest of the Caucasus as no worse than Britain's conquest of India (although again he seems to miss the irony of calling the invading nations "civilized" and their victims "semi-savage races"). Baddeley concludes his remarks with a welcome condemnation of this mentality:

> It comes then to this, that if once we allow Russia's claim to exact submission and obedience from the tribes; if, further, we admit the right of man to play the part of Providence in punishing the innocent with the guilty, and both alike with the utmost severity, then Yermoloff's justification is complete. Yet a tolerance so wide would vindicate not his misdeeds alone but the crimes of a Tamerlane, and, failing a reversion to Old Testament ideas of man's duty to man, Christianity must ever reprobate the one and the other.[42]

A man of the twentieth century, Baddeley ultimately sees through the rationalizations of imperialists such as Ermolov and condemns them. Unfortunately, the collective punishment he berates was to become standard operating procedure for the Russians.

Why did such viciousness become systemic among the Caucasus command? One answer lies in a dilemma the officers faced after the Napoleonic Wars. "For the generals," Vladimir Lapin writes, "the activity of diplomats, who were creating post-Napoleonic Europe, essentially meant farewell to their hopes of receiving further rewards."[43] There was more to it, though. Even if war in Europe were to break out again, the campaign of

1812 made it clear that Russia would suffer enormous losses even if victorious. On the other hand, Asia's military backwardness would make victory and glory easy. Even before he arrived in the Caucasus, Ermolov wrote, "We can't take a step in Europe without a fight, but in Asia entire kingdoms are at our service."[44] Ermolov reveled in his overwhelming firepower against which his opponents—particularly the mountaineers of Chechnya, Dagestan, and Circassia—were powerless to combat: "It is very interesting to see the first effect of this innocent means [cannons!] on the heart of man, and I learnt how useful it was to be possessed of the one when unable all at once to conquer the other."[45] In his quest for personal glory, Ermolov chose adversaries (victims might be a more appropriate term) who stood no chance against his superior weaponry, and he employed levels of brutality and inhumanity as yet unseen in the Caucasus. It worked, too: Ermolov's officers were decorated and promoted as their tactics became more devastating. Subsequent generations would emulate Ermolov's form of success.

Potto explains Ermolov's attitude toward the peoples of the Caucasus, whom former administrations had (at least theoretically) treated as sovereign nations with whom peaceful relations could be established:

> With the appearance of Ermolov in the Caucasus . . . the passive and ineffective politics of palliative methods of giving gifts to our enemies was replaced by active politics which didn't have as its goal a temporary and fragile peace, but rather total victory, complete subjugation of the hostile lands. . . . He looked upon all the peaceful and hostile tribes of the Caucasus Mountains, if not as already under Russian rule, then sooner or later destined to be, and in any case he demanded unconditional obedience from them.[46]

Baddeley summarizes Ermolov's ideology in similar terms:

> Yermoloff's central idea was that the whole of the Caucasus must, and should, become an integral part of the Russian Empire; that the existence of independent or semi-independent States or communities of any description, whether Christian, Mussulman, or Pagan, in the mountains or on the plains, was incompatible with the dignity and honor of his master, the safety and welfare of his subjects. On this idea was based the whole of his policy, every one of his

administrative measures, every movement of the troops under his command, and to the end thus clearly set up in his own mind he from the beginning devoted himself heart and soul.[47]

In other words, Ermolov's goal was to conquer and assimilate the peoples of the Caucasus, using every weapon at his disposal. His initial target was the South Caucasus, which was intended to serve as a base for further expansion into Iran and ultimately India. The North Caucasus, which offered little material benefit, had to be conquered simply because it was a barrier between Russia and its newly acquired territories to the south. Again, Potto summarizes the Russian position:

> Between native Russia and [Georgia] lay a single path of communication across an isthmus between two seas occupied by the Caucasus range, populated by unconquered tribes who blocked the path through the Caucasus Mountains with every means at their disposal. Obviously, if Russia's rule of the South Caucasus was to be permanent, it was necessary to compel the peoples occupying the Caucasus lands not to interfere with communications through those lands. And if the system of peace and gifts didn't achieve this goal, then one path remained for Russia, the path of war, regardless of how many victims it would demand.[48]

The North Caucasus peoples were of no use to Russia but only stood as an impediment to their free travel to the Christian lands of Georgia and Armenia. As such, the land was valuable but the people themselves were of no consequence; hence, Potto concludes with a justification for genocide.

Before his assault on Kabardia, Ermolov spent several years trying unsuccessfully to destroy the Chechens and Dagestani peoples, employing methods that would be used against the Kabardians with devastating results. In his comprehensive study of Russia's conquest of the northeastern Caucasus, Moshe Gammer notes that "Ermolov was well within the existing consensus" in his use of violence as the main tool in controlling the Caucasus, and that "if he exceeded it, he did so only in the severity of his measures, in the amount of force he used, and in his brutality and cruelty."[49] In fact, Bulgakov was at least as brutal as Ermolov. Ermolov's significance lay

Tribes of Circassia
and its Neighbors
1400 – 1855

Sea of Azov

RUSSIAN EMPIRE

Caucasus
Military Line
(begun 1735)

KUMA

MOZDOK

Lesser Kabardia

TEREK

Chechnya

Ingushetia

Greater Kabardia

MALKA

Ossetia

Karachay

Balkaria

GEORGIA

Refugee
Kabardians

KUBAN

URUP

Hamysh

KRASNODAR

Temirgoys

Egerukays

LABA

Besleneys

Cherchenay

Mahosh

Temirgoys

Bzyp

ABAZA

ABKHAZIA

Biedukhs

PSHISH

Abzakhs

Ubykhs

Coastal Shapsug

SOCHI

Hatukays

Shapsugs

ADAGUM

TUAPSE

Natuhays

ANAPA

NOVOROSSIISK

BLACK
SEA

0   20 mi
0   50 km

Rutgers Cartography 2012

in the prestige he brought as a hero in the War of 1812. He legitimized the barbaric tactics that led to Bulgakov's dismissal. The lack of any meaningful response by the emperor to Ermolov's atrocities assured subsequent commanders and their troops that no acts of cruelty would be punished. Not that Alexander, and even Nicholas I, didn't try to restrain Ermolov when his brutality exceeded all boundaries of humanity.[50] However, these reproaches never led to the sort of investigation that ended Bulgakov's career. More often, Ermolov's officers received honors for their massacres.

Ermolov's encounter with Kabardia began in early May 1818, when five Kabardians assaulted the line and afterward took refuge in the aul of Tram, about seven miles from Fort Konstantinogorskaya. The villagers were ordered to turn the party over, which of course would violate of the custom of hospitality. When the villagers' refusal was communicated to Ermolov, he ordered that the aul be annihilated. The Russians surrounded the aul at night, drove all the inhabitants out with only the shirts on their backs, burned the village, took all of the livestock and distributed it among the Cossacks. Afterward Ermolov warned the Kabardians that "this time I limited it to [Tram]; in the future I will show no mercy to convicted bandits: their villages will be annihilated, their property taken, their wives and children slaughtered."[51]

The villagers' response was predictable: they prepared to join the western Circassians and launch raids in reprisal. A series of letters from Ermolov to Pshi Tkhamade Kuchuk Janhote followed that reveal Ermolov's failure (or refusal) to understand the Kabardian point of view. In his first letter, written in June 1818, Ermolov takes a belligerent tone: "I ordered [the destruction of Tram] and forewarned you that in more than a year and a half of indulging in the foul and roguish acts of the Kabardian people, I vainly waited for the princes to realize how villainously they had betrayed their pledge of loyalty, which they had freely given, and having grown tired of enduring this insult to the authorities representing our great Sovereign, I will now use completely different methods than I have up until now."[52] A note should be made about the "pledges of loyalty." Whenever there was a skirmish, the Russians insisted the Kabardians deemed to be involved take such a pledge. Because they were too numerous to keep track of, by the time of Ermolov the Kabardians could only have perceived them as a meaningless formality to end Russian hostilities, at best akin to a truce. However, they worked well for the Russians. Any hostile act by the Circassians could be labeled a violation of one of the countless "pledges" and used as justification for a "punitive campaign." In any event, by the end of June a nationwide rebellion was brewing in Kabardia, and so in early July Ermolov wrote Janhote again:

> Having explained to you my intentions in my judgment of Kabardia, all of which was based upon the will of my great Sovereign, I commission you to explain them not only to your clan but to all the princes, landowners and peasants of Kabardia.
>
> It won't be difficult for you to explain to them that the great and merciful Sovereign wishes peace and happiness for the Kabardian people. My actions will be conducted according to His will. . . .
>
> I repeat, so that there will be no pranks before my arrival, I give you my word before I present my explanation that I have absolutely no thoughts of causing any harm whatsoever to the Kabardian people, who may remain completely calm. There is no danger in believing my word.[53]

After driving the inhabitants of Tram into the woods and threatening to annihilate their villages and slaughter their children, it's difficult to see how the Kabardians could trust Ermolov when he now promised that he had "no thoughts of causing any harm whatsoever to the Kabardian people." Not surprisingly, the Kabardians were unimpressed and continued their preparations to migrate into western Circassia. In late August Ermolov wrote Janhote again, now in an almost collegial fashion:

> I have heard rumors that the residents of Tram wish to migrate beyond the Kuban in order to commit banditry along our borders. Since they are dependent upon you, I hope that you can restrain them from this foolish intention, for they can never acquire through banditry what I can obtain for them if they remain peaceful residents of Kabardia. I punished them once for their hostile actions, in violation of their obligations, and I can be of use to them many times over if they would just refrain from mischief.
>
> . . . I wish you success and will always respect your worthy and diligent service, which you are continuing to carry out at the present time for the welfare of your countrymen.[54]

None of this had any effect, and so in October Ermolov arranged a meeting with the Kabardian pshis, where he returned to issuing threats, promising that the fate of Tram would be repeated if the Kabardians continued their "thievery."[55]

Believing Del Pozzo to be too conciliatory, Ermolov replaced him as regional commander with General Karl Stahl. Stahl arrived in the regional headquarters of Georgievsk in early 1819 and immediately began a campaign against the residents of Lesser Kabardia, accusing them of concealing fugitive Chechens. The pshis there denied the charges, pointing out (correctly) that they and their ancestors had considered themselves "forever inclined and loyal to Russia" since the split of Kabardia in the mid-sixteenth century.[56] Whether Stahl truly believed that the population of Lesser Kabardia was aiding the Chechens or not (and again, due to the tradition of hospitality, they would have had no choice in some cases), he found it a convenient justification for clearing the rest of the fertile right bank of the Terek River. The Chechens had already been driven back from the river and Cossacks were busy colonizing their land, and now it was the Kabardians' turn. After Ermolov annihilated a number of auls in 1820, most of the Lesser Kabardian pshis signed a pledge of loyalty and a promise to inform the Russians of any fugitives in their midst. Despite their surrender, in September Russian troops under the command of Major Taranovsky demanded that the Kabardians living on the Terek leave for the Julat highlands, threatening them with cannons when they hesitated.[57]

There was little more that the Kabardians could do after the plague had devastated the entire country. As Ermolov himself mentions in his memoirs, "The plague was our ally against the Kabardians, for having completely annihilated the population of Lesser Kabardia and devastated Greater Kabardia, it weakened them to the point where they were not able to gather in large numbers as they had previously."[58] Perhaps this is the best testimony to Ermolov's character: in the face of a disease that nearly wiped out an entire nation that had been a loyal ally of Russia for 250 years, he expressed no sympathy at all. For Ermolov, the plague was a tool, an ally. However, it had only partially destroyed the Kabardians, so Ermolov had to finish the job himself.

Ermolov and Stahl became occupied by affairs in Chechnya in 1819 while Kabardian raids increased in size and frequency.[59] By 1821 the situation was out of Russian control, forcing Ermolov to return to Kabardia in September.[60] In November he developed a plan to "pacify" Kabardia once and for all and submitted it to Stahl for execution:

> The onset of winter has stopped their ability to move on the Line and it will make their punishment more palpable and will be a most certain means of pacifying them. . . . Meanwhile, in order to keep them fearful of our raids and too occupied with their own safety to conduct raids on the Line, I consider it necessary to lead a small force into Kabardia that will not occupy any specific location but rather go quickly from one aul to another, particularly the lowlands where they take their herds of cattle and horses in the winter, where we can kill the cattle and steal the horses. . . .
>
> The primary goal of the expedition commander should not be battles or skirmishes but rather the elimination of the cattle and horses which, of course, they can't hide.[61]

Russian forces went through Kabardia in December and January, rustling thousands of head of cattle and horses and burning all the auls they came across. Despite Ermolov's order that "the punishment is to be carried out against armed men only," throughout the winter troops led by Colonel Kotsyrev destroyed every aul they came across.[62] They threw several thousand villagers out of their homes and in least one aul bayoneted all the men, women, and children.[63] The survivors of these assaults were forced to migrate to the lowlands during what turned out to be a very harsh winter and were given no assistance in building shelter. In his orders, Ermolov remarked that "the winter isn't so harsh or enduring in this land that it will be painful for the people to live in the open air for two months." Because this statement is so patently false that it borders on the absurd (the average December–January temperature in the Kabardia lowlands is -5 degrees Celsius), one can only assume he meant it as a joke for Stahl.[64] Prisoners captured during battle were either forced into military service or given to the Cossacks as slaves.[65] The livestock was given to the Cossacks, and the stolen horses were sent to breeders in central Russia.[66]

After the conclusion of the operation a major land redistribution project began. Ermolov gave the clans who fled to the mountains an ultimatum to recognize the Russian emperor as their sole sovereign and return to the lowlands. The landowners agreed to accept Russian rule but asked to stay where they were. Ermolov refused, and finally the majority of the clans agreed to be resettled on the left bank of the Terek.[67] The few Kabardian aristocrats who had remained loyal to Russia throughout the campaign were given huge tracts of land while the winter pasturelands of clans who fled to the mountains were given to the Cossacks.[68]

As brutal as this campaign was, it was only a preparation for Ermolov's own assault in the spring. Several divisions armed with heavy artillery crossed into Kabardia in late May and followed the river valleys, burning villages and rustling livestock.[69] Little organized resistance was met (there were very few Kabardians left), and the majority of the villagers fled to western Circassia. At the end of July the Russians returned to the line, while Ermolov conducted surveys to determine the best places to build a new military line right through the heart of Kabardia.[70] He wasted no time: although he sent his proposal for the new fortresses to the emperor only in late July, Baksan Fortress had already been built and others were under construction.[71]

Were Ermolov's actions and orders genocidal? Using definition of genocide in the UN Convention on Genocide, a very strong case against him can be made:

> Genocide means any of the following acts committed with intent to destroy, in whole or in part, a national, ethnical, racial or religious group, as such:
>
> (a) Killing members of the group;
> (b) Causing serious bodily or mental harm to members of the group;
> (c) Deliberately inflicting on the group conditions of life calculated to bring about its physical destruction in whole or in part;
> (d) Imposing measures intended to prevent births within the group;
> (e) Forcibly transferring children of the group to another group.[72]

Ermolov and his men violated all five of these categories on several occasions. There can be no argument that he killed innocent Kabardians; even Tsarist historian Vasily Potto admits as much. As for points (b) and (c), the wholesale destruction of auls and the vast scale of theft of cattle and other goods necessary for the Kabardians' survival was, in Ermolov's own words, intended to terrorize them. As an experienced officer in the Caucasus, he knew that forcing people into the elements in winter was a death sentence, one more painful than if he had simply massacred them. By destroying entire communities, he disrupted the Kabardians' social system, forcing them to flee and exist in such conditions that raising families was impossible. Finally, when the aristocrats who refused to submit fled to western Circassia, Ermolov sent their children, who had been taken as hostages in 1814, to orphanages or to the army.[73] Because of his actions as well as those of his predecessors, the population of Kabardia was reduced from three hundred thousand in 1790 to only thirty thousand by the 1820s. All of the survivors were in Greater Kabardia, since the entire population of Lesser Kabardia had either died or fled to western Circassia.[74]

Additionally, Ermolov was well aware that the plague had decimated the population of Kabardia. A campaign that didn't spare the elderly, women, or children and that left thousands of people without shelter in a particularly harsh winter was certainly designed to deal a death blow to the Kabardian nation. Ermolov's rapid colonization of Lesser Kabardia with Cossacks and Ossetians is clear evidence that he had no intention to allow the Kabardians to recover from their losses. Furthermore, as Safar Beituganov has argued, "the punitive expeditions were inescapably accompanied by the mass migration of Kabardian auls across the Kuban—more than sixty settlements between 1821 and 1822. The flight of the Kabardians across the Kuban, which was considered the border between the two empires, was in fact the first manifestation of the mass migration of the Circassians to Turkey."[75] Technically, Beituganov is correct: Ermolov's campaign resulted in the first forced migration to the Ottoman Empire. The fact the Circassians considered themselves independent doesn't alter that fact that, from the Russian perspective, the Kabardians were expelled from their homeland. Beituganov goes a step further, claiming that the process actually began in 1803 when clans hostile to Russia were forced to migrate from their lands close to the line to less desirable locations within Kabardia.[76] Forced migrations would follow the Circassians until 1878, when the Russians drove them from the Balkans.

Ermolov's actions after the campaign likewise damaged the very fabric of Kabardian society. He abolished the religious courts and created a provisional court in Nalchik, outlawed the custom of pur, required Kabardians to supply information about anti-Russian activities among their compatriots, and restricted the rights of the Islamic clergy while allowing Christian missionaries free access to the peasantry. He severely crippled the Kabardians' ability to conduct trade by enacting a strict visa system, and at the same time constructed fortresses and settlements that further disrupted the feeding of their herds.[77] Although the purported goal of these measures was to increase security for Russian and Cossack settlers, Ermolov knew very well that the consequences of these new regulations, particularly the restriction of land use, would be further crippling of Kabardian society.

Ermolov's destruction of what little remained of Kabardia was total. The reforms he instituted stripped the aristocrats of virtually all their authority and reduced them to subjects of the tsar. The Provisional Court in Nalchik, which dealt with all matters of any substance, was overseen by Russian officers (the first director being Kotsyrev). The court also had authority to send Cossack units into Kabardia and western Circassia on "police missions." One apparently progressive move was the exclusion of the pro-aristocratic Islamic clergy from the courts, which would seem to have been a step toward increasing the rights of the peasantry.[78] However, this turned out to apply only to major cases in which Russian law held sway; disputes between landowners and the peasantry continued to be decided "according to ancient [Kabardian] customs and rites," meaning under complete control of the aristocracy and clergy.[79]

One last chapter in this story shows how much the attitude of St. Petersburg had changed since Bulgakov's tenure. In the spring of 1825 the Kabardian aristocracy in exile made a final attempt to break Russian control by the rather extreme method of compelling their countrymen who remained behind to flee to western Circassia as well. Hoping to exploit the growing anger at the new regulations, a joint Circassian force of around 500 men prepared for an assault on Russian forces in Kabardia from an aul belonging to the Karamurze clan. Line Commander General Alexei Velyaminov learned of the impending assault and crossed the Kuban River into the Besleney lands. Attacking at night, Velyaminov's forces burned the suspected aul to the ground along with most of its inhabitants. Nearly everyone who survived the fire was slaughtered. Afterward the Cossacks counted 570 bodies, not including those killed in the fire. All the cattle and horses were stolen, and 139 villagers who survived were taken prisoner.[80] For his participation in the massacre, Ermolov recommended Major General Fyodor Bekovich-Cherkassky, a former Kabardian pshi, for the St. George's Cross for "an exceptionally brave enterprise, fulfilled in the most successful manner." Emperor Alexander rejected the request, stating that "if his behavior at the beginning of the assault merited a reward, he lost his right to it, since the action that was begun sensibly was concluded by the total annihilation of over 300 families, among which were primarily women and children who were not participating in the battle."[81] The emperor could still recognize barbaric behavior for what it was, but his attitude toward it had changed significantly. In 1810, such behavior had led to Bulgakov's dismissal, while in 1825 it was merely cause to withhold honors. It was only a temporary setback as well. Ermolov recommended Bekovich-Cherkassky for the award again in July, and this time Alexander approved the request.[82]

Despite the death of their leadership, joint Abzakh–Kabardian forces attacked Russian positions throughout the summer and broke into Kabardia. They caused significant damage but were unable to inspire an exodus into western Circassia. The Circassians continued to harass the Russians where they could, but by 1826 Kabardia was firmly under tsarist control.[83] Thus ended the first phase of the Russo-Circassian War, the conquest of Kabardia. The aristocrats in exile became known as the *beglye kabardintsy* (refugee Kabardians), and remained in western Circassia until they met their fate in 1864.

Despite his apparent success in Kabardia, Ermolov's tenure in the North Caucasus was an unqualified failure. His massacres of noncombatants, wholesale plunder of livestock, and dishonesty only inflamed hatred of the Russians in the North Caucasus. Whatever chance there was for a rapprochement was almost totally destroyed. In the east, the Murid movement was a direct consequence of his merciless attacks on the indigenous peoples, while in the west the Circassians were so enraged that by 1830 the Shapsugs declared war on Russia.[84] As Moshe Gammer concisely states, "one of [Ermolov's] legacies in particular, to which all Russian sources remained blind, proved to be very detrimental to his successors in their dealings with the mountaineers: his extreme brutality achieved results opposite to his intentions and made the natives immune to terror. Experiencing the worst, they were afraid of the Russians no more."[85] In a very real sense, Ermolov set in motion the mutual distrust and hatred that would end in genocide.

2

A Pawn in the Great Game

Having established contact with the Slavs, I have decided to place them in contact with the Circassians and Chechens as well, in order to give Prince Adam Czartoryski greater leverage with England. . . . The Circassians and the Asiatic peoples living between the Black and Caspian Seas are a tool in their hands through which they distress and frighten the Russians.
—Mihail Czaikowski

The destruction of Kabardia remained hidden from the world. When Ermolov conducted the raids that nearly annihilated the Kabardians, not a single European newspaper took notice. As the European powers were vying for supremacy in a post-Napoleonic world, there was little interest in an obscure corner of the Russian Empire, far away from any strategic resources or shipping routes.

Western Circassia was another matter. The Black Sea had been an arena of international competition for centuries, and while in the eighteenth century it was for all intents and purposes an Ottoman lake, Russia continually pressed for control of the northern shore. The first foothold was the Crimean peninsula, which the Russians annexed in 1784. The Circassians occupied two hundred miles of the Black Sea coastline east of the Crimea, and Russia was determined to take this strategic region as well. Once the Black Sea Cossacks settled the north bank of the Kuban River, St. Petersburg looked for an opportunity to expand southward into Circassia. At first the other major powers took no notice, but the Ottomans quickly realized the potentially mortal threat Russia posed to their troubled empire. They had been manipulating the Circassians themselves for decades in the vain hope that they could one day exercise genuine authority over Circassia, but by 1829 they realized this was never going to happen. In an effort to cut their losses they relinquished their claims to Circassia in the Treaty of Adrianople. Even this failed to draw much attention, but when Russia quickly exploited the weak position of the Porte (as the Ottoman government was known) to gain special rights in the Dardanelles, Great Britain saw its own interests in the Black Sea threatened. Suddenly European newspapers and politicians took up the Circassian cause, and some even called for military intervention. The issue was debated in Parliament, and it looked at one point as though Britain would go to war with Russia in order to establish a protectorate over the struggling nation. Agents lived among the Circassians, promising international support and urging them to escalate their war against the Russians. Ultimately, however, the British deserted Circassia. A few politicians continued to press for action, but Parliament wasn't in the mood for a major war. All that British intervention accomplished was to make the Russians determined to conquer Circassia as quickly as possible.

The Fiction of Adrianople

Between 1768 and 1829 the Russian and Ottoman Empires fought four wars. The immediate causes differed, but Russia used each one to extend its authority to the northeastern shores of the Black Sea. Catherine the Great first expressed this vision while discussing the goals of the first of these wars in November 1768: "On conclusion of peace we must demand free navigation on the Black Sea and in order to accomplish this we must try to establish ports and fortresses even before the conclusion of the war."[1] In each successive conflict, the western Circassians were used as pawns by both sides: Ottoman agents persuaded the Ubykhs, Shapsugs, and Natuhays to fight the Russians (and burned their auls when they refused) while the Russians demanded pledges of loyalty from the Hamysh, Mahosh, Bjedukhs, and other tribes on their borders (and burned their auls when they refused). By the war of 1828–1829, the Russians and Ottomans were fighting in the heart of Circassia, bringing devastation not seen since the raids of Tamerlane in the late fourteenth century.

On September 14, 1829, Russia and Turkey signed the Treaty of Adrianople. Article 4 contained the following stipulation: "All the coast of the Black Sea from the mouth of the Kuban to the wharf of Saint Nikolai inclusive shall enter into the permanent possession of the Russian Empire." Circassia was never mentioned by name in the treaty, although in the preface Emperor Nicholas I is described, among many other titles, as "the hereditary ruler and possessor of the Circassian and mountain princes."[2] This, of course, was nonsense: the Russian tsars had never been any sort of ruler of Circassian or "mountain" princes, and certainly had no hereditary claim to anything. As for transferring the coast of the Black Sea to Russian rule, the Turks did have a series of forts there, but by no means did they control the coast. The forts were trading outposts and places from which the Porte hoped one day to mount an assault on Circassia like the one the Russians were conducting from the north. Since, according to the treaties of Küçük Kaynarca (1774) and Jassy (1792), all land south of the Kuban River belonged to Turkey, when the Porte ceded the coast in the Treaty of Adrianople, St. Petersburg took that to mean all land north of the coast was now Russian as well.[3] This too was nonsense. Turkey's "possession" of Circassia under Küçük Kaynarca and Jassy was a de jure declaration that had no connection with reality, so the Russian assumption that Circassia was now under the jurisdiction of St. Petersburg was a fiction built upon a fiction.

In his memoirs, Russian officer Fyodor Tornau claims St. Petersburg saw Article 4 for what it really was—the removal of a legal barrier to the conquest of Circassia:

> [The Turks'] concession had meaning on paper only—in reality, Russia could rule the land ceded to it through force alone. The Caucasus tribes that the Sultan considered his subjects never obeyed him. They recognized him as the successor to Muhammad and the Padishah of all Muslims, their spiritual leader, but they paid no taxes and contributed no soldiers. The mountaineers tolerated the Turks who occupied a few fortresses on the sea coast because of common religion, but didn't allow them to interfere in their internal affairs and fought with them or, more accurately, attacked them mercilessly for any interference. The Sultan's concession was completely incomprehensible to the mountaineers.[4]

The Russians were sidestepping another legal barrier. By acquiring Circassia through their interpretation of the Treaty of Adrianople, Russia was violating Article 5 of the 1827 Treaty of London, in which the signatories (England, Russia, and France) agreed not to seek "any augmentation of territory" as a result of the Greek War for Independence. Since this is what caused the Russo-Turkish War of 1828–1829, Russia's acquisition of Circassia was a violation of the Treaty of London—even Caucasus Archeographical Commission chairman Adolf Berzhe, a staunch defender of the 1864 deportation, admitted as much.[5] In eliminating the Ottoman problem, the Russians had provoked the British.

By the time of Adrianople, the western Circassians and Russians were on the verge of a workable relationship, but it came about only after decades of fighting. It began in the 1790s, when the Shapsugs unseated their aristocracy. The Bjedukh and Hamysh aristocrats agreed to help the Shapsug pshis regain power, and after a series of failed attacks, Hamysh pshi Batcheri Hajimuke led a delegation to St. Petersburg to ask Catherine for help.[6] The empress granted his request and ordered Zakhary Chepega, *ataman* (chief) of the Black Sea Cossack army, to support the aristocrats.[7] On July 10, 1796, the Cossacks and their cannons joined the Hamysh and Bjedukh tribes against the Shapsugs in the Battle of Bziuk, about eleven miles south of Ekaterinodar (modern Krasnodar). Although the Shapsug forces numbered perhaps as high as ten thousand and the aristocrats had only one thousand men, the Cossack artillery threw the Shapsug cavalry into chaos.[8] After losing as many as two thousand men, the Shapsug infantry retreated.[9] It was a pyrrhic victory for the aristocrats, though, for the civil war continued until the Shapsug aristocracy gave up all their privileges at the Pechetniko Zafes in 1803.[10] By virtue of their success against the aristocrats, the Shapsugs became the most respected (and feared) tribe in Circassia. Russian intervention in the revolution turned the Shapsugs into the most powerful enemy the Russians had ever confronted in the Caucasus.

The situation deteriorated quickly. In 1798 Catherine's son Paul accepted Shapsug pshi Ali Sheretluke's petition to be accepted as a Russian subject, after which Sheretluke moved his villages to the north side of the Kuban River. In response, the Shapsugs increased their attacks on the Cossacks. At the end of 1799 Paul suddenly replaced Black Sea Cossack Ataman Kotlyarevky with Fyodor Bursak. This unprecedented move (the Cossacks had always elected their leaders) was immediately followed by

Bursak's request to be granted permission to cross the Kuban in order to carry out "punitive raids."[11] Paul granted Bursak's request and, beginning in summer 1800, Bursak led large Cossack parties into Circassia where he burned auls and stole cattle, making no distinction between hostile and pro-Russian tribes.[12] Throughout 1802 and 1803 the Cossacks massacred villagers, took prisoners to be sold as slaves, and stole large numbers of livestock.[13] The Circassians retaliated in kind. Finally, in December 1804, Bursak led thirteen divisions across the Kuban and, as Cossack historian Fyodor Shcherbina reports, "having covered the entire land of the bitter enemies of the Black Sea Cossacks in every direction," destroyed their homes, property, and food and forced them to accept Russian suzerainty.[14]

The Russians had never had any problems with the western Circassian tribes until the Black Sea Cossacks settled north of the Kuban. Their predecessors were the Zaporozhian Cossacks, who were exploited by St. Petersburg as defenders of the frontier with Poland. When they rebelled in 1708, Peter the Great decided to eliminate them.[15] The fact of the matter was that they were brigands who served a purpose during wartime but whose indiscriminate pillaging ultimately made them a liability. Even pro-Cossack historian Potto admits that "the Zaporozhian Sech . . . caused Russia nothing but misery with their raids on Turkey on Poland, which constantly threatened to tie it up in a new war with their neighbors."[16] By 1775 the Zaporozhians had been split up and scattered around Russia. General Potemkin converted one section of the Zaporozhians into the Black Sea Army during the Russo-Turkish War of 1787–1791, and after the war they petitioned St. Petersburg to settle the land north of the Kuban River. The region was relatively uninhabited after the Russians annihilated the Nogay Turks living there in the 1770s.[17] However, the Circassians had relied upon this area to graze their herds for centuries. Even before Catherine granted formal permission, the Cossacks were settling the land directly adjacent to Circassia.[18] The Cossack population north of the Kuban exploded in the 1790s, exceeding sixty thousand by the end of the eighteenth century.[19] As Thomas Barrett has aptly noted concerning this process: "The North Caucasus was a part of the fault line between Christianity and Islam that stretches from the Balkans through Central Asia. The Russian state tried to push that line further south by Christianizing the region, not so much through missionary activity, but by settling Christians there and getting rid of Muslims."[20] The Cossacks had played this role in the northeastern Caucasus for many decades. Of course, some had settled in the northwest as well, but they had relatively peaceful relations with the Circassians. There was a bit of theft here and there: Cossacks raided Circassians and other Cossacks, Circassians raided Cossacks and other Circassians, and Cossacks and Circassians raided Turks together. This was life in the North Caucasus, and no one had a problem with it.[21] What escalated the violence was the large influx of settlers after 1792, which cut off the Circassians from some of their traditional pastures. The rapid construction of military outposts certainly didn't encourage trust either: along the 170-mile frontier, the Cossacks constructed sixty posts armed with batteries and more than one hundred pickets.[22] As Potto notes:

> With the appearance of Russians all along the banks of the Kuban, a wall of Cossack settlements rose before the Circassians; the steppes north of the Kuban were closed off to them, and the Don disappeared into the inaccessible distance. At that point, everything that had nourished the Circassian soul for centuries, all its long martial experience and enterprise, strength and boldness became directed at those who were impeding them from spreading out into the Kuban lands, which had at that time become the stronghold of the Russian border and at the same time a bloody arena of countless conflicts.[23]

All of this happened just as the Cossacks interfered in the Shapsug civil war at Bziuk, and it was shortly afterward that violence dramatically escalated.

Even Bursak's raids couldn't destroy the peace altogether. By 1806 Circassians and Cossacks were once again living in relative harmony and the feudal tribes almost unanimously sided with Russia.[24] When the next Russo-Turkish war broke out that year, Caucasus commander in chief Gudovich gave orders to "try as much as possible to . . . flatter the ruling Temirgoy, Atuhoy, Navruz, and Mahosh princes and keep them allied with Russia," and directly warned Bursak "that under the current circumstances there is no need to take any action against the Kuban people."[25] Nevertheless, Bursak led his troops across the Kuban again and destroyed villages throughout 1807. Major General Gangeblov was finally sent to the line to see what Bursak was up to. At first Gangeblov joined in the brigandage;

in May, his and Bursak's combined forces destroyed all the auls along five river valleys, after which Gangeblov ordered a retreat over Bursak's protests.[26] None of these operations served any military purpose; even Potto admits that Bursak's raids of 1807 were "of absolutely no use to the Black Sea Province and only provoked the Circassians into further aggressive actions."[27] Altogether, almost two hundred auls were destroyed during the period 1807–1810. How many people died as a result of massacres, starvation, and exposure to the elements will never be known, but using Khan-Girey's estimate of two hundred persons per aul, at least forty thousand people were displaced by Bursak's raids.[28]

What was terribly sad about all this was that the Russians could have easily developed a close and lucrative relationship with the Circassians. After Bursak was gone many Russian civilian administrators had great success creating commercial ties between the two peoples. St. Petersburg established thirteen commercial centers in the northwest Caucasus in 1811 and even reached a formal trade agreement with the Natuhays.[29] In 1813 Rafael Scassi was placed in charge of developing commercial ties; after he arrived in the region, he attended numerous hases and concluded treaties that increased trade. The Circassians even sold the Russians much-needed wood for use in shipbuilding at Sevastopol. Scassi also supervised the creation of a major trading center at the mouth of the Pshad River south of Gelendzhik, which increased economic ties further. In the summer of 1819 tariffs were removed from the sale of salt, and new trading posts were opened in Kerch and Bugaze.[30] The Russians, however, had no intention of simply remaining trading partners. In 1821 Alexander I authorized "Regulations for Commercial Relations with the Circassians and Abazas," which, in addition to designating Kerch and Bugaze as official trade centers, enumerated precise legal procedures for Russo-Circassian commerce.[31] St. Petersburg's goal was to make the Circassians so dependent upon Russian trade that they could be coerced into incorporation into the empire. Thomas Barrett explains:

> Russian trade policy with the mountain people was directly connected to attempts to conquer the region through winning over, subduing, killing, or exiling the native inhabitants. Creating a salt dependency was one such tool. Forts or the central government

also issued periodic bans on selling weapons or materials used for making weapons such as iron and steel. By the nineteenth century, there was also a fair amount of scheming about how to draw the mountain people into the Russian orbit peacefully, through an expansion of trade.[32]

The Circassians had long understood what the Russians' goal was. The Natuhays expressed their opinion quite clearly when French traveler Édouard Taitbout de Marigny visited Circassia in 1813:

> The Russians . . . have always shown the greatest desire to take possession of our territory. . . . We nevertheless consented that they should enjoy the sacred right of hospitality, and that one of their vessels should approach Pshad [River] under the direction of Scassi, a merchant known to us for several years, who took a cargo of wood for building, in exchange for salt. This man promised to provide for all our wants by an advantageous commerce; but, far from thinking of our happiness, he who had received under our roofs bread and salt, has promised Russia to accomplish the ruin of our independence, and in order to succeed in this, he daily augments the number of his agents upon our coasts, which he causes to be visited by our soldiers; and we doubt not, but that commerce is the means which you employ in order to sow discord among our princes, and to form establishments, which, in case of need, you will change into fortresses.[33]

Despite the new regulations and the distrust, trade between the Circassians and Russians was vibrant throughout the 1820s.[34] This attracted the attention of Ermolov, who was interested only in conquest. Responding to Scassi's proposal for direct trade with the Circassians, Ermolov wrote in 1819: "I . . . find that the measures that Scassi proposes will never be of any real use to the administration, but will only result in extreme disconsolation for both the mountaineers and the Russians in their mutual trade, since the mountaineers, being generally untrustworthy, lazy, and uneducated, will remain in ignorance for a long time to come."[35] In 1822 Ermolov wrote Foreign Minister Karl Nesselrode in an attempt to undermine Russo-Circassian commerce, which was now thriving:

It's impossible not to feel respect for the government's intention to develop trade relations with the mountain peoples of the Kuban region, and through it to supply them with their essential needs, soften their severity, and moreover convince them of the benefits of ties with us, lessen the exclusive influence over them that the Porte exercises, and finally to bring enlightenment to the half-savage peoples. But the application of this splendid theory is very inconvenient, if not impossible. This project cannot be established among a people hostile to enlightenment, under the power of a foreign government, under an ignorant Muslim government![36]

Ermolov's warnings couldn't alter reality, however, and trade continued apace. Unable to stop Scassi through official channels, Ermolov took the law into his own hands and sabotaged relations between the Circassians and Russians through the only means at his disposal.[37]

In 1821 Ermolov sent Major General Mikhail Vlasov to take command of the army. At that point the Circassian campaign began to parallel Ermolov's devastation of Kabardia. Vlasov is described by Shcherbina as a brigand who "without doubt was ruled by military vanity and a thirst for rewards."[38] His first engagement with the Circassians was at the Battle of Kalaus in October 1821, when the Russians cornered the Circassian force in an estuary and killed perhaps 100 men with cannon fire, while perhaps 1,000 more drowned. Three days later, the Circassians returned to collect the bodies of their comrades and Vlasov ambushed them, using his cannons to kill another 250.[39] Nearly all of Vlasov's subsequent actions appeared to serve no military purpose at all. Between 1822 and 1824 he burned auls and rustled cattle, making no distinction between peaceful and hostile communities.[40] In two cases Vlasov destroyed the auls of Circassians who were loyal to Russia, and it was the second raid that ended his career. The victim, Natuhay pshi Sagat-Girey Kalabatluke, filed a formal protest that was supported by Scassi. An investigation headed by Adjutant-General Strekalov found Vlasov guilty and even prompted a reprimand from Emperor Nicholas I, which was almost unheard of by this point in the war: "It is clear that it was not just a contemptuous desire to gain a reputation for military excellence without real effort that motivated the destruction of the villages of some unfortunate victims, but also

unforgivable vanity and a shameful desire for profit."[41] Potto excuses Vlasov for his abuses by noting that everything he stole from the Circassian
auls "he gave to the Cossacks to improve their households and support
their orphaned children." He blames Vlasov's fall on Strekalov's ignorance
of the true state of affairs in the region and the machinations of Vlasov's
"enemies."[42] Shcherbina, certainly no friend of the Circassians, has a different perspective: "The finale was fitting for the vain general who, in his
pursuit of military glory, on the one hand forgot the interests of the people
he was sent to defend, and on the other viciously punished the Circassians with unnecessary severity for minor infractions as well as major
attacks, and occasionally for no reason whatsoever. The first group, the
Cossacks, he destroyed economically, and the second, the Circassians, he
drove to the extreme limit of hatred."[43] Shcherbina also notes that "Vlasov
conducted himself in this manner at the pleasure of Ermolov, who was a
zealous advocate of a war of devastation against the mountaineers and
generously rewarded the executors of his punitive plans."[44] So it appears
that, after being thwarted in his official attempts to stop Russo-Circassian
trade, Ermolov instructed Vlasov to carry out an unofficial campaign to
reignite the Circassians' hatred of the Russians. His attacks on clans that
were well-known Russian supporters—the Hamysh, Bjedukhs, and some
Natuhay aristocrats—seem to leave little doubt.

Vlasov's actions succeeded in creating a state of intense hostility
between the Circassians and the Russians. As collegial assessor Dmitry
Kodinets of the College of Foreign Affairs reported in May 1827 to General
Ivan Paskevich, Ermolov's successor:

> The innocent Circassians have been deprived of their property and
> have become animated by vengeance, in accordance with their cus-
> toms, and having assembled in a significant mass have caused dam-
> age to our lines.
>
> ... The actions of our troops under the command of General Vla-
> sov have incited in various ways hatred toward the Russians among
> the mountain peoples. Only the Natuhays remain consistently on
> our side despite the repeated renewals of despotic expeditions by
> the commander of the Black Sea forces, and they try by every means
> to restrain their neighbors from raids on our lands.

The Shapsugs, who are inclined more than the others to revenge, came in armed mobs to the Natuhay village of Pshad to steal the property of our merchants who had set up a trading post there, but they were repelled and punished by its residents, who are loyal to us, particularly Prince Indarluke, who risked his life in our defense, along with his sons. But this admittedly rare devotion to us did not save the Natuhays from a terrible disaster that befell them last year, at the beginning of 1826, when a large squadron of Black Sea Cossacks, led by General Vlasov, unexpectedly burst into their homes, and specifically into the auls of Natuhay Prince Sagat-Girey, and destroyed everything and stole whatever remained. This prince and his relatives have always been an example of continual loyalty to Russia; living for many years right along our border, Sagat-Girey considered himself in every sense one of our people, by his own choice, and at the very moment that our squadron was bringing death and plunder to his home, he was away at his relatives,' consulting with them on matters that were specifically for our advantage. The details of this event were communicated to the higher command at the time, immediately after which the General Adjutant of His Imperial Highness Strekalov arrived, and after a careful and extensive investigation found the Natuhays completely innocent, and placed all the injustice of this last expedition on General Vlasov. Sagat-Girey and his subjects were rewarded on this occasion as much as possible for the destruction they endured, and a new system of handling affairs with these peoples was established for precise employment.[45]

Despite the efforts of Ermolov and Vlasov to poison the situation, by 1826 the benefits of commerce had convinced many Circassians to move closer to Russia. Even on the eve of the Russo-Turkish War of 1828–1829, the Circassians continued to trade with the Russians.[46] In the same report in which Kodinets lambastes Vlasov, he is cautiously optimistic about prospects for peace:

Since [Ermolov's removal], our border has experienced unbroken peace, and this serves as inarguable proof that it is very easy to live in peace with these people, as long as we show them examples of justice and constancy in the preservation of the treaties we have established with them. . . .

We have been presented with the genuine hope that the Kuban peoples can live in complete peace and concord as close neighbors with the Russians, but the nonstop complications that this Mission faces from the Black Sea Command, its totally negative actions and its deliberate attempts to undermine the authority and the power of this Mission in the eyes of the mountain tribes must necessarily destroy our ability to continue to pursue our goals with the success we expect.[47]

The Treaty of Adrianople was the deathblow to Kodinets' hopes. Emperor Nicholas now viewed the Circassians as legally bound subjects and wasted no time preparing for the conquest of Circassia. Already in November 1829 he issued orders for a "change of the system of relations with the mountaineers beyond the Kuban."[48] The first step in this new "system" was the removal of Scassi as director of trade relations in preparation for the complete suspension of Russo-Circassian commerce.[49] The Circassians were no longer to be considered independent tribes to be dealt with through treaties and commercial cooperation but as imperial subjects to be ruled by governmental fiat. As eager as the Russians were to bring Circassia under complete imperial control, though, they quite literally had no idea what they were in for. General Grigory Filipson claimed that the emperor and his advisors "didn't even suspect that we were dealing with a one and a half million valiant, militaristic mountain dwellers who had never recognized any authority over them, and who possessed powerful natural fortresses at every step in their forest-covered mountain thickets." Filipson concluded that the emperor truly "thought that the Circassians were nothing more than rebellious Russian subjects, ceded to Russia by their legal sovereign the Sultan in the Treaty of Adrianople."[50]

The projects the Russian government subsequently proposed for incorporating Circassia into the empire are proof that it had no idea what it was up against. Foreign Minister Nesselrode created a committee to establish a "Trans-Kuban District," and in early April 1830 the committee drew up a preliminary plan for administration of Circassia. Under "positive measures," the committee proposed that the "most influential"

Circassian leaders should be invited to an assembly "under the direction of the Caucasus Line Commander," where that they would be informed that Emperor Nicholas, "generous in kindness and strict in justice, wishes to bring an end to the disorder in the Caucasus," and would be asked their opinions as to how "the Monarch's will" could most effectively be implemented. The rest of the report recommends in great detail how the new district was to be divided and the tribes incorporated into a single administrative unit. Under "negative measures," the committee recommended a complete blockade of the Black Sea coast to stop all Turkish influence in Circassia and to destroy trade: "with the annihilation of the opportunity to market prisoners and other fruits of their thievery, the Caucasus tribes will no longer find any benefit in continuing their rapacious raids into the Russian districts that border them as well as between themselves." A visa system was to be imposed to prevent free movement of Circassians in the empire, and markets were to be established in urban centers where the Circassians would be able to trade with Russians.[51]

If these plans hadn't had such tragic consequences, we could simply dismiss them as ridiculous. Despite three decades of almost nonstop hostilities, Nesselrode somehow believed that the announcement of "the Sovereign Emperor's" will would convince the Circassians to lay down their arms and submit to Russian rule. Likewise, the notion that a blockade impeding all trade would stop the Circassians' attacks could only be believed by someone who had not read (or believed) Kodinets' report of 1827 that placed the blame for Circassian raids squarely on the shoulders of the Black Sea Cossacks, not on any "rapacious" desire for booty. As for the proposal to assemble the "most influential" Circassians in a meeting with the Russian military command, it was fantastic on two counts. First, there were no Circassians who were influential beyond their own tribes—this had always been the central problem with Circassian attempts at self-government. Second, the Abzakhs and Shapsugs still considered themselves at war with Russia and were confident in their ability to defend their homeland. The only "disorder" they wanted an end to was the Cossacks' presence.

In response to the report, Paskevich commissioned General Bekovich-Cherkassky to assess the situation and draw up specific recommendations. Bekovich-Cherkassky, the same former Kabardian pshi who had slaughtered Kabardian women and children in the 1825 massacre of the Karamurze clan, submitted his report in fall 1830.[52] Bekovich repeated the Ermolov party line, warning that "by themselves, gentle measures that have not been preceded and supported by the force of arms are insufficient when dealing with half-wild peoples, and will remain insufficient and even harmful," and proposing "the occupation of the locations that serve as the keys to their livelihood," thereby "depriving them by force of arms of their most important means of survival."[53] In other words, starve the Circassians into submission. In his report to Nesselrode in June 1831, Paskevich enthusiastically supported Bekovich's plan and enumerated fourteen measures to enact it, most of which had already been in use for thirty years. The sole innovation was the order that, after "having caused the mountaineers to feel our might," Russian administration should be rapidly introduced.[54] How Paskevich, an experienced commander with intimate knowledge of the intractable situation in the Kuban region, could support a proposal so out of touch with reality is anyone's guess, but in any event, he was replaced later that year by Alexei Velyaminov.

The final act of this absurdist play was Emperor Nicholas's tour of the Caucasus in 1837. In anticipation of his trip the emperor ordered Sultan Khan-Girey, a Hamysh nobleman in Russian service, to prepare a detailed description of Circassia. Khan-Girey was a Circassian in the mold of Izmail-Bey Atazhukin, who understood Russia's military might and saw the only salvation for Circassia in an ultimate capitulation to St. Petersburg. Khan-Girey's father, Makhmet Krym-Girey, was an influential Hamysh aristocrat who sympathized with the Russians and migrated to the north bank of the Kuban in the late eighteenth century. There he worked as a mediator between the Russians and Circassians and eventually joined the Russian military. Krym-Girey suffered a typical Caucasus peacemaker's fate: he was murdered by anti-Russian elements among the Circassians. His will instructed Khan-Girey to go to Tbilisi and join the Russian army. Ermolov sent him to St. Petersburg, where he became one of the first North Caucasians to graduate from the Petersburg Military School. He served in the Russo-Persian War of 1826–1828 and the Russo-Turkish War of 1828–1829, after which he returned to his family's homeland in an effort to persuade the Hamysh to accept Russian suzerainty. Upon his return to St. Petersburg he decided to devote his life to the cause of peaceful unification of Circassia with the Russian Empire.[55] For the next five years he wrote a comprehensive study of Circassia and its people, and just as he was finishing the work, Nicholas ordered him to prepare just such a text. The final product, *Zapiski o Cherkesii* (*Notes on Circassia*), is the most comprehensive description of the Circassian people ever written. With it Khan-Girey hoped to persuade Nicholas to adopt a peaceful strategy for incorporating Circassia into the empire. He sent chapters from *Zapiski* to the emperor in May 1837. Some excerpts became available to Velyaminov as well.[56]

Most of the book is an ethnographical study, but the final section is devoted to methods for peaceful Russo-Circassian unification. Khan-Girey proposed that Russia exploit the feudal structure of the Circassian tribes to draw them into the Russian orbit. Once these tribes were peacefully incorporated and their material condition began to improve, the democratic tribes would see that their long-term interests lay in unification with Russia.[57] However, not only were none of Khan-Girey's proposals followed, but the final section of *Zapiski* in which he proposed his plan disappeared and has never been found.[58] There is no doubt that it was submitted with the rest of the text; he referred to this final section in his December 4, 1839, request for the return of his manuscript.[59] Realizing he would never get it back, he began to rewrite it. He also continued to work as a peacemaker in the Caucasus until 1842, when he died suddenly in Ekaterinodar at the age of thirty-four. According to witnesses, he thought he had been poisoned on the orders of anti-Russian pshis.[60] *Zapiski*, minus the final chapter, was discovered only in 1958 and was finally published in 1978.[61]

Khan-Girey played a central role in Nicholas's 1837 visit to the North Caucasus as well. In May 1836 he received instructions from the Ministry of War on his mission, which concluded:

His Majesty has affirmed the conditions to be demanded of the mountaineers for their submission:

1. Cease all hostile activities towards us.
2. Send hostages of your choosing. They may be replaced by others after four months, but only by approval of the Russian Administration.
3. Turn over all our deserters and prisoners living among them.

4. Refuse to accept anyone who has not submitted into their auls without informing the Russian Administration and refuse to grant asylum to abreks [renegades].

5. Refuse to accept horses, cattle and sheep belonging to anyone who has not submitted into their herd, and if such should occur, the entire herd shall be confiscated by our forces and additionally the subject residents shall be held responsible for such instances.

6. Assume responsibility for the passage through their land of all criminals who carry out nefarious activities within our borders, and for the return of our prisoners and for compensation for stolen cattle and horses.[62]

As always, several of the conditions were impossible for the Circassians to accept because they violated adyge habze. Additionally, after Vlasov's wholesale pillaging, the demand that the Circassians must pay "compensation for stolen cattle and horses" made, quite literally, no sense at all. However, unlike Tsitsianov and other commanders' impossible demands, this particular document doesn't appear to be an attempt to provoke violence but simply a product of total ignorance. Arguably even more surreal was the letter dispatched the same day to Velyaminov, which discussed Nicholas' planned visit to the North Caucasus "for the invitation of the mountain tribes, especially the numerous and warlike tribes of Circassia, to voluntarily announce their submission to His Imperial Majesty": "His Majesty has deigned to dispatch a trusted officer from his person to announce to the mountain tribes His Majesty's anticipated visit to the Caucasus so that they may be invited to take advantage of this unexpected event, which will not likely repeat itself, and dispatch to His Majesty deputies to announce their submission, and to impress upon them in any case the necessity of soliciting regular direct government by the Russian Administration."[63] One can only imagine how Velyaminov, an officer in the mold of Ermolov who had been fighting the North Caucasus peoples for twenty years, reacted to this bizarre idea. With few options available, Velyaminov ordered Khan-Girey to assemble a group of elders from clans that had already submitted to Russian rule to meet the emperor when he came to the North Caucasus in September. This experience finally impressed upon Nicholas the truth of the situation: the Circassians were overwhelmingly hostile to the idea of Russian rule. Not only that, the British were threatening intervention as well. Nicholas decided the only remaining option was to begin a full-scale war and conquer Circassia as quickly as possible.

The British Gamble with Circassia

British involvement in the Caucasus has generally been looked upon favorably by western scholars and Circassians alike. British agents in the Caucasus were treated as respected leaders by Circassian pshis during their time there and are remembered as patrons of the Circassian cause. A close examination of exactly what happened paints a more ambiguous picture and corroborates to some degree the Russian claim that British intervention only caused more suffering. Likewise, London's motivations were far from humanitarian. Involvement in Circassia was a risky geopolitical gamble to protect British economic interests.

The British had been wary of Russian expansion since the 1730s, when St. Petersburg drew closer to Persia. In 1797 St. Petersburg established a separate department to deal with the "Asiatic peoples" living in the Russian Empire, and through it Russia declared its right to conduct internal affairs without concern for international objections.[64] Perhaps as a sign of the maturity of Russia's newfound imperialistic arrogance, St. Petersburg rejected London's offer of mediation at the negotiations leading to the Treaty of Turkmenchay (1828), arguing that Persian affairs belonged to the sphere of its "exclusive interests."[65] All of this was disconcerting but still not enough to compel Britain to adopt an openly anti-Russian policy. The Treaty of Adrianople likewise raised eyebrows but only generated a few anti-Russian treatises that failed to gain much support.[66] However, the Treaty of Unkiar Skelessi (1833), which came after Russia rescued the Porte from a coup attempt by the Egyptian pasha Muhammad Ali, could not fail to be met with hostility in London, as John LeDonne explains:

> Should Russia feel threatened by Britain and France and invoke the treaty of Unkiar Skelesi, the Porte was bound to close the Dardanelles to their warships but was not bound to close the Bosphorus to Russian warships. That was the ominous novelty: the geographical

unity of "the straits" was abandoned in favor of its constituent elements. Russia gained the right to penetrate the straits and keep Britain out of them.

Britain thought it allowed both a fleet-in-being strategy in the Mediterranean and a fortress-fleet strategy in the Black Sea. It could not do both without challenging Britain's determination to return a Russian challenge with a challenge of its own.[67]

Russia's attempts to gain complete control of the Black Sea threatened a vital British route to Persia and India. After Russia seemed to have gained control over the Dardanelles, a flood of articles and treatises appeared that raised the possibility of British military action as a remedy for Russia's effrontery. It was in this alarmist climate that the Circassians' plight entered the consciousness of the European public and became an international issue.

It was easy to manipulate public opinion in favor of the Circassians. As early as the thirteenth century European travelers wrote descriptions of the peoples they encountered in the Caucasus, with the Circassians frequently taking center stage.[68] There were many references to Circassians in the 1700s and early 1800s in advertisements for cosmetics that played on the long-standing stereotype of the beautiful Circassian woman.[69] The Circassian man began to receive attention in the travelogues of the early nineteenth century, in which he was described as a semicivilized warrior, something to be admired but certainly not respected as an equal to a European man.[70] Circassia was a land of noble savages and mystical beauties but little else. It made a perfect pawn: strategically located, vaguely familiar to Europeans, and expendable.

The anti-Russian campaign threw the spotlight directly on Circassia almost exclusively due to the efforts of a young diplomat named David Urquhart. After having spent several years traveling in Anatolia, Urquhart used personal connections to gain access to the highest political circles in Britain in 1832. In 1833 he wrote a treatise concerning the potential benefits of increased Anglo-Turkish trade that the king himself found persuasive.[71] The book exaggerated the Ottomans' economic and political strengths and identified Russia as the prime villain in an otherwise promising scenario.[72] The following year Urquhart was sent to Istanbul, and there he met the equally Russophobic British ambassador Lord Ponsonby.

The two of them set out immediately to influence the British Foreign Office into taking aggressive action in the Black Sea (Ponsonby even went as far as to propose sending warships to Circassia).[73] In July and August Urquhart toured the Black Sea coast, where he came up with the idea of using the Circassians as a tool in his goal of driving back the Russians. Exactly what happened on this trip is hard to say: among other things, Urquhart claims to have met fifteen tribal leaders and nearly two hundred village chiefs, designed the Circassian flag, and helped them draft a petition to London for assistance. Given his penchant for exaggeration, his naïve certitude in the correctness of his positions, his Russophobia that bordered on the pathological, and his contempt for his superiors' instructions, his account must be taken with a grain of salt.[74] It is known that he did visit Circassia and returned with a petition for British aid that he almost certainly wrote himself. After his trip, he arranged for two other Britons, James Bell and John August Longworth, to visit the Circassians and encourage them in their fight against Russia. Bell and Longworth also gathered material for travelogues to be used to further influence British public opinion.

After returning from Circassia, Urquhart published a series of pamphlets called the *Portfolios*, which railed against Russia for its military actions in Poland and the Caucasus. This still wasn't enough to persuade London to enter the Black Sea and thereby nullify Unkiar Skelessi, so Urquhart took matters into his own hands. In November 1836, in collusion with James Bell and his brother George, he ran the blockade of Circassia that the Russians established in 1830 in the schooner *Vixen*. The Bell brothers only became interested in Urquhart's intrigues after the Russians began to interfere with their mercantile business on the Danube and apparently saw a war in the Black Sea as a convenient means of preoccupying St. Petersburg. According to G. S. Bolsover, Urquhart's hope was that the Russians "would confiscate the *Vixen* and embroil themselves with Great Britain," but "if they ignored the vessel, they would virtually abandon their claims to Circassia and enable the British government lawfully to support its inhabitants."[75] The Russians seized the *Vixen* and British journals "were loud in their denunciations of the latest example of Russian villainy,"[76] but Foreign Secretary Lord Palmerston feared open warfare and defused the situation. Urquhart was drummed out of civil service and subsequently accused Palmerston of being a paid Russian agent.[77]

The travelogues published by Bell, Longworth, and a third Briton, Edmund Spencer, did succeed in bringing the Circassian issue to the attention of the British public and in linking the Circassians' fate with broader issues of British security. Spencer, who claimed to be "no advocate for war," nevertheless warned that "the time has arrived when it is imperative upon us to place a barrier against the further advances of a power that threatens to become a dangerous rival—a powerful enemy."[78] He called upon Russia to respect the Circassians' rights "if she is, as she pretends to be, actuated by a desire to uphold the interests of nations, such as she professed to be at the pacification of Greece," while he lamented that "every consideration, whether of humanity or just policy . . . will, alas! I am afraid, be ineffectual," leaving war as the only option.[79] Oddly, Spencer encouraged Russia to colonize Circassia with "the industrious inhabitants of Europe," the very thing the Circassians were fighting against.[80]

James Bell makes a similar case in the preface to his memoir of 1840, arguing that the conquest of Circassia should be viewed in a larger geopolitical context: "However inconvenient it may be for the Government of Great Britain at the present moment to bring to solution the question, whether Russia has any claim whatever over the territory of Circassia, there cannot be a doubt that such a claim has no existence, in right or in fact, and that the independence of that country, not only as a fertile source of commerce, but as a check upon Russia's movements, is of vital importance to Great Britain."[81] Bell was far more than a writer. In his two years in the Caucasus, he attended hases, advised pshis, and made one promise of imminent international support after another. He describes many of his activities in his memoir, giving the reader the most detailed accounts available of what the British were telling the Circassians. For example, at the Adagum Hase of April 1838, when the Circassians asked what help England could be expected to provide, Bell answered: "The coast was considered as not appertaining to Russia, and consequently open to British commerce. . . . If another English vessel were taken by the Russians elsewhere than in the bay of Suguljak (and even the question as to that locality, I told them, I believed still undecided), the Government of England would interfere to demand restitution; the effect of which would be, to throw the trade entirely open."[82] Bell accurately stated the official British position that Russia's acquisition of the coast of Circassia was a violation of the

Treaty of Paris. His speculation on a future *Vixen* affair and England's reaction to it, however, was an outright lie. By 1838 the *Vixen* affair had been forgotten and Britain was involved in expanding trade with the Ottomans independently of the Straits question, while the Russophobes had turned their attention to Afghanistan. As a result of Bell's promises, the delegates voted to break all communication with Russia and take an oath of war.[83] While they very well could have done this anyway, Bell's deceptions at such a crucial juncture in Circassian history were inexcusable.

While the activities of Urquhart, Bell, and others were not officially recognized by London, there can be little doubt that these agents operated with the knowledge and approval of their government or, as Paul B. Henze notes, "they would not have persisted so long." Thus, Henze rightly argues, their efforts consisted of what are now known as "covert action operations."[84] Bell and Longworth encouraged the Circassians to unite with Imam Shamil and promoted unity among the Circassian tribes to create an effective military force, but to do so they incited them to attack and rob tribes who cooperated with the Russians and drive out suspected collaborators.[85] Thus the British, like the Russians and Turks before them, exacerbated the Circassian civil war that began with the Battle of Bziuk forty years earlier and made it less likely that the Circassians would be able to create a central government. This in turn was the very excuse Palmerston and others used to justify abandoning them after the Crimean War.

The truth of the matter was that the British were encouraging the Circassians to escalate their war with Russia by promising them a level of military support they had no intention of providing. One interesting piece of evidence of the British agents' exaggerated promises of aid is found in a letter from Caucasus commander in chief Alexei Velyaminov of June 6, 1837: "Four English agents in the mountains have been spreading the rumor that if military activities do not cease, as soon as word is received in Istanbul a united fleet of several European powers, the Turkish Sultan and the Egyptian Pasha—as many as 300 ships—with landing forces and the necessary artillery will set sail; that Sefer Bey Zanoko will arrive soon with a Shapsug delegation on two ships loaded with lead and gunpowder."[86] It's unknown whether this promise was actually made or if it was just a rumor, but it provides a clue as to how profoundly the British were deceiving the Circassians.

Ultimately the Russophobes in Parliament lost momentum and the agents went home. In the 1840s they teamed up with Polish exiles to incite both the Circassians and the Cossacks to war, but nothing came of any of these ventures. On the other hand, the Russian Caucasus commanders remained frightened of a potential British intervention and escalated their war against the Circassians. Additionally, British agents incited intertribal warfare and silenced any voices of compromise. At many hases in the 1830s where proposals for peace with the Russians were made British agents played an active role in undermining them.[87] As late as 1834 a large number of Circassian leaders were close to a permanent agreement with Velyaminov, but the interference of Bell and others sabotaged their efforts.[88] The death of Khan-Girey, a dedicated peacemaker whose respected position in the army made him invaluable to any effort at compromise, was possibly one consequence of British interference. In hindsight, the best hope for the Circassian people apart from Britain fulfilling its promise and sending massive military support was in some sort of negotiated peace with the Russians that would have ended Circassian independence—certainly a tragedy, but one in which the Circassians would not have been subjected to genocide. Although it's impossible to say what Urquhart's, Bell's, and Spencer's true feelings concerning the Circassians were, their actions risked the very existence of the Circassian nation while their primary concern was Britain's commercial interests in Europe, South Asia, and the Middle East. Their efforts in the Caucasus were a geopolitical gamble in which the Circassians were taking the full burden of the risks of failure. Once they left, the Russians escalated their attacks to a level of brutality unheard of before.

3

From War to Genocide

We must assume that we will need to exterminate the mountaineers
before they will agree to our demands.

—Alexander Baryatinsky

In concluding his description of the final conquest and expulsion of
the Circassians in the 1860s, Russian officer Ivan Drozdov tried to justify
the wholesale death and destruction that his army brought upon them:
"Mankind has rarely experienced such disasters and to such extremes,
but only horror could have an effect on the hostile mountaineers and
drive them from the impenetrable mountain thickets."[1] The final horror that Drozdov refers to was really just the culmination of an increasingly barbaric campaign against the Circassians. In the 1830s Russian
commanders had already gone beyond war crimes and were committing actual atrocities. It was a sign of frustration: Ermolov's campaigns
had only increased the determination of both the Circassians and the
Chechens to fight to the last man, and the army that had defeated Napoleon was held in check by "savages." It was also a sign of the changing
mindset of the Russian Caucasus commanders. In their minds the Circassians were no longer future subjects; they were eternal enemies who
had to be wiped out. It was only in the aftermath of the Crimean War
that the military resources were available to complete the conquest of
the region, and as soon as they were the Russians moved quickly to
drive the Circassians from their homes. After twenty years of increasingly brutal tactics, there was little that the field commanders would
refrain from doing.

Stalemate

An underground society called the Union of Salvation made a feeble attempt at overthrowing Emperor Nicholas I in 1825. The leaders of this group, known to history as the Decembrists, were hanged and the rest were exiled to Siberia. After several years the Tsar offered the would-be revolutionaries the option of service in the Caucasus. One person who took Nicholas up on his offer was Nikolai Lorer. Shortly after he arrived on the front line in 1837 he was invited to the office of the regional commander, General Grigory Zass: "After entering the general's office, I was struck by some sort of intolerably offensive smell, and Zass, laughing, ended our confusion by telling us that his people had no doubt placed under his bed a box with heads, and in fact he pulled out and showed us a huge chest with several heads that stared at us horribly with glassy eyes. 'Why are they here?' I asked. 'I'm boiling and cleaning them, and then sending them to various anatomical offices and my academic friends in Berlin.'"[2] Not all the heads went to Berlin immediately, however: "In support of the notion of [filling the Circassians with] terror that Zass preached, the heads of Circassians were constantly stuck on lances on a specially made hill at Prochny Okop, and their beards blew in the wind."[3] In creating a scene reminiscent of a famous anecdote about Vlad the Impaler, Zass claimed he was carrying on the tradition of Ermolov, who, "hanging people mercilessly, robbing and burning auls, was able only through these means to bring success to our side."[4] But, to his credit, Ermolov never collected human heads.

Zass's acts were emblematic of the direction the war took after Britain's intervention and the failure of Nicholas's visit. Caucasus commander Velyaminov himself offered a reward to his soldiers for the heads of Circassians, which he sent to the department of anthropology of the Academy of Sciences in St. Petersburg for study.[5] While Ermolov's generation considered the Circassians barbarians and unworthy of the rights accorded civilized men, Velyaminov and his successors denied the Circassians their very identity as human beings. This "harvesting" of Circassian heads for study also foreshadowed the infinitely more horrific practice of the Nazi medical experiments. In fact, an almost identical episode did occur during the Second World War. As Richard Rubenstein reports, "[University of Strasbourg professor August] Hirt wrote to [Heinrich] Himmler informing him that all nations and races had been studied by means of skull collections except the Jews. . . . Hirt advised that the Jews should be kept alive until a doctor could take down accurate statistics. Then they were to be killed and their heads removed with proper scientific care."[6] The Nazis were far more methodical and cold-blooded than the Russians, but the difference between Velyaminov's bounty hunters and Hirt's surgeons is only one of degree.

By the 1830s the Caucasus Corps, which had never been known for its professionalism, had become the dumping ground for criminals and political dissidents, commanded by officers who "were distinguished by a pathological ferocity that was so shameless that the central authorities often had to sharply check them."[7] Of course, the entire conduct of the Caucasus wars from the time of Tsitsianov was testimony to the Russians' contempt for the North Caucasus peoples.[8] They put little effort into understanding the differences between the various nations; indeed, the term "Cherkes" (Circassian) was used as a synonym for "mountaineer" as far away as Chechnya.[9] By the 1840s the Russians referred to the Circassians most frequently as *khishchniki*, which translates as "thieves" or "plunderers." Initially the term was used to describe parties of Circassians who attacked Russian fortifications, but now the Russians were using it in place of "Circassian" to describe everyone they encountered. Men, women, children, and the elderly were reduced in the Russian mind to bandits based upon their identity as Circassians.

Not all the brutality was as gratuitous as Zass's decapitations. After Nicholas's tour of the Caucasus, the Russians methodically searched for ways to deal a deathblow to the Circassians. Velyaminov abandoned the practice of burning auls during short "punitive" raids on nearby tribes and adopted Bulgakov's systematic destruction of homes, food, and flocks deep throughout Circassian territory. In the second half of the 1830s Velyaminov and his successors conducted such expeditions and by 1836 established a plan for the "gradual occupation of the lands of the mountain peoples" with "the Black Sea and other Cossacks."[10] This plan did not address what would happen to the Circassians once the Cossacks were settled on their land, particularly those who refused to accept Russian suzerainty. It's difficult to believe he expected them to live side by side with their conquerors after forty years of war. The solution to this problem would be left to the next generation of Russian commanders, who concluded that the Cossacks should simply replace the Circassians, who would be driven out or killed. The plan for genocide was already in place seventeen years before Nikolai Evdokimov began his ethnic cleansing.

Many of the expeditions resulted in little more than random destruction of auls and food supplies, or simply searching the mountains and finding nothing at all.[11] A somewhat more coherent effort was directed toward establishing a series of forts along the Black Sea coast. In spring 1838 General Nikolai Raevsky conducted reconnaissance missions south from Anapa, thirty miles east of the Crimean peninsula, and submitted a proposal for colonization that was quickly undertaken.[12] However, after attempts at moving inland did nothing but bring down large numbers of Circassians upon them, some Russian commanders concluded that the fortresses were useless.[13] In 1840 the Circassians and Abazas destroyed most of them, and in April 1841 they captured Fort Tenginsky in the center of the Black Sea Line.[14]

The only place where the Russians were successful was at sea, where the blockade managed to almost completely shut down foreign trade. This, coupled with a disastrous harvest in 1839, caused widespread famine.[15] Of course, starving the Circassians was the whole point of the blockade, but only to break their will. Shortly afterward Admiral Lazar Serebryakov took the strategy of forced starvation to its final extreme, proposing it as a method of mass extermination: "On March 21, 1841, I informed your excellency that conditions had never been more favorable for driving the Natuhays to the most extreme of conditions; that after the failure of the harvest of 1839 there was a general lack of food in the mountains; and that if forces attacked in the summer and destroyed all their harvest, by the following winter they would all be victims of starvation."[16] As Yakov Gordin has noted, ninety years later Stalin would use this very method to starve to death the Ukrainians opponents of collectivization in the Holodomor ("death by hunger") of the 1930s.[17] In this sense, Serebryakov may hold the dubious distinction of being the first modern military commander to formally propose genocide.

One very strange detail in military reports that deal with the destruction of homes and food is the absence of any mention of civilians. In the field notes of 1836, rarely does a page go by without mention of at least one aul being burned (forty-four were burned in October alone).[18] Sightings of Circassian parties on horseback are occasionally mentioned, but there are no references to women and children anywhere. It is clear in some reports that the auls had been abandoned, but occasionally the aul is said to have been taken "without resistance."[19] In one case, troops under Colonel Milenty Olshevsky burned two occupied auls, but again there was no mention of what happened to the villagers.[20] Through this systematic neglect of the human victims of their campaigns the Russians reduced the war to a bureaucratic procedure. It is also at this time that the term *ochishchenie* (literally, "cleansing") begins to appear in field reports in reference to the expeditions into the mountains. This focus on the land rather than the people who occupied it made genocide inevitable. It is true that the civil administration still saw the Circassians as future subjects while the military command considered them irreconcilable enemies. However, both branches of the Russian leadership were convinced that this strategic land had to be incorporated into the Russian Empire. The military commanders had already decided that the Circassians hated the Russians too much to ever become subjects of the Empire, so they worked toward their destruction. Once they concluded that the Circassians would be eliminated in any event, they began to treat them with increasing levels of brutality. Velyaminov, Zass, Serebryakov, and others were the pioneers who laid the ideological and tactical foundations that Nikolai Evdokimov would employ in the 1860s to commit genocide.

One reason why the Russians turned to genocide as a solution to the Circassian issue was that they could never develop a coherent plan for subjecting them to Russian rule. Although Raevsky's efforts to conquer the Shapsugs in 1838 met with total failure, in January 1839 Russian minister of war Alexander Chernyshev proposed virtually the same plan.[21] The Russians were to take points along the Black Sea coast and, with the assistance of naval power, establish fortifications. From there Russian forces, backed by Cossack reinforcements, would "undertake the pacification of the Circassian tribes in the interior through the occupation of the area between the Kuban, the sea, and the Gelendzhik Line."[22] Chernyshev expected Circassia to be conquered through this approach by 1841. The problem was that Chernyshev doesn't indicate the precise means to be used to compel the Circassians to surrender. St. Petersburg was still unaware of how impenetrable the mountains were, how many Circassians lived there, and how determined they were to preserve their freedom.

The Circassians themselves were confident in their ability to hold off the Russians indefinitely. The military successes of Shamil in Chechnya gave them new hope, so when the he suggested joining forces, many Circassian leaders agreed. Shamil wasn't interested in Circassian independence. As the third imam of the *ghazawat* (holy war) declared in response to Ermolov's excesses, his plan was to create a pan-Islamic state across the North Caucasus. His large army had proven itself capable of defeating the Russians in battle, but the key to victory was the creation of a unified front from the Caspian Sea to the Black Sea. In the spring of 1846 Shamil led an army of twenty thousand into Kabardia to seize the Georgian military highway and unite with the Circassians, but all this did was ignite a civil war and prompt a new round of Russian pillaging.[23] Then, with only slightly more success, he sent a series of *naibs* (deputies) to western Circassia to unify the tribes into a single fighting force. In May 1842 his first naib, Haji-Mohammad, was able to gain the allegiance of the Shapsugs, Natuhays, and Ubykhs but made little progress elsewhere.[24] He did, however, start a military reform that resulted in the Shapsugs and Natuhays developing standing militias to enforce *hase* decisions by 1846, and this in turn led to the Adagum Zafes in February 1848, where plans were drawn up for the creation of a standing army.[25]

After Haji-Mohammad's death in May 1844, Shamil sent Suleiman Efendi as his replacement. Rather than help the Circassians organize an army, Efendi tried to persuade them to send their best fighters to Chechnya. Naturally, this proposal met with total failure, and Efendi left shortly afterward.[26] Shamil's third naib, Muhammad Amin, arrived during the Adagum Zafes and gained the allegiance of most Circassian tribes in less than a year. He frequently resorted to military force to ensure the loyalty of "peaceful" tribes such as the Egerukay, Mahosh, and Temirgoy, and to coerce Shapsugs and Natuhays who had not adopted Islam into abandoning paganism and Christianity. Amin continued Haji Mohammad's work of organizing a standing army with mixed results: by mid-1851 he had lost a series of series of battles and control of Circassia, but his forces regrouped and he had regained the allegiance of most of the tribes by the spring of 1853. When the Crimean War began, the Circassians seemed to be close to creating a unified state, albeit one that was now under mortal attack.[27]

Betrayal

The war Urquhart wanted finally came in 1853. Once again, Circassia appeared to have sincere supporters who would help them in what was now the final stage of their struggle for survival. As it turned out, geopolitical calculations on the part of England and France left them empty-handed once again and even placed St. Petersburg in a better position than before the war to drive the Circassians from their homeland.

It's really no surprise that the European powers didn't take Circassia's dilemma seriously. Revolutionary movements were appearing all over Europe: the peoples of Palermo, Venice, Lombardy, and Piedmont were rising against the Austrians; the Balkan peoples were challenging the Ottomans; and the Poles were rebelling against the Prussians. In such a political climate, Circassia's war for survival with Russia must have seemed of little significance. Still, a small group in England remained dedicated to the project of focusing the war on Circassia, thereby liberating the nation and, more importantly, creating an obstacle to Russia's complete control of the north coast of the Black Sea. Edmund Spencer returned to the region in 1851 and published a new memoir in 1854 in which he argued for direct intervention. By landing in Circassia, Spencer wrote, England and France would have an ally numbering in the tens of thousands who knew the terrain well. Although he based his case for intervention on economic concerns, predicting that, if the Russians gained complete control of the North Caucasus, they would soon take Iran, Turkey and perhaps India, Spencer wove a humanitarian plea for the Circassians into his argument:

> Surely if there is a spark of humanity or justice to be found in the cabinets of the two great Western powers, whose united action at the present moment is sufficiently powerful to control the destinies of the world, it is time to put an end to this most unjust and barbarous war. . . . They are fully aware that Russia has not the shadow of a right to the sovereignty of the Caucasus, yet they hesitate to perform an act of justice; but now that she has thrown at their feet the gauntlet of defiance, the honour of their respective countries calls for a vigorous and decisive course of action; and their first movement ought to be to declare Circassia and the whole Caucasian isthmus independent—a tardy act of justice, but totally consonant with international law.[28]

Spencer followed his appeal with an ominous prediction of the consequences, should England fail to defend the Circassians:

> On the contrary, if, slumbering in fancied security, we should still
> hesitate to pursue the bold line of policy dictated to us by the pres-
> ent crisis, it is highly probable that in a few years, when the gal-
> lant inhabitants of the Caucasus shall be subdued or, what is more
> likely, exterminated, their country incorporated with the Russian
> empire, and Persia and Turkey chained to the chariot wheels of the
> conqueror on his march to India, our children will bitterly regret the
> pacific tendencies of their forefathers.[29]

British supporters of Circassia had reason to believe the French would be
enthusiastic about the prospect of running Russia out of the Caucasus. Paris
had been dabbling in the region from at least the time of the Russo-Turkish
War of 1787–1792, when dozens of military specialists served alongside the
Turkish army. In the first decade of the nineteenth century both France
and England signed treaties promising financial aid to Turkey and Iran in
their anti-Russian campaigns in the Caucasus.[30] The French also understood the economic potential of commerce in the Caucasus and were working to obtain preferential trading rights with the Circassians during the
mid-1800s.[31] At the outbreak of the Crimean War, however, French interests were elsewhere. Intent on both expanding his influence in the Levant
and achieving a dominant position on the European continent, Emperor
Louis Napoleon was content to antagonize Russia over obscure questions
of religious privileges for Christians living in the Ottoman Empire. While
Lord Palmerston was still promoting an aggressive agenda in the Black Sea,
Napoleon was clearly out to get as much as he could for as little effort as
possible. Furthermore, while the British public was becoming enthusiastic
toward their nation's involvement in what seemed to be an inevitable war,
the French people were overwhelmingly opposed.[32]

The Russians had all but surrendered the Black Sea coast before the war
even began, abandoning their fortresses entirely in early 1854 in response
to rumors that the Circassians were preparing a major assault.[33] The Russians had insufficient troops in the region to engage in a full-scale war and
had Chechen leader Shamil and his forces to contend with as well.[34] The
Ottomans increased their generally anemic assistance to the Circassians

and sent Sefer-Bey Zanoko, an elderly Circassian aristocrat who had been living in Istanbul, as their choice of leader of the Circassian forces.[35] English, French, and Turkish officers treated him as the legitimate head of Circassia when he arrived in Sukhumi, Abkhazia, but rather than unify the Circassians, this created a split in loyalties.[36] Muhammad Amin still had a good deal of support and was not interested in a power-sharing arrangement. Rather than working together, the two pretenders to Circassian rule spent much of their time fighting each other.[37]

Palmerston was certain England could use the war to deprive Russia of both the Crimea and the Caucasus and worked to influence public opinion in his new position as home secretary. However, in December 1853 Lord Granville suggested a raid on the Russian fleet in Sevastopol, and Napoleon quickly endorsed the idea. When Palmerston presented his final plan to the cabinet in March, it contained no reference to the North Caucasus, although he still had grandiose plans in the Black Sea and hoped that Sevastopol would be the first step toward driving Russia from the coast.[38] In March 1855 the British Navy took what might have been a preliminary step in that direction, bombarding Novorossiysk ten miles south of Anapa on the twelfth and the thirteenth. Realizing the hopelessness of the situation, the Russians abandoned both Novorossiysk and Anapa, leaving the entire coast of Circassia open to British contact with the Natuhays and Shapsugs. However, the Turks installed Zanoko in Anapa, who drew his support from the Bjedukhs and Abzakhs.[39] When the British asked to occupy the fortress at Anapa that summer, Zanoko refused, citing Circassian sovereignty.[40] In one of the greatest blunders in Circassian history, Zanoko deprived his people of their last chance for international support. In September and again in December, he attempted to mount his own offensives but was driven back on both occasions.[41] After the fall of Sevastopol on September 8, Louis Napoleon wanted to move into Eastern Europe and seize more territory as bargaining chips in future negotiations for peace. However, France was suffering from inflation and facing possible unrest; Napoleon's inner circle and nearly the entire French population were eager to get out of the war immediately. The French drew up a peace proposal, and since the Ottomans were militarily exhausted, the British faced the choice of concluding peace or fighting Russia alone. In November Palmerston reluctantly agreed to begin the peace process.[42] Napoleon's proposal was delivered to

St. Petersburg, and the new emperor, Alexander II, after conferring with his ministers, decided to seek a way out of the war.[43]

The Circassians' fate was sealed in the negotiations leading to the Treaty of Paris in 1856. The British representative, the Earl of Clarendon, insisted that the Kuban River be the border between Russia and Turkey, but France and Turkey both agreed with Russian representative Filip Brunnov that the Treaty of Adrianople set the area south of the Kuban (i.e., Circassia) as Russian territory. Thwarted on that front, Clarendon then tried to stipulate that Russia would not be allowed to rebuild fortresses on the Black Sea coast, but again France supported Russia.[44] An amnesty for nationals who fought on the side of the enemy was included, but it was extended only to nations Russia had previously controlled; because the Circassians had never been under Russian control, they were excluded. In effect, the treaty granted Russia tacit approval to deal with the Circassians as they wished: the Circassians' land was declared Russian territory, but the Circassians themselves were denied the rights of Russian subjects. When the treaty was debated in Parliament in May, both Palmerston and Clarendon countered conservative challenges on the Circassia question by claiming (falsely) that Britain had never been in contact with the Circassians and that they had no desire to be under Turkish rule.[45]

While the Porte's decision was probably based on the realization that it would never rule Circassia, the reasons for France's opposition to British proposals on Circassia are unclear. John Curtiss argues that only Britain was strongly motivated to continue the war. Russia would never have agreed to terms dictated by Britain alone, and not only did France not have any good reason to continue the war, public opinion also left Napoleon little choice but to sue for peace.[46] On the other hand, J. B. Conacher claims that there is evidence that Russia would have made concessions if the French had supported Clarendon.[47] Certainly, the French never showed any interest in North Caucasus throughout the war, and since Napoleon faced the threat of domestic violence, it's no surprise that Britain found itself standing alone in defense of the Circassians. As for Palmerston and Clarendon's comments in Parliament, they were of course attempting to defend a treaty they couldn't change against political attacks. In any case, with the conclusion of the Treaty of Paris, the British—after twenty years of promising support—walked away from the Circassians and left them to their fate.

The Aftermath of Crimea

As if things weren't going badly enough, at the end of the Crimean War a new power struggle broke out between Muhammad Amin and Sefer-Bey Zanoko. Amin continued to press for an alliance with Shamil under the Islamic banner, while Zanoko promoted Circassian national unity. Although Amin had more support on the ground Zanoko had the backing of the Porte and international recognition. In May 1856 Zanoko convinced Amin to travel with him to Istanbul and ask the Porte to choose a single leader. It was a trick, however, for as soon as Amin left, Zanoko moved rapidly to establish complete authority and asked the Porte to officially recognize him as the leader of Circassia. The Porte refused, Amin returned, and the two continued to wrangle. In the middle of all this, an international force led by Teofil Lapinski arrived in February 1857 to help the Circassians, although it failed miserably.[48] Some European agents remained in Circassia, but they could do little more than watch as the tragedy unfolded.

On the other hand, the Crimean War left the Russians well situated to complete the conquest of Circassia. Just before the war, thirteen new Cossack stanitsy were established, and in May 1857 construction of Fort Maikop was begun.[49] From there the Russians were able to rebuild the decrepit Labinskaya Line, following the Laba River into the heart of Circassia.[50] More importantly, the Russians increased their military presence in the North Caucasus by shifting the entire Crimean Army to the Black Sea Coast.[51] To support these troops, St. Petersburg interpreted a provision in the Paris Peace Treaty that allowed it to keep a small fleet in the Black Sea in the most liberal fashion possible.[52] Novorossiysk, a commercial port that was leveled in the war, was rebuilt to accommodate warships, and the Russian navy was able to bombard the Circassians along the coast while the army pressed them from the mountains.[53] Finally, because of Shamil's surrender in 1859 and the conclusion of the war in Chechnya and Dagestan, the Russians were able to move the Left Wing army to the Kuban, increasing overall troop strength by 1860 to approximately seventy thousand men.[54] The Labinskaya Line was rapidly reinforced with new troops, and by 1860 the entire Laba River valley was full of Cossack stanitsy while the native population was completely driven from the right (eastern) bank. The Russians now had enough troops to completely surround the Circassians.

There was still no concrete strategy, though. Unlike the northeastern Caucasus, where Imam Shamil was looked upon as leader, in the northwest no single person carried sufficient authority to negotiate on behalf of all the Circassians. There could be no definitive "surrender." At the same time, while England and France were currently too concerned with affairs in Europe to pay attention to the Caucasus, St. Petersburg feared that this could change very quickly.[55] It was in this context that Commander in Chief Alexander Baryatinsky placed General Nikolai Evdokimov in charge of military operations in 1860.[56]

Unlike Ermolov, there is little written on Evdokimov, and he left no memoirs himself. Historians such as Semyon Esadze and Rostislav Fadeev describe his military accomplishments, and Berzhe praises his "brilliance" repeatedly, but virtually nothing is said of his character or ideology. One account of Evdokimov that does reveal something of the man is that of Milenty Olshevsky, commander of the reserves in Kuban Oblast during the final campaign. Olshevsky was a veteran of Velyaminov's expeditions of the 1830s but subsequently had been involved in administrative affairs for some time before being reassigned to the Kuban. In his memoirs, he describes Evdokimov as an opportunist who "was never picky in the means he employed." He notes that "Baryatinsky was well-acquainted with Nikolai Ivanovich's military prowess, but also knew about his shortcomings," and that "having chosen him as his colleague and the director of the conquest of the eastern Caucasus . . . Alexander Ivanovich looked askance at his passion for personal gain."[57] Another revealing portrait is painted by Mikhail Venyukov, a unique figure in the final chapter of the genocide in the Caucasus. After completing his studies at the Imperial Military Academy in 1856, Venyukov became a geographer and traveled throughout Siberia before arriving in Evdokimov's headquarters in late 1861. Venyukov devotes a chapter in his memoir to what he observed in the Caucasus, and gives a perspective not found in any other account. He was clearly appalled at what he saw happening and had little respect for Evdokimov, whom he describes as contemptuous of his commanders and determined to drive the Circassians from Russia entirely:

> I can't help but remember a conversation with Count Evdokimov. . . . He took me to task for indicating the Bjedukhs on an ethnographical map of the Kuban region in 1862.

"When do you plan to publish this map?" He asked me.

"I don't know; that will depend on the Geographical Society; most likely at the end of next year (1863)."

"Well, you should know, most respected sir (this was the Count's usual epithet for a subordinate), that if you wish to make your map of current interest, then rub out the Bjedukhs. There, in Petersburg, they talk about humaneness, interpreting it falsely. I consider humaneness to be love for one's country, for Russia, her deliverance from enemies. So what are the Bjedukhs to us? I will expel them, like all the remaining mountaineers, to Turkey."[58]

This sheds an interesting light on the plan Evdokimov presented to Baryatinsky for the conquest of Circassia. On the one hand, he proposed the same strategy he used against Shamil: roads and fortifications would be rapidly constructed, followed by Cossack stanitsy. The stanitsy would be placed close together and linked by crossroads so each would have immediate support from several directions if threatened. Meanwhile the troops would canvas the mountains in search of auls and food supplies, which would be burned, and livestock, which would be seized. The Circassians would be hemmed in and left without food or shelter, and would have no choice but to surrender. In the Circassian case, Evdokimov proposed a measure that was not taken in Chechnya: all the natives—Abazas and Nogays as well as Circassians—would be deported either to the lowlands north of the Kuban River or to Turkey.[59] This is what Venyukov's map was meant to reflect. The Bjedukhs had agreed to be resettled north of the Kuban. However, as we can see, Evdokimov never had any intention to relocate the Bjedukhs or any of the Circassians to the lowlands.

Having been given permission to conduct perhaps the first ethnic cleansing in modern history, Evdokimov moved quickly. On June 20, 1860, Russian forces surrounded the Besleneys and drove four thousand families from their homes. Esadze claims the majority then voluntarily migrated to Turkey, but Olshevsky provides a different interpretation, stating that they "were sent to Turkey by the force of our arms in spring 1861."[60] Evdokimov then turned against the Natuhays and Abzakhs. The Russians had never had serious problems with the Natuhays, who occupied themselves with commerce, and they had very little contact at all with the mountain-dwelling

Abzakhs until they began to encroach on their land.[61] The Abzakhs agreed
to Russian demands in November 1859 and signed a truce with Evdokimov.
However, Olshevsky claims the treaty was a ruse to give the Russians time
to move more troops into the area and prepare for total conquest. An official report of 1864 corroborates this.[62] Likewise, Drozdov recalled that after
Muhammad Amin's surrender at the end of 1859, Russian negotiations
with him were intended only to allow them time to prepare for a massive
assault on Circassia.[63] Drozdov saw no battles throughout 1860 and noted
that during this time the Circassians became "quite good neighbors," but
he still approved of Russia's plan to destroy them, asking "would it be possible to have a half-savage republic within the borders of the Empire?"[64]

The Russians tried to conceal their determination to force the vast
majority of Circassians to Turkey from the Porte, framing the early deportations as short trips to Mecca.[65] In actual fact, the Russians used the
Mecca pretense as a way of stranding as many Caucasians as possible in
Turkey. In 1859 approximately 2,500 people traveled there to see what
the conditions were like, but when they arrived Russian officials confiscated their passports. The Ottomans, apparently becoming wise to the
Russians' scheme, began petitioning St. Petersburg to limit the number
of immigrants. By April 1860 the Porte was requesting that the Russians
restrict emigration, if not stop it altogether. Baryatinsky refused and tried
to persuade St. Petersburg that it would be in Russia's interest to allow
all the Circassians to immigrate to Turkey as long as they weren't allowed
to return. The results were quick in coming and did not bode well for
the huge numbers of Circassians who were to be deported over the next
four years. In early 1860 Russian consul A. Moshnin reported to St. Petersburg that the Circassians' situation was dire and that the Turkish government was not responding to their needs. Even Evdokimov wavered in his
determination to deport the Circassians as quickly as possible. In April
1860 he wrote to Prince Grigol Orbeliani of the "disastrous condition of
the mountaineers who immigrated from the Right Wing to Turkey" and
suggested that since Turkey was unable to accept further immigrants,
the process should be halted altogether.[66] This was only temporary. By
June he was petitioning to allow 442 Kabardian families to emigrate, and
bluntly stating that "as far as the threat that all the population might
emigrate, even if this were to be accomplished this would, in addition to

delighting us, bring us another real benefit: it would liberate us from a people who wish us ill."[67]

After seeing what awaited them, many Circassians wanted to return home. Baryatinsky admitted that refusing to allow Circassians to return was "technically illegal" and acquiesced to the requests of many of the early deportees. However, he suggested that those who returned should be settled "far from the Caucasus" among Cossack communities.[68] Those Circassians who belonged to "subjugated" tribes were to be "immediately sent to the interior of Russia for permanent settlement," while Shapsugs and Ubykhs were to be taken prisoner and offered in exchange for Russian prisoners. "If after three months the exchange doesn't occur," the Circassians were to be "sent to Siberia for permanent settlement." The Cossacks were none too happy with the plan to settle Circassians in their communities. Furthermore, a special committee determined in June 1861 that "settling natives of the Caucasus within Russia, in places that do not correspond with their way of life, neither from the point of view of climate or culture, will lead to their certain death."[69] Nevertheless, by the fall of 1861 a protocol for settlement of Circassians returning from Turkey stipulated that those who had accepted Ottoman citizenship, who had overstayed their passport, or who "didn't receive their passports separately under their own name," would be refused permission to return. Only those Circassians who had not sold their property prior to their departure would be allowed to return to the Caucasus (but they had all sold their property), and then only if the local administration "found it convenient to settle them in their former homes." Otherwise, they would be sent to locations in central Russia and Siberia, where they were to "surrender immediately to the local military command."[70] Financial assistance was authorized only for those too ill to work.[71] Thus, the establishment of a special regime for the Circassians, which would continue to treat them as a hostile force long after the war was over, was begun prior to the mass deportation of 1864.

Irma Kreiten's excellent analysis of the chicanery involved in this entire charade shows that "the pilgrimage topos was used in an inverse way in order to curb back-migration." The Turks didn't officially agree to accept the deportees but rather allowed them to enter Turkey "under the pretense of travelling to Muhammad's tomb."[72] The Russians issued the Circassians temporary passports, which meant that the Russian government had no right to stop the Circassians from returning home. To sidestep this legal problem, St. Petersburg used the argument that, since the Circassians chose to sell their property before leaving and since they took their entire families, their true intention was to adopt the citizenship of a foreign state. By this logic the Russian government wasn't guilty of issuing passports under false pretences. Instead, so the argument went, "the 'mountaineers' . . . left their homeland under the pretext of pilgrimage, hiding their true intentions from Russian authorities." St. Petersburg therefore claimed it was not obliged to honor their passports.[73]

War Minister Dmitry Milyutin put the process of deporting the returnees to central Russia on hold in late fall, stranding thousands of people without food or shelter. "These mountaineers," Baryatinsky's adjutant prince Grigol Orbeliani pleaded in December 1861, "bloated from starvation, barely alive, their children dying, are willing to go anywhere, even Siberia, if it would save their families from starvation." He made a case for allowing the Circassians to return to the Caucasus, arguing that "the disaster they suffered in Turkey will serve as a lesson for them" and would make them happy to accept Russian rule.[74] Evdokimov rejected Orbeliani's suggestion, insisting that all returning Circassians must settle in either Orenburg or Stavropol Oblasts, and that those who hadn't returned yet had to agree to those terms.

Evdokimov clearly defined his notion of "convenience" when deciding whether to settle Circassians in their former homes: such a condition did not exist. One problem was forty thousand Natuhays, who had agreed to Alexander's terms and were still living close to the Black Sea coast. In early 1862 Evdokimov decided to drive them out regardless of their submission, arguing that the "settlement of Cossacks and the total removal of the native population" were "essential" for the defense of the Black Sea coast. He suggested they be encouraged to emigrate: "if the Natuhays wish to take their entire society to Turkey, then not only will we not stand in the way, but will use all available means to achieve it at any time."[75] In fact, already in 1861 Evdokimov was using "all available means" to intimidate the Natuhays off their land, and Olshevsky writes that it was Evdokimov's policy of appropriating their land and giving it to Cossacks that caused the Natuhays to "voluntarily" immigrate to Turkey.[76]

The one voice in favor of compromise with the Circassians was Caucasus staff commander General Grigory Filipson. His reasoned and humane opinion was unwelcome in the company of Baryatinsky, Milyutin, and Evdokimov when the four met on October 15, 1860, to make a final decision about how to deal with the Circassians. According to Milyutin, Filipson argued that

> large scale operations against the Shapsugs and the Ubykhs would only drive these populous tribes to rage and might even provoke the interference of the western powers, particularly England, which did not recognize Russia's right to the eastern shore of the Black Sea. In Filipson's opinion, gentle measures in coordination with Muhammad Amin would achieve the same level of submission gained from the Abzakhs and Natuhays, solidifying our control of the region only through the establishment of several fortifications and roads, the establishment of an administration in line with their way of life and morals, and uninhibited trade with Turkey etc.[77]

Milyutin dismissed Filipson's "illusions," openly wondering how, after having served thirty years in the Caucasus, he could fail to see that the Circassians were contemptuous of "humaneness and gentleness." It is difficult to see how Milyutin could possibly know the Circassians' attitude toward "meekness" and "humaneness" when all the Russians had dealt them over several decades was wholesale destruction, pillaging, and acts of gross inhumanity. For his part, Milyutin repeated the argument that the deportation should take place as rapidly as possible to avoid international intervention: "The hostile position of Europe and particularly England, it would seem, should lead to a conclusion completely opposed to Filipson's proposal: this very hostility has provoked us to take definitive steps to protect ourselves, without wasting time, from foreign interference."[78] After Filipson presented his case, Evdokimov forwarded his plan for expelling the Circassians from the mountains.[79] The plan was then sent to a commission in St. Petersburg for consideration. The commission objected to Evdokimov's plan in the strongest terms, postulating that "the mountaineers . . . would prefer death to settlement on the steppes. . . . This [plan] would lead not to their submission, but to their extermination."[80] Nevertheless, Milyutin had already decided to go ahead, and he convinced Alexander to approve it on May 10, 1862.[81] On May 22 a committee was created to oversee the deportation of the Circassians, although the Russians, fearful of British intervention, packaged it as a plan for the Cossacks to colonize the "Kuban region."[82] As for what to do with the Circassians who refused to emigrate, Kreiten has discovered a document from 1863 in which Milyutin openly states that "if it is not possible to civilize the mountaineers, then they have to be exterminated."[83] In November 1863 Baryatinsky wrote Milyutin with a similar proposal:

> The coastal peoples, having been squeezed out, fully perceive their powerlessness and there is no doubt that they would submit to us if there was an actual place to settle them. But seeing as the mountaineers' desire to remain on the coast runs contrary to the accepted plan for the pacification of the western Caucasus, which requires we move them far from the coast, as well as the fact that the climate and terrain along the coast and the customs of the people who have lived there until now are so alien to life on the Kuban steppe, we must assume that we will need to exterminate the mountaineers before they will agree to our demands.[84]

The public efforts to conceal the true nature of the Russian plan, along with statements concerning the possible necessity to "exterminate" the Circassians demonstrates that Milyutin, Baryatinsky, and other decision makers were prepared to commit mass murder if necessary.

Milyutin's report of the meeting raises another interesting point. Filipson commented that the attendees were concerned only about the Shapsugs and Ubykhs, which meant that the rest of the Circassian nation was no longer considered a major issue. True, the Shapsugs and Ubykhs represented the majority, but the other tribes that Evdokimov drove out—the Abzakhs, Besleneys, Bjedukhs, Cherchenays, Egerukays, Hamysh, Hatukays, Mahosh, and Temirgoys—don't seem to have been a concern at the October 1860 meeting. Venyukov confirms that the Abzakhs were not only peaceful but helpful, reporting that in fall 1861 they "had friendly relations with us and regularly brought hay, chickens, eggs and so on to sell us. . . . I don't know how we would have fed ourselves if it hadn't been for the Circassians."[85] The assault on the Abzakhs was not prompted by any security concerns, but rather was based on Evdokimov's decision to rid the mountains of all its inhabitants.

Despite the peace treaty, Drozdov's division conducted raids throughout 1859 in Egerukay, Mahosh, and Abzakh lands, burning auls and running off the residents.[86] Drozdov describes a raid in December: "Dawn, the troops move toward the targeted aul, shouts of hurrah!, shots, the glow of burning huts, the cries of children, the wailing of women—what could be more terrible, more effective than this picture?"[87] After the survivors fled to the woods, Drozdov's unit burned the aul, leaving the villagers to fend for themselves in the dead of winter.[88] Such raids were abandoned in favor of large military operations in early 1860, when a Russian force attacked the Shapsugs on the south slopes. According to Olshevsky, their mission was to "annihilate the people living in the area, to make roads and crossroads through the forests" and military roads to the headwaters of the Sheps River. There fortifications would be built from which further actions could be conducted.[89] The rapidity of the Russian conquest sent the Circassians into a panic: throughout 1860, clans from the Besleneys, Temirgoys, Mahosh, Egerukays, and refugee Kabardians surrendered and were deported to the lowlands.[90]

In January 1861 Drozdov's battalion set out from Maikop, and even though the temperature dropped to -30 degrees Celsius, the Russians spent the entire winter and spring cutting roads. By May they reached the Egerukays, Mahosh, and Temirgoys who had fled the deportations of 1860. In violation of the Treaty of 1859 the Russians began cutting down the Mahosh forests, building roads and stanitsy and gradually driving the Circassians farther and farther into the mountains. While Filipson's troops kept Circassian tribes from communicating with one another, the army drove out the Besleneys from the left bank of the Laba, both violations of the treaty.[91] Word of the Russians' breach of the truce and their rapid progress reached the most distant Circassian tribes, and on June 25, 1861, a hase was held in Sochi where the representatives decided to create a unified government and petition the European powers again. One last delegation, including both Ottoman and British representatives, promised the Circassians international recognition by London, Paris, and Istanbul if they would unite against the Russians.[92] In response the Circassians built a *mejlis* (parliament) in Sochi, but troops under the command of General Kolyubakin came almost immediately and destroyed it.[93] Once again, the European powers did nothing.

Meanwhile, Evdokimov assembled the Verkhne-Abadzekhsky detachment to drive the rest of the Circassians from their homeland. This enormous force, numbering forty thousand, moved out from Maikop to run out the rest of the Abzakhs.[94] Abzakh elders came to Evdokimov and asked him to stop building roads and forts on their land, promising to live in peace and accept Russian suzerainty as they had agreed according to the Peace of 1859. In reply Evdokimov moved his troops into the Abzakh lands, accused them of violating the truce, and told them that if they wanted peace they would have to accept whatever form of government he chose to impose upon them. The Abzakhs asked if a deputation could be sent to St. Petersburg to confirm this was the government's intention, but Evdokimov refused. He finally allowed them to send the deputation to Baryatinsky in Tbilisi. When the deputation arrived, Baryatinsky was seriously ill (as Evdokimov knew), but Orbeliani confirmed that Evdokimov was acting on the orders of St. Petersburg. However, Orbeliani, one of the more humane officers in the Caucasus, suggested that they petition Emperor Alexander himself when he arrived in the region in the fall. The Caucasus commanders did not expect this, and they quickly moved to sabotage this last attempt to stop the ethnic cleansing of Circassia.

In St. Petersburg, Milyutin worked to influence the emperor into rejecting any proposal the Circassians made. In a letter to Alexander of September 10, the defense minister dismissed the deputation as a trick and a last resort by a defeated people:

> According to correspondence from Prince Orbeliani, a union recently created between three peoples who until now have not submitted to our rule—the Shapsugs, Ubykhs and Abzakhs—have sent a delegation to Tiflis for negotiations, and this delegation wishes to present itself to Your Majesty during Your trip to Kuban Oblast. . . .
>
> Long experience has sufficiently taught us how little real meaning any negotiations and treaties can have with the mountain peoples and how their conception of the conclusion of peace differs from our demands for submission. In this regard the peoples of the western Caucasus are less able than any others to obey any treaties. If a union really exists between them, then in this case these tribes are too accustomed to independence and discord, too little acquainted with civil order and authority to be assured that their submission is genuine.
>
> Therefore, it is my belief that the arrival of this deputation of the so-called Circassian tribes cannot have any results. This fact serves only one purpose: to clearly demonstrate the inescapable position

in which the tribes of the western Caucasus have now been placed, owing to the threatening advance of Cossack settlements on them. The mountaineers see the imminent and unavoidable end of the century-long war; they feel that the mighty Cossack population will completely crush them. . . .

With all this in mind, may I be so bold as to say that the appearance of the deputation and their peaceful overtures must not have the slightest influence on our plan of action in the western Caucasus. We must persistently continue to settle the region with Cossacks, for I cannot withdraw my longstanding view that, once the Cossacks have squeezed the natives from the mountains, we can permanently rule the region, create peace there and no longer be in danger of losing the Caucasus at the first break with the naval powers.[95]

Back in the Caucasus, Evdokimov was continuing with the conquest of Circassia unabated, rapidly constructing roads, forts, and settlements.[96]

Alexander arrived in Taman, forty miles northwest of Anapa, on September 23. According to Esadze, more than five hundred Circassians turned out to ask the emperor not to expel them from their homeland. He describes a touching (and unlikely) scene in which the Circassians laid down their swords, fell to the ground, and swore their fealty to the emperor.[97] Alexander continued his tour, eventually visiting the Nizhne-Abadzekhsky detachment on the twenty-seventh. The deputation arrived and met with Olshevsky, who counseled them on the accepted manner of presenting a petition to the emperor.[98] The next day the deputation, led by Ubykh representative Haji Berzege, met with the emperor. Alexander agreed to accept the Circassians' submission on condition that they fulfill all the administration's demands, including the return of Russian deserters. Venyukov, who was present, reports what happened next:

> After the Sovereign's gracious reception of the delegates, Count Evdokimov became frightened by the idea that the mountaineers would accept the Emperor's proposition and remain on their land "under Russian protection," which he didn't want to allow, having already made up his mind to expel them from the mountains to the last man. Aware of the Asiatics' naïveté, he ordered Colonel Abderrakhman [an ethnic Circassian], with whom he was close, to go to

them that night and convince them that they could now demand everything, even the withdrawal of our troops beyond the Laba and the Kuban, and the dismantlement of our fortresses.[99]

The statement Berzege gave the emperor the next day wasn't quite as belligerent as the one Abderrakhman had urged them to write, but it was a far cry from the declaration of submission Olshevsky had advised. It began by enumerating Russian violations of the Peace of 1859, followed by an offer of peaceful coexistence if the Russians would stop building roads and fortifications in the mountains and would take care in locating new Cossack stanitsy so that Circassian herding routes wouldn't be disrupted—essentially the same things the Circassians had been asking for since the 1760s.[100] Alexander was offended and gave the Circassians a one-month deadline to decide whether they wished to move to the lowlands, "where they will receive lands that will permanently be in their possession and where their civil government and courts will be maintained," or to immigrate to Turkey.[101] Whether the final form of the petition was influenced by Abderrakhman or not is unclear, but Venyukov was convinced that it was Evdokimov's plot that sabotaged the meeting. As for Abderrakhman, Venyukov admits that he couldn't tell if he believed Evdokimov or was a co-conspirator in the count's "insidious" plan "to dupe . . . his countrymen."[102]

The Circassian reaction was mixed. Evdokimov claimed that the Shapsugs and Abzakhs continually wavered between accepting resettlement in Russia and deportation to Turkey,[103] while Olshevsky reports they were prepared to fight to the last man: "The majority of the Abzakhs and Shapsugs living in the mountains didn't want to hear about immigration to Turkey. This majority included the careless youth and the 'baygushi,' i.e. people who had, so to speak, neither house nor home. 'We'll fight and die to the last man, but we won't leave our forests and mountains,' they shouted, worked up by the Ubykhs."[104] Nevertheless, after the October 1861 deadline set by Alexander, some of the Abzakhs, Shapsugs, and Ubykhs quietly prepared for emigration. The Temirgoys, Mahosh, and Egerukays argued among themselves at first, but, seeing that they were surrounded by Russian troops, surrendered and prepared to go to Turkey.[105] However, hundreds of thousands refused to move, confident that their traditional refuges in the mountains and canyons would protect them as they had so many times in the past.

4

1864

The state needed the Circassians' land, but had absolutely no need of them.

—Rostislav Fadeev

Ethnic Cleansing

The final Russian assault on Circassia began at the beginning of November 1861.[1] Estimating the remaining population of Circassia at two hundred thousand, the Russians assembled sixty-five combat battalions, twenty-five Cossack divisions, and one hundred cannons.[2] Mortally afraid that the British would interfere once they found out what he was doing, Evdokimov conducted the campaign with frantic speed. He was merciless even with his own men, driving them so hard that at one point they were close to mutiny. When he was informed that the men were dying from the furious pace, his response was "then let them die at work!"[3] The Cossack settlers suffered from Evdokimov's obsession as well. Many were brought in from parts of Russia quite different from the Caucasus and had no idea how to survive in the mountains. Furthermore, Evdokimov didn't bother to establish supply and communication lines before moving further on. The settlers, who were for the most part unarmed, were quickly blockaded by Circassian forces and suffered nearly daily attacks.[4] They quickly became so terrorized that they even stopped tending their fields and driving their herds, and as a result they and their animals starved.[5]

Evdokimov's callous disregard for the lives of Cossack settlers and his own troops was nothing compared to the brutality to which he subjected the Circassians.[6] Reports abound of massacres throughout the final campaign, some for revenge and others for expediency's sake. In an example of the former, in April 1862 the army gathered at the headwaters of the Fars River, forty miles northeast of Sochi, and attacked the Circassians and Abazas there. The battle continued up the mountains, where the Russians encountered a large Circassian contingent and were forced to retreat. In retaliation, the Russians slaughtered hundreds of other Circassians they came across who had run out of ammunition. According to Drozdov, "The mountain was covered with the corpses of bayoneted enemies . . . the soldiers were so embittered that it was hard to stop them."[7] However, the Russians more frequently found it expedient to use their cannons indiscriminately. In one instance, General Tikhotsky's men, who were building roads along the Belaya River in late June, bombarded the forest where the Circassians were hiding after their auls had been burned. Likewise, in September Evdokimov led the army up the Kuban and bombarded a Circassian aul across a gorge. Most of the residents fled into the forest, which Evdokimov bombarded for six hours straight. It was around this time that Drozdov heard that the Circassians "were taking oaths to die to the last man and let the Russians pass their corpses to their native auls."[8] Numerous massacres followed in which Circassian fighters were apparently making good on their oath. In one case hundreds of Circassians sacrificed themselves to cannon fire to allow "thousands" to escape.[9] Russian troops combing the mountains and destroying auls were repeatedly attacked by Circassian forces that stood their ground even when being showered with cannon fire.[10] Drozdov witnessed a battle in spring 1863 in which unarmed Circassians charged desperately, "literally throwing themselves on our bayonets, where they died."[11]

By the fall of 1862 Evdokimov was organizing his main unit, the Dakhovsky Detachment, for the next assault into the mountains while the Crimean Army was moving east from Anapa along the Black Sea coast.[12] The Natuhays there put up a fierce resistance, but by the end of 1862 most of their lands were occupied by Cossack stanitsy. "Their situation became intolerable," Berzhe recounts, "and Count Evdokimov, completely understanding it, found a brilliant way out of it by granting the free immigration to Turkey for those who didn't wish to accept Russian rule."[13] In an attempt to portray Evdokimov as a humanitarian who only wanted the most hostile Circassians sent to Turkey, Berzhe quotes a letter of September 17, 1862, in which Evdokimov wrote:

> The deportation of the tribes who refuse to surrender to Turkey . . .
> is without a doubt an important national measure that facilitates

the conclusion of the war in the shortest time possible, without
major problems on our side; but, in any case, I always saw this measure as an aid to the conquest of the western Caucasus that would
be possible without driving the mountaineers to despair, and would
provide a way out for those who would prefer death and destruction
to Russian rule.[14]

The unspoken implication was that, if need be, the Russians wouldn't have
hesitated to kill all the Circassians if they had continued to defend their
homeland.

In the beginning Evdokimov concealed his plan to drive all the Circassians to Turkey despite Alexander's promise to grant them land north of
the Kuban. As the campaign progressed, the entire Caucasus Command
adopted the position that the only acceptable number of Circassians in
the empire was none. In September 1863 Caucasus staff commander Alexander Kartsov argued (falsely) that since the Abzakhs repeatedly violated
the 1859 treaty, they couldn't be trusted anywhere within Russia's borders:

It has become obvious . . . that no matter what conditions of submission the mountaineers agree to, this submission will continue only
as long as the mountaineers wish to agree to it, and the first shot on
the Black Sea, or even some sort of forged letter from the Sultan, or
the appearance of a self-appointed pasha could start a war. Even if
we occupied the mountains with fortresses and connected them with
roads we would always have to keep a huge number of troops at the
ready in the mountains, and there wouldn't be a moment's peace.[15]

Kartsov concluded that "the measures taken against the mountaineers
may seem brutal, but they were compelled by bitter need. Fifty years of
experience has convinced us that there can be no peace with a people who
have no government and who don't even have the conception of the rep-
rehensibility of theft and banditry."[16] Likewise, on October 4 Evdokimov
unambiguously argued for the deportation of all Circassians to Turkey:

I have had the honor to report to Your Excellency about the value
and necessity of uninhibited dispatching of the natives of Kuban
Oblast for settlement in Turkey. . . . By force of arms, of course, they
will finally submit to our demands and settle where we direct them,

but after settling in their new locations they won't soon forget their former way of life and, because of their naïveté, will easily believe any promises that are generously made to them by Turkey. As long as military forces are here and the police keep various rumors from spreading, the native population will no doubt remain peaceful, but as soon as some pretext appears for foreign interference, naturally the intriguers in Constantinople will continue to keep the large native population here under observation and will direct all their efforts toward inciting them in a more or less hostile manner toward us. With this in mind, we will have to keep extra forces in the region, take special precautions and establish a special surveillance regimen in the western Caucasus and, consequently, spend excessive funds. Even the most insignificant circumstances that occur when we're not well-prepared can suddenly increase governmental expenses in Kuban Oblast. A rumor about some inconsequential acts of banditry by a small group of youths will undermine faith in the peace and security of the region.[17]

Evdokimov's emphasis on the cost of keeping the region secure was due to the emperor's ambivalence toward financing the deportation.[18] Alexander feared a huge outlay if large numbers of Circassians were deported, and in this letter Evdokimov was trying to convince the emperor that the cost of allowing the Circassians to remain would exceed the expense of deporting them.

By early 1863 the war was all but over, and further Russian actions can only be described as ethnic cleansing of a civilian population. Although the Shapsugs, Abzakhs, Ubykhs, and others continued to hold out throughout the year, Drozdov recalled that "the enemy, physically exhausted after tremendous losses suffered in frequent bloody battles with us, seeing our success in colonization and the mass of troops hemming them in everywhere, began to fall morally as well."[19] By May the Russians completely occupied the heart of the Bjedukh lands and were moving on the Abzakhs. Some Circassians came to the Russian camp to surrender while others stopped fighting and merely looked on from the woods as the Russians advanced. According to Drozdov, those who did surrender were given the choice to be settled where the Russians ordered them or to go to Turkey:

"the latter group, which constituted the majority of the population, were burning with hatred of us to the last minute, so much so that they didn't even try to conceal their feelings, expressing it in curses and generously heaping them on us—the involuntary cause of their deportation."[20] Venyukov provides a different picture:

> The war was conducted with implacable, merciless severity. We went forward step by step, irrevocably cleansing the mountaineers to the last man from any land the soldiers set foot on. The mountaineers' auls were burned by the hundreds, just as soon as the snow melted but before the leaves returned to the trees (in February and March). We trampled and destroyed their crops with our horses. If we were able to capture the villagers by surprise we immediately sent them via convoy to the shore of the Black Sea, and farther, to Turkey. . . . Sometimes—to the credit of our troops, rarely—there were atrocities bordering on barbarity.[21]

Likewise, General Zabudsky stated in August 1864 that "the population, consisting of people of all the tribes, exclusively given to theft and plunder, were driven from the Krai [District] through force and under convoy conveyed to the sea coast."[22]

In the summer and fall of 1863 the Russians met with very little resistance, mostly parties of fewer than fifty who had to be satisfied with capturing a horse or a few head of cattle, or occasionally wounding or killing a Russian soldier.[23] As Evdokimov reported, "the military actions carried out by the army of Kuban Oblast during the summer of this year have placed the mountaineers of the north face in an inescapable position, and have deprived them of not only the possibility, but even the hope of engaging us in battle."[24] By August the Abzakhs, "driven to extremes," were begging the Russians to allow them to remain in their homes until October so that they could harvest their grain, but Evdokimov refused.[25] In September the Russians occupied the Urup Valley in eastern Circassia and chased the Hamysh, Khan-Girei's perennially pro-Russian tribe, to the peaks of the Caucasus Mountains, where they were trapped. Most fled over the ridge, and by late summer Evdokimov's army crossed the mountains and started driving them toward the coast.[26] Because he had refused to allow them to stay until their crops were ready to harvest, they had very little food with them.

However devastating Russian actions had been throughout summer 1863, it was the fall campaign that showed the extent to which Evdokimov was willing to sacrifice Circassian men, women, and children to achieve his goal. The operation became even more methodical and thorough: a unit would travel up a river valley in search of auls, and the Circassians would flee into the woods. The Russians would burn the auls and any food they found, round up all the livestock, and go back down the mountain. There they would wait for a week or two and then travel even farther up the river valley in search of any makeshift huts the Circassians had built and would burn them. This process would be repeated two or three times until Evdokimov was satisfied that everyone was either dead or driven out.[27] This brings up an interesting point. In his field reports, Evdokimov regularly omits statistics on Circassians sighted or captured while meticulously recording other details. This stands in stark contrast to his description of Circassian attacks on Cossack stanitsy, in which he lists the approximate number of Circassians, locations, expeditions to find the attackers and rescue captured Cossacks, and so on. For example:

> On June 24 a party of bandits numbering approximately thirty surrounded the livestock and horses that were being tended by eight men near Egerukovskaya Stanitsa and seized 23 horses that belonged to a reserve battalion of the Dagestansky Squadron, the support artillery squadron for Company No. Four, and three officers. They made off quickly across the Belum. Despite intense searches by cordon troops from the Belorechenskaya Line all the way to Kurdzhinskaya Stanitsa, as well as by the reserves of that stanitsa up and down the Kurdzhips, the bandits weren't found. During this attack two of our men of lower rank were killed and one was taken prisoner.[28]

Compare this account with a typical description of an operation in an aul:

> On August 24 seven battalions, three dragoon squadrons, and one hundred Astrakhan Cossacks armed with six cannons crossed the Pshish early in the morning across from Shirvanskaya Stanitsa, went into the Shekots River Canyon, and setting up camp four versts beyond the stanitsa, started clearing the forest in all directions. This continued until the twenty-ninth.

During this time enemy auls in the region were burned.

A large number of Abzakhs gathered near the detachment but took no hostile actions.

On the evening of the twenty-ninth the detachment moved to a new position three versts farther along Shekots Canyon.[29]

The obvious question—what happened to the Abzakhs who gathered?—is never answered. Also, what does Evdokimov mean by "a large number?" Were there women and children? How many auls were burned? Were they occupied at the time? Evdokimov never answers these questions.

In other reports, Evdokimov mentions numbers of Circassians found, but in equally cryptic terms:

> Between October 19 and 26, in view of the total expulsion of the natives from the Abinsky Squadron's territory, the following movements were planned: in the forest around Krymskaya Stanitsa from the Abinskaya and Litkhirskaya Rivers to the Khablskaya, and then to the south along that road. . . . Several columns followed this route, penetrating into the most hidden places and forcibly cleansing the Cossack lands of the natives. During the operation forty-seven people of both sexes were taken prisoner.[30]

The area Evdokimov describes is about two hundred square miles in the heart of Shapsug territory. There should have been more than forty-seven people there, so the comment that the columns "forced the natives to vacate the Cossack lands" (zastavili tuzemtsev ochistit' kazach'i zemli) raises the questions: what happened to all but the forty-seven who were taken prisoner? Evdokimov also frequently mentions that people "of both sexes" were taken prisoner, but he never mentions children. Nearly all the reports resemble these two: Evdokimov rarely mentions where the prisoners wished to go, and when he does, he simply states with one exception they all wanted to go to Turkey. Considering the detail in Evdokimov's field reports in other aspects of the campaign, his failure to include these types of statistics or even explain what happened to the Circassians seems odd, at the very least. This also makes it impossible to say exactly what happened in the mountains. Were there more massacres? How many bodies did the Russians find? What did they do with the women, children, and elderly who were too weak to travel? These are questions that will most likely remain unanswered.[31]

In driving the Circassians to the coast between October and December 1863, Evdokimov knew very well that he was sending them to their deaths. As a regiment commander under Velyaminov in the 1830s, he had seen the extreme weather along the coast, the perpetual wind, and the frequent devastating storms. In late September he was warned directly of the consequences of forcing a migration in the fall when he visited his troops in Abzakh territory:

> While I was with the squadron, the Abzakh elders came to me on the twelfth to surrender, and requested permission to remain in their homes until spring 1864, but I categorically rejected this request. On my way back to Stavropol from the Pshekhsky Detachment, in Terskaya Stanitsa, where I was stopping for the night, on the thirteenth the most respected representatives of all the Abzakh clans once again approached me with a pledge of unconditional surrender, and explaining all the burdens of migrating just as the winter was about to set in, they asked to be allowed to stay in their current homes under any conditions the administration felt were necessary. In order to lighten the Abzakhs' burden and create order among them so that they would accept and fulfill our demands, I am sending them a pristav with special orders. I will report to the high command on how this situation resolves itself.[32]

Despite being told of the imminent suffering and death that they would face if they left their homes in the fall, Evdokimov still forced the Abzakhs out. By his own admission, these were people who "had never exhibited any military opposition" and always complied with Russian demands.[33] He expelled unarmed, peaceful civilians and sent them where he knew a majority would likely die solely because of their ethnic identity as Circassians. Additionally, he and Grand Prince Mikhail, who had assumed the position of Caucasus commander in chief after Baryatinsky's retirement, ordered that Cossack stanitsy must be constructed immediately, so that the Circassians would have no place to return to and would be trapped on the shore just as winter hit.[34]

Evdokimov's frantic pace continued throughout the fall, leaving a massive trail of devastation. By early November the Circassians managed to put together enough men to engage the Russians in battle, in part because the Ubykhs allied with the Jigets, an Abkhaz tribe. The Ubykhs themselves are a particularly tragic case: the Russians weren't even sure where they lived until 1840, when the Ubykhs attacked Nagavinskaya and Holy Spirit forts, which the Russians had unwittingly built on Ubykh land near Sochi.[35] After that, the Ubykhs became the Russians' implacable enemies. Evdokimov had been forewarned on October 18 that the Shapsugs, Ubykhs, and Jigets were preparing to attack, and by early November the Russians were moving along the coast toward the Ubykh lands. The battle took place on November 9 and 10 and ended when the Ubykhs ran out of ammunition and the Russians bayoneted those who didn't flee. Two more battles were fought on November 19 and December 10, after which the Russians captured sixty-four "people of both sexes" and took six hundred head of cattle.[36]

Those who hid in the mountains hoping to evade the Russians faced a slow death. French agent A. Fonville described conditions there:

> We met several Abzakh parties who were fleeing the Russians. These poor people were in the most pathetic condition: barely covered in rags, driving their little herds of sheep, their only source of nourishment, ahead of them, men, women, and children followed each other in silence, leading a few malnourished horses that were carrying all their household wares and anything else they managed to take along. . . . Such starvation raged that the unfortunate inhabitants, driven to extremes, ate tree leaves. This abject poverty gave rise to typhus, which resulted in a horrific number of deaths. . . . The starvation was horrific; many poor souls died from it, and we were unable to lend any support to the mountaineers; we were in extremely straitened conditions ourselves and frequently suffered deprivations. Without food, without shelter, we most frequently stayed in the woods and under cliffs, becoming victims to all sorts of foul weather. Sometimes an aul would take us in, but we avoided that out of fear of catching the diseases that were wiping out entire communities. In one aul, eight people died of typhus in the short time we were there.[37]

Russian authorities were well aware that Evdokimov's campaign was resulting in massive deaths among those who fled. According to one report, the Circassians' "attachment to their land up till now is so powerful that they frequently flee into some sort of dark ravine, where they die of starvation or the elements, rifle in hand, so that they may fire their final shot at the Russians for expelling them."[38] How many died in the canyons will remain unknown, but certainly the vast majority of the victims were women, children, and the elderly.

Catastrophe on the Coast

Those who were captured fared little better. Already exhausted, starving, and no doubt terrified at what was to come next, they were driven to the coast, surrounded by Russian cordons. Fonville describes the operation: "The inhabitants of the auls came running out of all the places where they had lived, which were subsequently occupied by the Russians, and their starving parties went through the country in different directions, leaving their sick and dying on the path. Occasionally entire groups of emigrants froze to death or were carried away by snowstorms, and we frequently noticed their bloody trails as we passed. Wolves and bears were digging in the snow and pulling out human corpses."[39]

The coast offered little refuge. The Circassians arrived just as one of the worst winters in recent history hit the Black Sea. In late December Kartsov wrote ambassador to Istanbul E. A. Novikov about the tragic conditions, describing the Circassians as "ruined, without food, without money and even without clothing."[40] Drozdov described similar conditions in the Sochi River valley, where his troops captured forty men, women, and children. The prisoners, "barely covered in rags, fell from exhaustion; mothers held their dead babies in their arms. Our hearts wrung with pain looking at these unfortunate souls, but we couldn't help them."[41] Despite it all, the Russian troops continued driving more Circassians to the coast, making things worse.[42] Although he was repeatedly informed of the catastrophe, Evdokimov refused to take any steps to relieve the situation—to allow the Circassians to return home and build dwellings, for example—and instead complained, "I wrote to Count Sumarokov as to why he keeps reminding me in every report concerning the frozen bodies which cover the roads."[43]

The Circassians had become one of the first stateless peoples in modern history. The Treaty of Paris had inadvertently created the situation: it declared Circassia a part of Russia but did not accord the Circassians the same rights as Russian subjects. The Russians could deal with them as they wished, and St. Petersburg chose to treat them as an enemy population occupying Russian land. Although the Ottoman Empire agreed to accept them, they were not yet Ottoman subjects while on the Black Sea coast and were technically out of the jurisdiction of any state. Deprived of all rights, they were at the mercy of the Russian military and had no way of seeking aid or justice.

Officially, the Circassians were to be dispatched from Novorossiysk, Anapa, Taman, and Sochi, but in fact the entire northeastern coast was covered with refugees throughout the spring and summer of 1864.[44] The first wave of boats left Trabzon, Turkey, in early January, the worst possible time of year on the Black Sea. The Circassians were dying in large numbers from typhus and smallpox, and the epidemics followed them into the boats. There the cramped conditions spread the diseases even more quickly than on the shore.[45] Not only refugees but entire crews were wiped out. After a Russian captain and crew met this fate in April, the Russians refused to transport any more on state-owned ships and left the rest of the deportation to the Turks and private vessels.[46] Evdokimov investigated the possibility of hiring ships to transport the Circassians, but his quibbling over fees delayed the exploitation of private boats for several months.[47] However, he apparently requested no food, water, or medical help.

Olshevsky describes the refugees' situation while awaiting deportation: "Conditions worsened daily for the Abzakhs and Shapsugs awaiting deportation to Turkey. At last their situation reached a desperate state, when everyone living along the coast of the Black Sea as well as between the main ridge and the Kuban were crammed into the mouth of the Tuapse River, the only point designated for departure to Turkey."[48] Just as the worst of the winter storms began to hit, more Shapsugs, Abzakhs, and others from the north side of the Caucasus ridge were forced down to the mouth of the Tuapse. Thousands of people were pressed together around Fort Velyaminovskaya "in the open air, constantly pierced by a cold wind, flooded by frequent rains, suffering from lack of provisions and lacking hot food." Olshevsky watched as "children, women and the elderly fell seriously ill and died, primarily of typhus and dysentery"; he described the shore as one giant graveyard.[49] Upon hearing these reports, the emperor asked Grand Prince Mikhail to inspect the situation. After a two-week stay on the coast, Mikhail covered up the catastrophe, reporting that there was no illness and that the Circassians had plenty of food and water.[50]

Olshevsky reported that the skippers, "particularly the Turkish," overloaded their boats and that many died from the crowded conditions. He placed part of the blame on the refugees themselves, "who . . . employed force and craftiness, and paid exorbitant fees to get onto a departing ship."[51] However, he affixed the ultimate responsibility for the disaster on Evdokimov: "Why did it happen that . . . the Abzakhs and Shapsugs, who were being driven from their homeland, suffered such horrific sufferings and deaths? It was exclusively because of the hurried and premature movement of our troops to the sea prior to the spring equinox. Had the Dakhovsky Detachment moved a month or two weeks later, this would not have happened."[52] As soon as the Abzakhs and Shapsugs had cleared the shore, more refugees appeared. By late March the crowd at Tuapse alone approached twenty thousand.[53]

Even as this catastrophe was unfolding, Evdokimov continued his campaign in the southernmost reaches of Circassia. Throughout January he annihilated Ubykh auls, leaving the villagers without shelter in what he himself described as "a severe winter."[54] Weather forced him to retire to a stanitsa for a short time, but by February he was again driving Abzakhs to the coast in heavy snow.[55] On March 31 his troops defeated the Ubykhs on the Godlikh River, after which the Russians were able to colonize the entire Sochi River valley.[56] As they moved into Qbaada Meadow, the Russians encountered a joint Ubykh-Jiget force on May 27. After their defeat in what turned out to be the final battle of the Russo-Circassian War, the Ubykhs and Jigets surrendered and prepared for deportation.[57] On June 2 [Old Style May 21[58]], Evdokimov determined that there were no more Circassians in the region and declared a day of celebration.[59]After a parade, a banquet was held on Qbaada Meadow at which Grand Prince Mikhail made a toast to the Kuban Cossacks and handed out medals for their victory.[60] According to Drozdov, "During the last part of 1864 and all of 1865 the battalions went back through all the conquered areas, driving out the mountaineer vagrants who remained, sacking the last den of Khakuchi bandits on the southern slope," and he concludes his memoir with the triumphant declaration, "in the mountains of Kuban Oblast now you might run into a bear or a wolf, but not a mountaineer."[61]

A Nation at Sea

Virtually every Russian officer and historian blames the Turkish skippers for the large numbers of deaths during the actual transportation. Archival materials show that while some Turkish captains deliberately overloaded their ships and cared little for the welfare of their passengers, there is much more to the story.

First, the primary blame must fall on the Caucasus military command, particularly Evdokimov, for insisting on completing the entire process as rapidly as possible. Those in charge showed no concern for the suffering and loss of life that would result or for the social, economic, and physical destruction that the deportation would cause in Anatolia. Evdokimov's letters to his superiors are filled with a sense of urgency, and he repeatedly stresses the need to accelerate the deportation, despite the Ottomans' repeated reports of the disaster that was taking place on their shores.[62] Even when October 1864 was chosen as a cutoff point for deportations for safety's sake, Evdokimov successfully argued to extend the deadline two weeks.[63] Even then, he kept shipping the deportees off throughout the winter, and in late December the Porte again petitioned the Russians to stop the deportation on humanitarian grounds.[64]

The Russians did little to help the Circassians make the journey safely. On May 17, 1863, Alexander ordered that those who chose to emigrate should pay their own way.[65] The Caucasus Commission pointed out that most of them had no money at all and convinced the emperor to give the refugees one hundred thousand rubles.[66] Initially funds were intended to go both to those being deported to the Kuban region and to those being sent to the Ottoman Empire. In January Evdokimov argued that the Circassians settling in Russia should be given material provisions and all the funds should be assigned to those leaving for Turkey.[67] In doing so, Evdokimov was not acting out of concern for the welfare of the deportees. He knew that all the funds would end up in the pockets of the skippers transporting the Circassians, and in fact much of it probably ended up in the hands of Russian officers. In April Evdokimov reported to Kartsov that "I am unable to keep track of an accurate distribution of the commission's funds," and requested that officials should be sent to the deportation points to deal with the issue.[68] It's unclear whether Evdokimov's request was granted, but for military personnel answerable to no one to distribute one hundred thousand rubles to stateless people who had no rights was not a formula for equity. How far would one hundred thousand rubles go anyway? Berzhe estimates it could be divided among approximately 470,000 deportees but qualifies this by adding that the total number of deportees was probably "significantly greater."[69] Taking Berzhe's guess, each Circassian would receive twenty-one kopeks, assuming all the money made it to the deportees.[70] The fees for transport averaged five rubles per adult, which meant that St. Petersburg's "help" was insignificant.[71]

The boats were indeed overloaded, with as many as three hundred persons squeezed onto ships designed to carry no more than a few dozen, so "there was not only no place to walk, but even lie down and sleep."[72] However, not all the boats were Turkish: according to one register, of thirty-seven ships that arrived at Novorossiysk between August and October, twenty-four were Turkish and thirteen were Russian.[73] Another register, dated May 29, 1864, lists fifteen Russian, eight Greek, and one Turkish, Moldavian, German, and British vessel each.[74] The Russians themselves were in charge of the deportation and certainly had some control over how many people were put on a ship. Some, sharing Evdokimov's concern that the British could put a stop to the deportation at any moment, most likely compelled the Circassians to board, just as other officers were no doubt moved by humanitarian concerns and felt that the massive suffering on the shore warranted taking the risk of overloading the ships. Greed was certainly responsible for some of the irresponsible behavior on the part of the Turkish captains, but as Bedri Habiçoğlu suggests, the skippers of some small fishing vessels barely capable of such a voyage had to have been motivated at least partially by sympathy for their coreligionists.[75] As for Olshevsky's claim that the Circassians themselves were to blame, not only were they helpless against the elements, disease, and lack of food and water on the coast, they also feared deportation to central Russia and even enslavement. This was mentioned in an official report of early 1864 as the primary reason the Circassians struggled to get onto the boats as quickly as possible.[76]

Nevertheless, the Porte, which seems to have been playing some sort of double game, deserves some of the blame for the disaster. Berzhe claims that beginning in 1859 Turkish agents were urging the Circassians to emigrate, and in July Russian ambassador Alexey Lobanov-Rostovsky asserted that Turkish emissaries were spreading rumors in Circassia that the two empires were exchanging their Christian and Muslim subjects.[77] On the other hand, Lobanov-Rostovsky mentioned in that same report that Ottoman minister of foreign affairs, Ali Pasha, had requested that the Russians slow down the deportation process. As late as fall 1863 the Turks were sending proclamations to Circassia urging them to stay and fight, promising the arrival of an international force, but in June 1864, just as the volume of immigrants was overwhelming Ottoman officials throughout the empire, the Porte issued a proclamation encouraging more to emigrate.[78] Whether or not Turkish agents really were agitating in the North Caucasus, the proclamation of 1864 is evidence of the Porte's gross irresponsibility. While it's likely that those Circassians who were actually given a choice would have chosen deportation to Turkey over deportation to the Kuban, the Porte proved itself to be either unconcerned about or oblivious to the consequences immigration would have for the refugees.[79]

After being driven from their homes, one painful task remained for the Circassians before they could board the ships: sell their belongings, mainly to the Russians who had just driven them out. In one final act of exploitation, the Russians bought up the Circassians' goods and livestock "for next to nothing," offering the deportees a fraction of the value of their animals and weapons, telling them the weapons would be forbidden in Turkey.[80] Even Evdokimov admitted that his soldiers were exploiting the Circassians' situation to obtain goods at far less than their market value.[81] What little they made from the sale of their possessions was immediately taken by the skippers for transportation. Evdokimov ultimately convinced St. Petersburg to pay for only the "very poorest" Circassians' travel expenses (although nowhere does anyone ever define "very poorest"), and even then only provided a maximum of two rubles per person, less than one half the fee being charged.[82] Such was the Russians' frugality that there were reports of Circassians being forced into selling one person out of every thirty into slavery to finance their own deportation.[83]

Evdokimov, Kartsov, Milyutin, and Grand Prince Mikhail wrote each other quite a bit during time of the deportation, but they didn't waste any time discussing the Circassians' suffering. Their main concerns were to minimize official expenses, to ensure that sick Circassians were transported on Turkish ships only, and to finish the deportation before the Ottomans demanded it stop.[84] Even in fall 1864, when there were so many corpses on the shore at Tuapse that Staff Captain Smekalov frankly stated, "I have no data because it's impossible to gather up [the dead],"[85] General Zabudsky's report is concerned with other issues: "In his report, Major General Geiman explained that the Khakuchis and the remnants of other tribes from the south face among them that have been squeezed to the shore by the Dakhovsky Detachment have been unable to find means to make the sea journey, and could very easily return to the mountains."[86] Around the beginning of September a single medic was dispatched to deal with the tens of thousands of ill deportees at Novorossiysk after the vast majority had already been deported.[87]

The last 10,600 Circassians that the Russians acknowledge remained at Novorossiysk for the winter of 1864–1865 faced the same fate as their fellow citizens the previous year, but rather than come to their aid, the Russians told the Ottomans to send either supplies or more ships to transport the deportees.[88] The Turks were able to take 6,000, leaving 4,600 stranded for the winter. Fortunately for those who remained, Olshevsky, the only high-ranking officer with any compassion, was in charge. He arranged for them to live with Cossack settlers until it was safe to travel again, thus avoiding another much smaller humanitarian disaster.[89]

How severely did the entire process cripple the Circassian nation? Only rough estimates can be made, but considering Berzhe's claim that 470,000 was a significant underestimate of the numbers deported, and Turkish demographer Kemal Karpat's estimate of 2 million between 1856 and 1876, we can safely say between 600,000 and 750,000 actually made it to a ship to be sent to Turkey during 1864.[90] If just 10 percent of the people driven to the coast died there (almost certainly an underestimate), the figure rises to between 660,000 and 825,000 people who made it to the shore. As for those who died en route from the mountains to the Black Sea coast, and keeping in mind a report that only 370 out of one party of 600 made it to the shore, a 10 percent death rate for this part of the journey is again extremely conservative.[91] This would mean that a minimum of between 726,000 and 907,500 Circassians were sent down the mountains. If we add to that another 10 percent who died hiding and fleeing from the Russians, the figure rises to between 798,600 and 998,225. Add to that the

Circassians who died as a result of battles with Russians over the last years of the war, and a potential population in 1860 of 1.25 to 1.5 million is not unreasonable. This means that, even with the most conservative mortality estimates, at least 625,000 Circassians died during Evdokimov's operations. Assuming an 1860 population of 1.5 million and an annual growth rate of 2 percent, the current population of Circassia would be approximately 30 million. The actual Circassian population worldwide, by contrast, is between 4 million and 6 million, with only 700,000 living in the Russian Federation.

The Case for Genocide

Did Russian actions in 1863 and 1864 rise to the level of genocide? While there were massacres, there was no coordinated effort to slaughter the majority of the Circassians. Also, the Russians didn't express any desire to exterminate the Circassians in their entirety based on their ethnic identity; indeed, men of Circassian ethnicity served under both Ermolov and Evdokimov, and tens of thousands were in fact given the option of settling in Russia. However, if we examine Evdokimov's ethnic cleansing and deportation operation in light of the UN Convention, it becomes clear that Russian actions constituted genocide.

According to the UN Convention, for an act to be considered genocidal it must be "committed with intent to destroy, in whole or in part, a national, ethnical, racial or religious group." Much debate has been conducted over the meaning of "intent," and as Robert Gellately and Ben Kiernan explain, frequently such arguments confuse "intent" with "motive":

> If a colonial power, motivated by conquest of a territory, or a revolutionary regime with the aim of imposing a new social order, in the process destroys all or part of a human group, does that constitute genocide? Not according to most popular definitions of intent. But in criminal law, including international criminal law, the specific motive is irrelevant. Prosecutors need only prove that the criminal act was intentional, not accidental. A conquest or a revolution that causes total or partial destruction of a group, legally qualifies as intentional and therefore as genocide whatever the goal or motive,

so long as the acts of destruction were pursued intentionally. In this legal definition, genocidal intent also applies to acts of destruction that are not the specific goal but are predictable outcomes or by-products of a policy, which could have been avoided by a change in that policy. Deliberate pursuit of any policy in the knowledge that it would lead to the destruction of a human group thus constitutes genocidal intent.[92]

A similar situation occurred in the Irish Potato Famine of 1846–1848, another event that has been labeled genocide by some researchers. Particularly pertinent to the Circassian case is Richard Rubenstein's discussion of intent and culpability concerning British assistant secretary of the Treasury Sir Charles Edward Trevelyan's decision to withhold readily available corn from the peasantry:

> Genocide is always a means of eliminating a target population that challenges an economic, political, cultural, religious or ideological value of the politically dominant group. Whether Trevelyan and his government planned mass death in Ireland is irrelevant. The famine could only be grasped as an "opportunity" to eliminate the Irish peasantry if the British government was prepared to accept mass death as part of the price of achieving that end. Had the government wanted to avoid mass death, its leaders would have elected other policies in the crisis. This they did not do.[93]

In other words, although Trevelyan and other British officials withheld food from the Irish peasantry primarily due to economic considerations, the subsequent starvation would serve the secondary purpose of eliminating a potentially hostile population.[94] The fact that the British didn't actively massacre the Irish is irrelevant: by denying them food, they condemned the Irish to death just as surely as if they had killed them outright. Evdokimov's campaign in Circassia had the same goal, although it was stated openly: to "liberate us from a people who wish us ill."[95] The main difference in approaches is that Trevelyan allowed a natural disaster to take its course while Evdokimov's troops actively induced starvation through the destruction of auls and existing food supplies. His was a deliberate policy designed to cause suffering and death among the entire population.

Although the stated motive was to compel them to surrender, Evdokimov certainly knew that the actions of his troops could not possibly lead to any other result than massive numbers of fatalities. The deaths of tens of thousands of Circassians were "predictable outcomes or by-products" of Russian actions: driving weak and starving people down a rugged mountain range in winter to a harsh coastal area with no food or shelter and no immediate means of transporting them. Upon being notified of the mounting catastrophe, Evdokimov not only failed to take action to alleviate the situation but actually exacerbated it by driving more refugees to the shore. By ordering the rapid construction of stanitsy, he also ensured that they would have no place to return to in order to find shelter. Likewise, Grand Prince Mikhail's false report about conditions could have no other motivation than to ensure more Circassians would remain trapped on the coast, where he knew they would die.

The case has also been advanced that the Russians did not deliberately inflict on the Circassians "conditions of life calculated to bring about its physical destruction in whole or in part," as the Genocide Convention phrases it, on the shores of the Black Sea. Rather, so the argument goes, the tragedy was a terrible accident due to the unexpectedly large numbers who wished to emigrate.[96] As the archival and eyewitness evidence demonstrates, this argument has no merit. Evdokimov and other commanders openly stated their intention to drive as many Circassians from the Caucasus to Turkey as possible. Evdokimov operated with the knowledge that thousands would die as a result of his policy, yet he followed through with it. Building on this fiction, Russian historians also argue that the government offered Circassians fertile farmlands to settle on and that they "voluntarily" rejected the offer, but this simply wasn't true. Olshevsky provides a vivid description of the so-called fertile lands the Tsar offered the Circassians:

> The squares of Ekaterinodar were impassable because of filth and swampiness. This occurred because of the frequent rains. . . . Illnesses, especially fever, due to the miasmas hidden in the swamps and quagmires in the city itself and the surrounding bogs and reeds . . . heat and suffocating air, from poisonous fumes rising from the bogs and swamps; throughout the year they were not only impassable, but difficult to move in due to mud and quagmires.[97]

Moving away from Ekaterinodar the countryside became more lifeless and yellowed. After passing Elizavetinskaya Stanitsa there were swamps and sandy fields filled with silt. Just after the Kopyl-skaya postal station was a kingdom of mosquitoes.[98]

Nikolai Lorer gives a similar description of the lands to which the Circassians who remained were directed: "All of the Black Sea region was surrounded by impassable swamps and flooded lands. Myriads of mosquitoes and flies swarm in the reeds and plague every living thing horribly. . . . In spring and fall there was such deep mud in the streets that communications were broken, and in some streets people even travelled in boats."[99] Because the Circassians had been driving their herds throughout the region for generations, they certainly knew what sort of land they were being offered. Furthermore, since the Russians had repeatedly violated treaties for decades, the Circassians had no reason whatsoever to believe in Alexander's promise that they would be given "permanent ownership" of the lands onto which they were settled. The fear of ultimate deportation to Siberia must have been another concern, since many Circassians had already been sent there.[100] There were also rumors that those who agreed to be relocated would be given to Russian soldiers as slaves.[101] Perhaps this is why many saw death at bayonet point and cannon barrel preferable to surrender, and why the few who were really given a choice preferred exile in Turkey. After seeing and hearing of Russian massacres during the campaign, they saw it as the best way to ensure that their families survived. This was hardly a "voluntary" choice, even in the cases where the Circassians weren't simply driven to the coast.

Two other definitions of genocide under the Convention are relevant in the Circassian case. First, there is no doubt that the Russians imposed "measures intended to prevent births within the group" upon the Circassians. By driving them to the coast, they were ensuring that the family life of the people deported would be grievously affected. Running entire families out of their homes in the winter and forcing them to walk down treacherous mountains to an open sea coast wouldn't simply disrupt their ability to procreate but would kill the majority of their children. "Causing serious bodily or mental harm to members of the group" is a form of genocide under the Convention, and this was a central part of the Russian strategy. In the words of Adolf Berzhe, "Evdokimov's plan was to base the conquest of the western Caucasus on the Kuban Caucasus Army, and by means of military lines and new settlements continually pressure the mountain tribes until it became completely impossible for them to live in the mountains."[102] In other words, the intention was to terrorize the Circassians: starve them and leave them without shelter. As Drozdov put it, "only horror could have an effect on the hostile mountaineers."[103]

The Circassian genocide was also one of the first examples of modern social engineering. Rostislav Fadeev called the conquest of Circassia "one of the most vital tasks in Russian history," and Berzhe concurred that only with the deportation of the Circassians could Russian security be permanently ensured.[104] Emperor Alexander had a more ideological vision, claiming in June 1861 that Russia was destined to "forever establish in [the Circassians'] place a Russian Christian population."[105] This notion of creating an entirely new order comes close to the concept of revolution as described by Eric D. Weitz, which requires a purge of some sort in order to create the new society: "the enemies have either to be reeducated, expelled, or murdered."[106] Fadeev states his case for deportation of the Circassians in nearly the same terms: "The Circassians, owing to their position along the coast, could never be firmly consolidated into Russia as long as they remained in their homeland. . . . The reeducation of a people is a centuries-long process. . . . It would have been exceedingly stupid to hope to transform the feelings of almost half a million barbaric people, independent from time immemorial, violent from time immemorial, armed and defended by impenetrable mountains."[107] Reeducation being impossible, expulsion became the preferred option, although the Russians didn't hesitate to drive the Circassians to their deaths and occasionally massacre them. The Russians looked for a way to force them out without killing every last man, woman, and child, although judging from correspondence between Evdokimov, Milyutin, and the commanders in Tbilisi, they were prepared to do so if need be. Future social engineers would either find no such option or simply choose the path of mass murder without bothering to consider other methods, but the Russians were their direct predecessors.

Another aspect of Weitz's article that is relevant to this case is his observation that "revolutions of the twentieth century invariably deploy the powerful metaphors of 'cleanness' and 'purity.'"[108] Throughout the reports of the campaign, Evdokimov describes the forced migration of the Circassians with the words "*ochistit'*" and "*ochishchenie*," literally "to cleanse" and "cleansing":

> The cleansing of the latter canyons of natives required a large number of soldiers . . .[109]

> Through all these actions of the Dakhovsky Detachment, the entire mountainous and inaccessible areas between the sources of the Belaya and Pshekha rivers were cleansed of natives.[110]

> In order to further squeeze this population and cleanse the land of the natives as much as possible . . . on the fifteenth of November three columns advanced to the mouth of the Defan.[111]

> On the first, second, third and fourth of December several columns went from the source of the Defan along the upper and middle reaches of the rivers annihilating the population, after which, having ascended along the Shapsugo and crossed over into Psekups Basin, they cleansed the left bank of this river of natives.[112]

One hundred and thirty years before the Serbian phrase *etnichko chishenie* became infamous around the world, Evdokimov had already conceived of the notion of "ethnic cleansing." His concern was the land, and the Circassians were little more than a pestilence to be removed.

5

A Homeless Nation

We are abandoning our Motherland, but she will never abandon our hearts.

–Circassian song

The Other Shore

The death and disease that beset the Circassians on the Black Sea coast followed them to Anatolia. Impoverished and ill, the deportees quickly learned their ordeal was far from over. In December 1863, after only a handful had arrived, Russian consul in Trabzon A. N. Moshnin reported that the refugees were dying so fast that "at the nearest cemetery . . . dead Circassians were buried so quickly and carelessly that the last rain uncovered the graves and hungry dogs ate off the hands and feet of the dead."[1] As tragic as this scene was, things would only get worse as the deportees began to arrive in large numbers.

Although it was the Russians who drove the Circassians from their homeland, the Ottomans were responsible for the disaster on their shores. Their offer to take in the Circassians was not strictly humanitarian: they had several reasons for wanting them to immigrate. Anatolia had been suffering from a population shortage for most of the nineteenth century, and large areas of potentially arable land went undeveloped. It was hoped that the Circassians could colonize these areas and increase agricultural output. Also, because the Ottomans were losing territory from all directions, their tax base was steadily declining. The new population would be a source of additional revenues that could be used to enact the reforms the Ottomans had recently developed and hoped would save the empire. Memories of Circassian Mamluk rule in the Middle East from the fourteenth to the sixteenth century were still alive as well. They had given the Circassians a reputation "for military efficiency, if not often ruthless ability," and the Porte hoped to exploit them to control its own rebellious populations.[2] Circassians were also experienced at fighting the Russians and knew the Caucasus well. They and other immigrants from Dagestan and Chechnya would make excellent additions to the armed forces in case of a future war against Russia. The Porte also hoped that, as refugees, the Circassians would be grateful and become loyal subjects, serving as models for less cooperative peoples in the empire.[3] Finally, some Circassians could be settled in Rumelia and Bulgaria as a counterweight to the Christian populations there who were clamoring for independence.

Unfortunately, the empire had serious problems that made a successful integration of large numbers of refugees unlikely. Three wars with Russia in the nineteenth century had depleted the army, leaving the Porte incapable of defending much of its empire in the best of times. Establishing and maintaining peaceful relations between the Circassians and the peoples among whom they were settled turned out to be a task that required large numbers of well-trained troops, and the Ottomans didn't have them. Additionally, after the Crimean War the Russians started a massive colonization effort in the Crimean peninsula. Through intimidation and economic pressure they forced the majority of the Crimean Tatars to emigrate from their homeland, and between 1856 and 1860 perhaps as many as one hundred thousand immigrated to the Ottoman Empire. This placed a tremendous strain on the communities where they were settled, primarily the Balkans where large numbers of Circassians were also sent.[4] In settling the Tatars, the Ottomans already proved themselves incapable of dealing with large-scale immigration: food, shelter, and medical support were all insufficient, and thousands of Tatars and natives died. Naturally, the people of the Balkans were fearful when a second wave of refugees began to arrive.[5] This animosity made success even less likely there.

The cultural challenges facing the Circassians were enormous. While the Crimean Tatars spoke a language very similar to that of the Turkish Ottoman population, the Circassian language was completely unrelated to Turkish. This made it much more difficult to incorporate them into society wherever they were settled. The Circassians were traditionally pastoralists who never had a central government and instead used the martial code of adyge habze to regulate their lives.[6] The survivors who made it to the Ottoman Empire were the hardiest and most determined of their people, and had survived as long as they had through the use of violence. The trauma of being forced from their homes and witnessing the gruesome deaths of their loved ones on the journey had to have taken a psychological toll on them that we cannot even begin to imagine. Placing them on farms and expecting them to forget adyge habze and adapt to agricultural life turned out to be a herculean task. In addition to all this, the Circassians had no direct experience with European powers other than Russia. The Circassians must have assumed that the Russians' tactics in war—wholesale slaughter of villages, organized banditry, and so on—were accepted European practices in wartime. When crises arose in their new homes, some Circassians responded according to the Russian model. The European community was aghast, and the Circassians unwittingly earned a reputation for barbarity that followed them wherever they went.

The Ottomans were indeed incompetent when it came to settling the Circassians, but the Russians did all they could to deceive them about to the volume and pace of deportation. In 1859, even as the Tatar experiment was making it clear that undertaking mass immigration too rapidly was risky, the Russians began negotiating with the Ottomans about Circassian migrations. Initially they promised that no more than fifty thousand people would be sent and that the process would be gradual.[7] The first migrants, mainly wealthy Kabardian aristocrats, arrived in 1860 and 1861 and were quickly settled in new locations, but the forced deportations of 1863 quickly overwhelmed the Ottomans. They repeatedly asked the Russians to slow down the flow of immigrants, but St. Petersburg responded that thousands of Circassians were already at the beach and that if the Porte did not accept them at once they would be driven inland, resulting in a great deal of bloodshed.[8] The Ottomans asked the Russians to at least wait until after winter 1863–1864 to begin the mass deportation, but already in December five thousand Circassians had arrived at Trabzon, and more people were being forced to the shore and loaded onto boats.[9] Ambassador Novikov told the Porte that since the majority of the Circassians were "hostile," there was nothing St. Petersburg could do. Kartsov's reply was more cynical: "the Turkish government itself engendered hostility toward the Russians and friendliness towards Turkey. The deportation is the result of these actions, and therefore the Caucasus Command is powerless to stop the mountaineers from going to Istanbul."[10]

Many who boarded ships never arrived. The number lost at sea will forever remain unknown, although eyewitnesses reported multiple instances of ships sinking. Among the very few recorded incidents, 100 people drowned when a ship sank at Ereghli, and 174 lost their lives when a ship ran aground at Inebolu.[11] According to another report, of 2,718 Circassians put on a ship bound for Cyprus, 839 died during the journey.[12] Sometimes crews threw overboard anyone who appeared to have a contagious disease. There were also cases of apparent sadism: in one incident people were tied up and thrown overboard from a ship bound for Cyprus, and the bodies that were recovered showed signs of mutilation.[13] Those who were fortunate enough to survive the journey found that the Ottomans were completely unprepared to deal with the half million or more sick and starving people who arrived.[14] The shortfall of resources was so great that at one point the British ambassador at Istanbul proposed unsuccessfully that the British government supply either financial or material aid. Donations were solicited and received from private citizens as well as the sultan, the grand vizier, and other government officials, but it was far from enough. What funds did arrive were embezzled on a massive scale.[15] In just a single case, one auditor found that 60,000 kuruş (£1,200) sent to the town of Geyve had been pocketed by the local administrator.[16]

There was no place to set up quarantine zones at first, sanitary conditions quickly deteriorated, and disease continued to spread as it had on the Circassian shores. The refugees were put in makeshift camps or left in the open air.[17] According to one report, five hundred to seven hundred people died daily at Samsun, and in February 1864 there was so much disease and so many poorly buried bodies that many residents of Trabzon abandoned the city.[18] On June 22 Moshnin wrote: "At the beginning of the deportation there were 247,000 people in Trabzon and its environs, and 19,000 died. Now 63,190 remain. About 180–250 people die every day."[19] French doctor Sulpice Fauvel estimated that two-thirds of the refugees died from disease in 1864.[20] Nor was the epidemic limited to the refugee camps: wherever the Circassians were settled, the native population and foreign consuls began to suffer from disease.[21] Even the cattle the Circassians brought were diseased and may have been responsible for a plague in

Trabzon Province in 1865.[22] In the face of all of this, Moshnin continued to recommend rapid deportation, and even proposed that Turkish vessels be allowed to carry contraband to Russia if the skippers would agree to bring Circassians back.[23]

Desperate to clear Trabzon, the authorities sent the refugees farther inland to places "famous for their unhealthy climates."[24] Mismanagement and corruption by local bureaucrats coupled with food shortages and disease brought the Circassians to abject poverty in short order.[25] Many were reduced to begging or menial chores, and some even sold their children into slavery, perhaps believing they had a better chance of survival.[26] Others, primarily young people who lost their parents and had no other options, turned to banditry to survive. This created fear throughout the empire that Circassians would start pillaging wherever they were settled.[27] Conflicts between refugees and natives broke out frequently. Those same corrupt officials who embezzled funds that were meant to avert this tragedy subsequently blamed the problems on the Circassians.[28] Many refugees petitioned the Russian consuls, promising to accept any conditions, including conversion to Christianity, for permission to return home, but these petitions were uniformly rejected. So desperate were the Circassians that on more than one occasion they laid siege to Russian consulates.[29] They finally began to flood into Istanbul, which they saw as a sort of "promised land" where a real life was possible. In July 1864 the Porte told officials in Trabzon a crisis was looming, but the governor there claimed he couldn't stop them. By October more than fourteen thousand Circassians had arrived, overwhelming the city's resources. Several ships were sent to Trabzon, and the Circassians were once again forced on board and taken to even more distant destinations. Nevertheless, the flow of refugees to the capital continued from Samsun and elsewhere.[30]

The Ottomans ultimately settled the Circassians in a line from Sinop on the Black Sea to Antakya on the Mediterranean, about 250 miles north of Beirut. Many settled on the Uzunyayla plateau in central Anatolia, and from there some moved to underpopulated areas nearby that had agricultural potential.[31] Requests for settlement and resettlement came in faster than the government could handle, so the Porte arbitrarily declared that those who had already been located were "permanently settled."[32] Nevertheless, petitions continued for at least twenty years, and groups of

Circassians would often flee from the places they'd been settled in search of friends and relatives.[33] Homeless and technically in violation of Ottoman law, many resorted to begging and banditry. Even those who remained where they were settled were left on their own to find a means of survival. Most were able to establish new homes, but others were forced to resort to marauding simply to survive. In addition to the panic over Circassian pillaging, the natives were afraid that the refugees would bring smallpox and would start the slave trade. The Porte tried to control the situation but was only partially successful; as a result, the stereotype of Circassians as bandits was reinforced, even though it was only a small minority that was actually involved in banditry.[34] Fear of Circassians became so great that Muslim and Christian communities alike protested whenever a plan was announced to move Circassians into the region.[35]

The Circassians' reception in the Balkans was no better. Abzakhs had already begun to arrive in May 1863 and were sent north along the Black Sea coast and west into Bulgaria.[36] By June 1864 there were more than 100,000 Circassians in the coastal cities of Constanta and Varna. Smallpox spread among the Circassians, and soon the beaches were transformed into mass graveyards. A quarantine zone was set up, but it was easily evaded through bribery, allowing disease to move inland. From Constanta and Varna the refugees were ultimately sent farther up the Danube to Shumen, Adrianople, and ports along the river that were supplied with little or no provisions.[37] In July another 60,000 Circassians arrived in Constanta and Varna and were sent west into Bulgaria, Serbia, and Kosovo.[38] All in all, there may have been as many as 250,000 Circassians in the Balkans by the end of the summer. To get an idea of the demographic impact, the population of the region was between 3.5 and 4.5 million, which meant the refugees represented between 5 and 7 percent of the entire population. This was on top of the 100,000 Tatars the Balkans had just absorbed.[39]

The British and French complained repeatedly that the Porte had settled the Circassians in Rumelia to increase the Muslim population in a predominantly Christian region, and there is some evidence that the Circassians were spread throughout Bulgaria as a potential force to suppress nationalist uprisings.[40] It must certainly have appeared to the Christian population of the region that this was the purpose of so many Muslims being settled in their midst, and this contributed to tensions between the two groups.[41] At the very least, settling Circassians among Slavic Christians who were in the nascent stages of rebellion was reckless, and in this sense the Ottomans must share some of the blame for the massacres of Turks, Tatars, and Circassians that took place during the Russo-Turkish War of 1877–1878. However, while the Circassians did have poor relations with their Slavic neighbors, Sarah Rosser-Owen has found evidence that animosity of the Bulgarians was at least partly the work of Russian agents. She also notes that the interethnic problems were overstated by foreign observers and that there were ample instances of interethnic cooperation.[42] Abdallah Saydam also gives an alternative explanation for the why the Porte placed the Circassians in Rumelia. In their correspondence, many officials involved in the immigration believed that it was a place where the Circassians could be quickly settled onto productive land.[43] The Russians were aware that there wasn't enough land in Anatolia to settle all the deportees and agreed that they would have to be permanently placed elsewhere.[44] The logical choice would have been the Balkans because the other Ottoman-held lands would have required a much longer sea journey and resulted in even more deaths. As for the British and French protests, Saydam notes that in the 1850s thousands of Crimean Tatars were transported to Rumelia on British and French ships with no objections coming from London or Paris. He postulates that by the 1860s, since the British were encouraging the Bulgarian independence movement, the portrayal of Muslim immigration to the region as an Ottoman plot to stifle Christian aspirations for independence served the their narrative well.[45]

The entire burden of supporting the refugees fell on the villagers themselves. Ottoman policy was to settle in villages no more than one Circassian family for every five Turkish families so that the Circassian families would be assimilated. This policy meant that Circassian clans and even individual families were broken up and settled far from one another.[46] On the other hand, Circassians were frequently given priority for the best land, which naturally caused resentment. Foreign observers claimed that in some places in Bulgaria residents had even been forced to give up their homes to Circassians.[47] Compounding the problem was an investigation that found that the land distribution had been manipulated by corrupt local officials. The Ottoman government proposed a radical redistribution project that did nothing but cause more conflicts between older and newer settlers and generate a string of lawsuits.[48] Other unforeseen problems cropped up: in one case in the 1870s, land given to the Circassians in central Bulgaria disrupted the cattle industry and caused a severe economic crisis. And of course there were uprisings: in May 1867 so many Circassians in Kosovo rebelled that hundreds of troops had to be brought in.[49]

Despite the troubles, most Circassians began to integrate themselves into Ottoman life. Very early on they began applying for positions in the government and law enforcement. Beginning in 1860 Circassians and others from the North Caucasus were given opportunities to enroll in military colleges as well as technical institutes. The North Caucasus peoples thus became well integrated into the civil structures of the state and society very quickly. The Ottoman government created several Circassian cavalry regiments, usually with a five-year term of duty. At the same time the Ottomans did what they could to destroy the Circassians' traditional way of life. They tried to break the influence of tribal leaders, often by exiling them far from their people.[50] Many of their customs were outlawed. Resettlement petitions were rejected more and more frequently, and the Circassians had no choice but to learn Turkish and become members of communities where they were distinct minorities. The process of assimilation had begun.

The First Balkan Ethnic Cleansing

If someone were to suggest that, after all they had been through, nearly half of the Circassians who survived deportation would again be chased from their homes and subjected to starvation, exposure, and massacre, one might think it was nothing more than a cruel joke. Unfortunately, this is what happened during the Russo-Turkish War of 1877–1878, when the Circassians in Rumelia were expelled from their new homes, along with their Tatar and Turkish neighbors.

> The proceedings of the Russians and Bulgarians in Bulgaria and Roumelia have convinced the Mohammedan inhabitants that it is the deliberate intention of Russia either to exterminate the Mussulman population by the sword, or to drive it out of the country. . . .
>
>   The shocking outrages which, there can scarcely be any doubt, have been committed upon them, either by the Russians or by

Bulgarians under their protection, have struck terror amongst the Mussulman populations. They are now flying, as the Russians advance, to escape the fate of their brethren, and are seeking refuge in the Turkish fortresses and Istanbul. . . . I saw yesterday several large steamers filled with these unfortunate creatures—men, women, and children. They arrive here in the utmost distress and misery, having abandoned or lost all they possessed in the world. It is feared that this great crowd of fugitives in Istanbul, which will be daily increased, may lead to disorders in consequence of the feelings of indignation to which their presence and their sufferings may give rise among the Mahommedan inhabitants of the city, or that, as was the case when the Russians expelled the Circassians from their country, the crowding together of so many starving persons may cause a dangerous epidemic.[51]

British ambassador to Istanbul Austen Henry Layard wrote this letter in July 1877, while the Russians were still on the borderlands of Rumelia. As the invasion progressed, the suffering described by the ambassador increased tenfold.

By the 1860s the same nationalism that swept across much of Europe earlier in the century had infected the Bulgarians. Of course, centuries of Ottoman misrule had given them more than enough reason to rebel. Sentiments got out of hand, and radical elements massacred around one thousand Muslim villagers in May 1876.[52] In response the Ottomans created bands of irregular troops called the *başıbozuks* to put down the rebellion and defend Muslim villagers. Some of these units were Circassian, and their response was predictable. All too familiar with massacres perpetrated by Slavic Christians and acquainted with only one method of response, they turned against the Bulgarians with a fury. Fanning the flames of ethnic conflict were Bulgarian partisans, who would burn a Circassian village in order to provoke retaliation and as an excuse for the Bulgarians to petition the western powers for intervention.[53] Of course, the act of Slavic Christians burning their villages could not but fill the Circassians with even more horror and rage, and the violence escalated. Plunder, rape, and murder were committed by both sides throughout 1876, acts that became known as the "Bulgarian Horrors." However, since the British supported the Bulgarians, only one side of the story was told in Europe, and the brunt of the blame for the "horrors" unfairly fell on the Circassians.[54]

The European powers delivered an ultimatum to the Ottomans demanding what would have amounted to a secession of the Balkans. The Porte refused, and Russia declared war in April 1877. The Ottomans knew they had no chance of victory and ordered an evacuation of the Balkan provinces.[55] The Russians moved quickly through Rumelia, and a horrific ethnic cleansing ensued. When the Russians encountered villages with mixed populations, they would disarm the Muslims, give the weapons to the Bulgarians, and incite them to slaughter their neighbors.[56] When there were no Bulgarians, the Russians would simply massacre the entire village. Cities such as Varna and Rusçuk were subjected to cannon bombardment, and hospitals and medical stations flying the Red Cross were the prime targets. In the face of these atrocities, tens of thousands fled into the wilderness. The ethnic cleansing wasn't limited to Muslims; Jews and Armenians were raped, murdered, and forced to run for their lives as well.[57] Thousands of Circassians fled from their new homes, but some refused to go without a fight. Reports of "bands of armed Circassians" roaming the Balkan countryside sent the already overwhelmed Ottoman government into a panic, but the Circassians quickly saw the hopelessness of their position and fled.[58] Those who managed to remain behind were driven out in 1879 as part of a policy of the Russian-backed provisional government to force them to emigrate.[59]

Throughout July the roads were covered with starving refugees.[60] By midmonth they were arriving in Adrianople, many of them "mutilated and wounded by the Bulgarians."[61] One French observer reported seeing children with bayonet marks, including a five-year-old girl who was "literally covered with lance and sabre wounds."[62] Judging from the reports, this was only the tip of the iceberg. Russians, Bulgarians, and particularly Cossacks raped, tortured, and massacred fleeing Muslims "with no regard for age or sex."[63] The reports were so horrific that at first Ambassador Layard didn't believe them, but on the first of August he assured the British foreign secretary that atrocities were being committed:

> The Porte has published many detailed statements on the subject, but as they are open to suspicion of being exaggerated, I have

thought it better not to forward them to your Lordship. There now can be little doubt that the Cossacks and the Bulgarian Christians, by whom they are accompanied, are burning Mussulman villages, driving away their inhabitants, and in many instances slaughtering them. The evidence to this effect appears to be perfectly clear, and coming from many independent and trustworthy witnesses, can scarcely be called in question.

It would scarcely be proper to accuse Russian Generals and the Russian Government of deliberately encouraging or sanctioning the extermination of the Mahommedans of Bulgaria; but I fear that there are influential persons who believe that the only way to Russianize Bulgaria, and to reduce the province to a complete state of dependency on Russia, is to destroy or remove the whole Mussulman population from it. . . . Constanta, Varna, Adrianople, and many other cities and towns, are full of refugees who have escaped the Cossack lance and Bulgarian knife to die of famine and disease.[64]

Layard also suggested that the Russians were attempting to instill so much hatred between the Christians and Muslims that they could never live side by side again. Justin McCarthy postulates that the Russian military command ordered the massacres in order to "spread fear among Turkish villagers, which would cause them to flee the advancing Russian armies" and would thereby hinder Turkish military operations.[65] However, massacres continued even as the Muslims fled.[66] If the Russians were trying to frighten the Muslim population into fleeing in order to block roads and distract the Turkish army from military concerns, then why would they attack and kill the fleeing refugees? Perhaps the Russians realized that, in contrast with the Circassians who had been sent across the Black Sea, these people could easily walk back to their to their old villages. Therefore, they escalated their tactics from simple deportation to wholesale slaughter. It also raises the question: if this is how the Russian military behaved in full view of international observers, then what did they do in the mountains of Circassia, hidden from the eyes of the world? Particularly interesting in this regard is a telegram from Akhmed Pasha to the Ottoman interior minister on July 9, 1877, that reports "the enemy is seizing defenseless villages and, after having destroyed them with cannon fire, is massacring the defenseless villagers. They are committing outrages upon the women, after which they are put to death."[67] Likewise, on July 14 the British consul at Adrianople reported that Russians were burning villages and "killing the inhabitants."[68] These last two reports in particular place Evdokimov's failure to report what happened to the Circassians in villages that were burned in 1863 and 1864 in a new and ominous light.

As the Russians advanced throughout the fall and winter, the Muslims fled further south and fell victim to starvation, disease, and the elements just as the Circassians had in the Caucasus. The mass exodus

> took place in the depth of a bitter Turkish winter. Thousands per-
> ished of cold and famine. Mothers, driven to desperation, deserted
> their half-frozen children. Sick people lost their protectors and were
> left to die, or were thrown on the scanty bounty of others nearly as
> unfortunate as themselves. . . . Most of those who escaped crossed
> the mountains, and at length reached Gumurdjina, which was the
> farthest point to which the Russians penetrated. Hearing there was
> safety to be found here, 80,000 refugees at one time occupied the
> Caza of Gumurdjina. Of these, in three months, 10,000 were carried
> off by disease, exposure, etc.[69]

One can only imagine the psychological impact this would have had on the Circassians, who had barely survived an identical tragedy brought upon them by the same nation only fourteen years earlier.

The Porte's attempts to relocate the Circassians from Rumelia were met with suspicion and fear. The memory of Circassian bands preying on Turkish communities after the first round of relocations in the 1860s had tarnished all Circassians with the label of bandit. No one wanted Circassians to settle in their regions. When forty thousand were placed in Adapazarı, forty miles east of Istanbul, a deputation complained to Ambassador Layard that they "lived almost in a state of siege." Layard promised to look into it with the help of Sir A. Sandison. However, Sandison "was scarcely surprised to hear of the excesses committed by the Circassians, as these people, having been hunted out of Europe, and having been deprived of all they possessed, had been sent into Asia without any provision having been made for their maintenance and support. The consequence naturally was that they were compelled to starve or to rob, and they, not unnaturally, chose the latter alternative."[70] The Ottomans couldn't make any provisions because they were nearly bankrupted by the war and the task of dealing with hundreds of thousands of indigents. In March 1878 there were 180,000 refugees in Istanbul, 50,000 of which were Circassian. The government was laying out a huge sum every day in order to feed these people and had to call upon charitable organizations to help supply food and clothing.[71] This, coupled with the loss of the entire Balkan region as a tax base, ensured that the disaster the refugees faced in Istanbul would follow them into the provinces.

As the Circassians in the Balkans were being driven from their new homes, their compatriots in Anatolia were fighting for a chance to regain their homeland. At the outbreak of war the Turks formed twenty-eight Circassian cavalry squadrons that played a key role in what would become known as the Abkhaz diversion. On May 12, 1877, about one thousand Circassians landed at Gudauta, Abkhazia, and began arming the local population. The Russian commander panicked and, after the Turks began shelling Sukhumi on May 14, the Russians evacuated the city. The Circassian operation, combined with the assault on Sukhumi and a second Circassian landing south of Sochi on May 23, forced the Russians to divert troops from the main theater of the war but was doomed to failure. The Circassians and their local allies did manage to harass the Russians over the next two weeks, and word of the expatriate landing reached Chechnya. Inspired by these developments, a Chechen named Haji Ali Bey declared himself imam, and a brief renewal of the Caucasus War ensued. As for the Circassians, once the Russians had beaten back the Turkish army and it became clear that the issue was no longer the capture of their former homeland but rather the defense of the Ottoman Empire, they deserted in large numbers.[72] So ended the Circassians' first attempt to regain their homeland. It wouldn't be their last.

6

Survival in Diaspora

Where Circassians settled on Turkey's frontiers, the cemeteries grew
faster than the trees.

—Suleiman Pazif

In 1881 British captain Claude Conder arrived in Amman during a campaign against Druze tribesmen. The town had been uninhabited as
recently as 1876, and Circassian migrants were just beginning to reclaim
the ancient site of Philadelphia.[1] Conder described the physical and psychological damage the settlers were suffering and painted a less than
hopeful portrait:

> The Circassian colony at Amman is one of several planted by the
> Sultan in Peraea. These unhappy people, chased from their homes
> by the Russians, and again driven from their new settlements in
> European Turkey by the late war, are now scattered in the wilder-
> ness, where land has been assigned them to cultivate. They have,
> however, the listless and dispirited look of exiles who find it impos-
> sible to take root in the uninviting district to which they have been
> sent. Hated by the Arab and the Fellah, despoiled of money and pos-
> sessions, and having seen many of their bravest fall or die of starva-
> tion, they seem to have no more courage left, and will probably die
> out by degrees, or become scattered among the indigenous popula-
> tion. Our appearance at Amman at once aroused their apprehen-
> sions. They believed us to be the pioneers of a Power which was
> about to seize the country, and anxiously inquired whether they
> would be allowed to remain where they were in case of an English
> or French occupation. It was in vain that I protested that our work

had no connection with politics. The Emir begged hard to be made
the confidant of a secret which, he insisted, we knew, and I was at
length obliged, in order to get rid of him, to express the opinion,
that whether French or English took Syria, there was no reason to
suppose his settlement would be disturbed, or that he would (as he
seemed chiefly to fear) be given up to the tender mercies of Russia.

It is from such incidents, not less than from the faces of the dead
looking skyward on the field of battle, that a man may judge of the
sorrow which is brought upon the weak and poor by the restless
ambition of conquering races.[2]

Despite the overwhelming challenges and the bleak prospects for success,
the Circassians survived. Less than twenty years later, Miss A. Goodrich
Freer passed through quite a different town:

A sudden turning at the ford of a rapid stream revealed the town of
Amman, lying in a narrow valley between low but precipitous hills.
Most of us were utterly unprepared, after six hours of riding across a
lonely tableland, to find an orderly town of 10,000 inhabitants, of an
aspect so superior to anything we had seen since leaving Jerusalem,
or even, so far as the actual town is concerned, to Jerusalem itself,
that an explanation seemed necessary, and the statement that the
population was Circassian was, geographically, an added perplexity.
The houses, built partly of mud brick and partly of ancient material
like those of Madaba, were well placed, most had porticos and bal-
conies, and some were enclosed with well-swept yards.[3]

As time passed, the Circassians who settled in Syria, Palestine, and particularly Transjordan established a good life and even prospered. At the same
time, the process of assimilation took its toll and put up barriers between
the migrants, their homeland, and each other.

The voyage of the Austrian steamer *Sphinx* was a grim portent of the
coming trials. In March 1878, after having been chased out of Rumelia,
about three thousand Shapsugs once again found themselves at sea headed
for unknown territory. Intending to land at Latakia, Syria, a storm washed
forty people overboard and forced the ship to seek refuge in a Cypriot port.
There several hundred more were killed when the ship caught fire.[4] Those

who succeeded in making it to Syria were held in the same primitive conditions as they were on the Black Sea coast, the Turkish shores, and the refugee camps in Greece and Istanbul. Utterly disillusioned, many asked if they could return to Rumelia and live under Christian rule. Some Turks were granted permission, but the European powers refused to allow the Circassians to return.[5] Once assigned a new location, the refugees had to cross desert terrain the likes of which they had never seen to reach the wilderness where they would have to build their new lives.

As always, the Porte had more than the welfare of the refugees in mind. Shipping them to Syria would have two benefits: the settlers could reclaim barren land and add to the agricultural output of the empire, and perhaps more importantly could serve as a stabilizing force in the region against the Bedouins and Druze. With this in mind, the Porte sent tens of thousands of Circassians to Syria and Transjordan, where they became true pioneers.[6] There was no government and certainly no law enforcement. The lands given them were technically Ottoman property, but the Bedouins considered the Circassians squatters on their pastures and appropriators of their springs. It was also clear that the Circassians had been sent there as agents of the Sultan and were loyal Ottoman subjects. Because Arab nationalism was on the rise, such people could not be met with anything other than suspicion. The Circassians also looked different, dressed strangely, and, like many minorities, kept to themselves. A few may have known some Turkish, but at first none spoke anything but the most rudimentary Arabic. Their traditions frequently conflicted with Arab mores too. For example, traveler Jane Hacker mentioned that the Arabs were horrified when they saw Circassian men and women dancing together at celebrations. Sometimes trouble became too much and the Porte would intervene and even round up particularly aggressive tribes, but for the most part the Circassians were on their own.[7]

To be fair, the Porte did attempt to settle some refugees in the more hospitable areas near the coast in Lebanon and Palestine, but stories of Circassian "atrocities" in Bulgaria had reached the Christians of Lebanon, making conflict likely if Circassians were settled there. Farther south, Palestine was just being claimed by Eastern European Jews as a safe place for emigration from Russian chauvinism, and the Sultan thought it wise not to settle more Muslims in that particular region.[8] Nevertheless, a few Circassian villages were established there in 1878. In 1918 Arthur Ruppin reported on the progress they had made, noting that "they have introduced advanced agricultural methods and are skilled in animal husbandry." In contrast to the stereotype of Circassians as lawless bandits, Ruppin described them as "cleanly, diligent, and courageous."[9] Around four thousand Abzakhs and Shapsugs live in two Israeli villages today. Seeing the Arab/Israeli conflict as ethnically rather than religiously based, the Circassians have remained neutral. The Israeli government has granted them many rights, including instruction in the Circassian language after sixth grade and a great deal of cultural autonomy.[10] However, the vast majority of the Circassians deported from the Balkans settled in Syria and Transjordan.

Syria: "The Siberia of Turkey"

The Circassians' new home in Syria was not a pleasant one. The Syrian provinces were among the most troubled in the empire, with Arab nationalist fervor growing and Bedouin, Druze, and Maronite communities demanding independence. The idea of using North Caucasus exile communities as a barrier between these unruly provinces and the Ottoman heartland had already occurred to the Porte: in the mid-1860s thirteen thousand Chechens were settled in eastern Syria to repel Bedouin and Kurdish attacks. The Chechens' fate did not bode well for the Circassians: disease, war, and desertion had killed or driven off all but five thousand by 1880.[11] The Porte hoped that establishing an entire line of Circassian villages would create a major military force that could repel nomadic attacks and protect the empire's heartland.[12] How many Circassians actually arrived in Syria is impossible to say. The Russian consul believed that more than forty-five thousand arrived throughout 1878 while Turkish researcher Izzat Aydemir puts the figure at seventy thousand.[13]

Before they could be dispersed throughout the Syrian *vilayets* (provinces), however, the Circassians had to be temporarily housed in the port cities. Their undeserved reputation had preceded them, and local authorities at Beirut, Acre, and elsewhere often refused to allow the refugees ashore, and in some cases even ordered the ships back to sea. Those who were allowed to disembark were left in the open air with the bare minimum of provisions.[14] An outbreak of smallpox in 1878 and multiple outbreaks of malaria made it difficult to convince local chiefs to accept the Circassians and settle them inland.[15] Very few of the refugees had anything of value, so the Wali of Damascus levied a tax to provide food—always an effective way to create resentment. Even then the refugees began to starve, and some resorted to banditry while others were forced to sell their children. Thousands more flooded into Tripoli demanding to be sent back to Istanbul.[16] Most were sent on to settle in Aleppo, Alexandretta (modern Iskanderun, Turkey), Homs, Hama, Damascus and its environs, and Transjordan. Much of this land was very poor; even experienced agriculturalists would have had a tough time. The Ottoman government didn't supply enough seed and equipment, and many starved to death in the first years.[17] Driven to extremes, some refugees fled back to Anatolia while others stole to survive. Several colonies failed as the settlers either died or left for more successful communities.

Settlements were particularly concentrated on the Golan Heights. A relatively inhospitable place with rocky soil, cold winters and frequent high winds, the region was abandoned when the Circassians migrated there in 1873 from Sivas in Anatolia and took up their former occupation as pastoralists. A few hundred Balkan refugees joined them in early 1878. Passing through the area at the time, British traveler Laurence Oliphant provides a good description of the Circassians in the first stages of building their future cultural center, Quneitra:

> About 300 Circassians were busily engaged in the first stage of building a village for themselves. They had chosen a site which had evidently been that of a town at some former time, for large square blocks of stone were abundant. Those who had not succeeded in getting a roof over their heads were temporarily sheltered by roughly improvised tents, and all were hard at work making a new home for themselves. . . . They were quite amiable so far as we were concerned, but were too busy to bestow very much attention upon us, and their residence in Bulgaria had accustomed them to the sight of specimens of Western civilization, so that we were no novelty. The women and children were hoeing and weeding in the newly-made gardens. The men were either hauling stone in creaking arabas drawn by bullocks—a sight which must have been altogether new to the neighboring Bedouins, who had never seen a wheeled vehicle in their lives—or were building the walls of the houses.[18]

Oliphant visited the village chief, Ismael Agha, and learned that there were approximately three thousand colonists in seven villages who, "although they had only been there a few months, were already establishing themselves in comparative comfort."[19] After his visit, Oliphant reflected on the undeserved reputation of the Circassians:

> The Circassians have such an evil reputation, that to undertake their defence, even with the Turks, is an ungrateful task; but I know few races who possess such noble qualities, though they have been subjected to experiences which have tried them beyond their power of endurance. It is probable, if a few Highland clans had been dotted about the southern counties of England a hundred and fifty years ago, and told to provide for themselves, that their former habits of life, combined with the absence of any sufficient means of subsistence provided for them by Government, would have resulted in their taking what did not belong to them.
>
> The chronic condition of warfare in which the Circassians had always lived, engaged in a lifelong struggle for independence against an overpowering enemy, developed in them sanguinary instincts, to which, in fact, they owe their successful resistance during so many years; while the methods by which the Russians conducted the war were precisely those which they themselves were accused of using in Bulgaria. The severity of the order of the Russian general commanding in Circassia, immediately prior to the Crimean war, is a matter of history; and the people could not therefore know the extent to which they were outraging civilized instincts by following the example of their Christian enemies. There can be no doubt that the exasperation following their conquest and expatriation, their extreme poverty and distress, and the close contact into which they were brought in Bulgaria with people of the same race and religion as their hated and traditional foes, proved a combination of influences more powerful than a high-spirited and almost totally uncivilised people could resist; but they are capable of the strongest personal attachments, and of the most generous and chivalrous instincts. If their ideas as to the value of life and the sacredness of property differ in degree from those of Europe, it is not because by

nature they are greater murderers and plunderers than other people, but because they have lived under circumstances which made murder and robbery the necessary conditions to their existence.[20]

Oliphant was somewhat surprised when he learned the Circassians were worried about the Bedouins, but their concerns were well justified: in August 1880 the Bedouins launched a major attack. The Circassians held their villages, forcing the aggressors to withdraw and agree to an armistice, but other tribes were determined to drive the Circassians out, and attacks became a way of life. Nearly all the villages were quickly militarized and were usually able to defend themselves. Frequently the Circassians had to fight two tribes at the same time, and, while they were generally better armed, their numerical inferiority led to many casualties. Such feuds continued until the mid-twentieth century.[21]

The Druze were a particularly threatening force. Just as the Circassians were settling in Syria, this eclectic religious minority was reaching the limits of its tolerance of Ottoman rule. Because it was now well known that the Circassians were brought in partially to maintain order, the Druze saw them not simply as squatters but as an enemy to be wiped out. Throughout the 1880s parties of Druze warriors attacked the newcomers' villages. In 1889 a truce was arranged, but it fell apart in 1894 when a band of Druze attacked a Circassian wedding party and killed the bride. As often happens, this isolated event was the catalyst that triggered a full-scale war. In late May a Druze army of perhaps ten thousand attacked the village of Mansour but were driven off by a combined Circassian force.[22] Despite the efforts of Circassian elder Khosrow Pasha to resolve the conflict, the Druze continued to mount attacks. In fact, the Druze weren't waging war against the Circassians per se but against the Ottoman Empire itself. The decisive battle began on November 19, 1895. A two-thousand-man Druze army was met by a joint Circassian–Bedouin force led by Mirza Bey. In the heat of the battle, an Ottoman cavalry division arrived to reinforce the Circassians, and the aggressors fled. The Druze, who after all were only defending what they believed to be their land, suffered tremendously for their attacks. The Ottoman forces followed them into their heartland and burned their capital. Then they joined with the Kurds and burned a number of Druze villages. The Ottomans forcibly disbanded all Druze military units, after which they called in reinforcements and devastated them in one final massacre.[23]

Despite all the problems, the settlers successfully reclaimed the long-abandoned Golan Heights. Orchards sprung up and the land was quickly cultivated. By the turn of the twentieth century, the ruins of Quneitra had grown into a city of 1,300 with a standing police force and a telegraph line to Damascus. Arab, Armenian, Greek, and Turkish merchants came and set up shop, and the town became a thriving trading center. Still, the Circassians there and throughout Syria lived a deliberately isolated existence and continued their own customs. The aristocracy maintained its authority for decades, and the hase remained the primary governing mechanism. The Circassians operated their courts independently of Ottoman authority and would tolerate no interference.[24] They also never forgot their homeland. Reporting on his travels in Syria in the 1890s, Russian anthropologist Aleksandr Eliseev wrote of the Circassians' yearning for home: "The Circassians still miss their homeland terribly and reminisce about their native mountains, and these precious memories that they brought from the Caucasus are probably why these desperate cavaliers and cutthroats have accepted this mild Russian traveler with such honor and glee that you could never doubt the sincerity of these children of nature!"[25] Likewise, in 1906 Russian consul in Damascus Samsonov wrote: "I have never once heard that the immigrants are satisfied with their situation and have no desire to return to the Caucasus."[26]

However, things were no better in their homeland. Many Kabardians chose to emigrate throughout the 1890s and were sent directly to Syria. The last such group, numbering around 1,500, landed in Alexandretta in 1905 under the leadership of Anzor Talostane and was the cause of some turmoil. They had been promised financial aid, and when it failed to arrive they began to clamor for justice; soon a rebellion seemed imminent. At the same time, the Circassians who had arrived in Syria in the 1870s were also on the verge of rebellion. They'd been granted a ten-year release from taxes and military service, and—not surprisingly— there was trouble when the Porte announced the end of these privileges in March 1888. Many simply refused to pay their taxes, while others demanded that they be permitted to return to Russia. The standoff festered until February 1904 when Damascus Wali Nazim Pasha attempted to conduct a census to establish a taxation system once and for all. In response, the Circassians demanded more fertile land.

Nazim Pasha realized the gravity of the situation and explored the possibility of sending the Circassians back to the Caucasus, but the Russians refused. In September 1905 Khosrow Pasha, who by now had emerged as the first post-deportation Circassian statesman, convinced his compatriots to stay where they were and submit to taxation. This didn't placate the Kabardian newcomers, however. Nearly 250 of the settlers attacked the vilayet administrative building in March 1906, and this finally convinced the Porte to take the Circassians' problems seriously and create a special commission to address the issue. Even then there was little improvement, although Khosrow Pasha and Mirza Pasha, another respected Circassian leader, continued to press for assistance.[27]

Despite the minimal help they had received during their first years in Syria, the Circassians remained loyal to the Porte when World War I broke out. Not only did they successfully protect the Hejaz Railway, they also moved into the Anatolian provinces and defended the Ottoman rear lines.[28] However, with the Arab revolt of 1916 many Circassians saw which way the wind was blowing and joined the rebels, fighting alongside them until French motorized units crushed them in 1920.When the French Mandate was established in 1922, the Circassians hoped for some sort of recognition as an official minority, but France's main concern was protection of the Christian communities. Therefore, religion was made the determining factor in what constituted a "majority" or "minority," not ethnicity or language. The "national" majority, Sunni Arabs residing primarily in the urban centers, was in the throes of nationalist fervor and was determined to create a state united by the Arabic language. Benjamin Thomas White has even observed that "it was probably easier for arabophone religious minorities to join that 'majority' than it was for non-arabophone Sunni Muslim groups: Circassians, Kurds and Turks."[29] Furthermore, the Circassians' experience in the Ottoman army made them valuable to the French, who actively recruited them to serve in the paramilitary Troupes du Levant. Viewed as mercenaries by the Arabs, Circassian participation in the Troupes ensured that they would continue to be distrusted during the mandate's authority.[30]

The French did allow the Circassians to take steps to protect their culture. In 1927 a group of intellectuals led by Amin Samgug established the Circassian Society for the Assistance of Education and Culture and began the task of preserving the Circassian language. The society opened its first school in Quneitra in 1933. In 1927 and again in 1929, Samgug's group asked the League of Nations to grant the Circassians autonomy as a national minority in Syria, but was rebuffed both times. However, there were many Circassians who favored greater integration into Syrian society and actively opposed Samgug. When France recognized Syria's independence in September 1936, the pro-Arab faction tried to paint Samgug's group as collaborators with the colonialists. On September 9 pro-Arab Circassian youths clashed with Samgug's supporters, and in the aftermath Samgug's group was ordered to disband. He formed a new society, Jolan, which petitioned the Soviet Embassy in Paris to allow a mass repatriation to the Caucasus. After being turned down again, he disbanded Jolan and confined himself to cultural and educational activities until after the Second World War.[31] Other Circassians continued the fight, however. In 1938 the Circassians of Homs and Hama petitioned the Syrian parliament for autonomy. When their request was rejected, they sent the League of Nations a long statement enumerating the difficulties they had faced since their deportation and requesting special recognition. The problem was that the league feared that granting the Circassians' request would prompt demands from Kurds, Turkmens, and other minorities.[32] The league was willing to approve only one of the petition's ten points, which concerned the instruction of the Circassian-language in schools.[33]

Despite many Circassians' active support of Arab nationalists during World War II, at the end of the war an anti-Circassian campaign became so violent that many Circassian officers and cultural figures had to leave the country. Samgug jumped back into the fray, pleading to the government that autonomy was the only way to preserve the peace. Something akin to a zafes was called, at which the pro- and anti-Arab factions clashed over strategies. The pro-Arab group argued that autonomy would only alienate the Circassian community further, and that the Circassians should openly declare themselves Syrian citizens. Ultimately, Samgug's idea was voted down, although a significant minority chose to petition the Soviet Embassy for permission to return to the Caucasus. Not surprisingly, the Soviets rejected the idea. The Circassians remained a suspect minority until their enthusiastic participation in the Arab-Israeli War of 1948.[34]

It was also in 1948 that the Circassian Benevolent Society, which had been shut down for years, was allowed to resume its cultural activities. Realizing that their political voice was going to continue to be silenced, many young Circassians joined the Communist Party as a step toward repatriation to the Caucasus. As it turned out, however, the multiple military coups following the Arab-Israeli War worked in the Circassians' favor. Sami al-Hinnawi's brief dictatorship in 1949 established the Circassians and other minorities as a central force in the military. His successor, Adib Shishakli, used Circassians as the core of his personal guard. By 1965 two-thirds of the Syrian Army was composed of ethnic and religious minorities.[35] In 1963 the Circassians, who occupied important posts in both the military and administrative branches of the government by this time, threw their support behind the Ba'ath Party. They finally established a secure position for themselves until the Arab Spring of 2011–2012.

As if all they had been through wasn't enough, the Six-Day War of 1967 once again put the Circassians in the middle of a conflict simply because they lived on strategically important land. By the 1960s Quneitra had become the undisputed cultural and economic capital for the Circassians in Syria, with around sixteen thousand living there and in the surrounding villages. Thanks to their efforts at reclaiming the abandoned region, more than ninety thousand people lived on the Golan Heights in 1960.[36] When the Israelis invaded in June 1967, nearly everyone fled. Thinking that they would be allowed to return after hostilities were over, most left all of their possessions behind.[37] Those who remained were intimidated into leaving: civilians were rounded up and threatened with automatic rifles, village elders and their relatives were summarily executed, and homes were ransacked.[38] Circassian eyewitness Mahmud al-Hajj Ahmad describes the occupation of his village, Ayn Ziwan:

> After six days of war, the Israeli army entered the village and began searching for weapons and Palestinian fighters. They came to our house looking for one of my relatives, a Palestinian refugee from 1948. He wasn't there, but my father asked me to go to Damascus to warn our Palestinian relatives. . . . I sneaked back into the village. Israeli patrols were all over. Some patrols left the citizens who remained in the village more or less alone, but the behavior of others was very bad.

They came to our house a second time. My father was sitting in the guest room with a friend, and the Israelis accused him of being a combatant. He said, "I'm not young enough to be in the military." The head of the patrol pointed a pistol to his head, and said, "You may not be in the military now but you were in 1948." In fact, my father had fought in 1948. He got a piece of shrapnel in his head. When the patrol left our house, my father said that we had to leave, especially the young men.[39]

So the Circassians were expelled at gunpoint once again. Just as they did when deported from the Caucasus, they had to sell their livestock for next to nothing and run for their lives. Once again they sought shelter in public buildings, this time in Damascus. Charitable societies did what they could, but many people, particularly the elderly, died shortly after their arrival. Tent cities established for the refugees slowly turned into residential areas with permanent structures.[40]

Immediately after they had driven off the residents, the Israelis bull-dozed the villages on the Golan Heights in preparation for colonization. They built many of their own settlements but took over Quneitra as it was. According to the disengagement agreement of May 1974, the city was returned to Syria, but before abandoning it the Israelis leveled it. All that the Circassians had built over the previous ninety years was destroyed. The refugees in Damascus were offered the opportunity to return, but even if there had been something to return to, most of them had already found employment in the capital. The largest, most unified center of Circassian culture in exile had been eradicated. The next generation of Circassians grew up in urban areas and lost the sense of community their forefathers had tried so hard to build.[41] Some refugees from the Golan Heights left Syria altogether, settling in small groups in Jordan, Saudi Arabia, and Western Europe. One group took up an offer by the United States to move to Paterson, New Jersey, where Circassians who evacuated the Caucasus with the Germans had been placed after World War II. A small but steady flow continued from Syria and Jordan throughout the 1970s and 1980s, and the New Jersey community has now grown to around five thousand. Through the efforts of the Circassian Benevolent Association, founded in June 1952, these migrants have been able to maintain their identity and pass their hopes on to their children. Some of those children, raised in an atmo-sphere of American political activism and espousal of social justice, would become the most determined champions of the Circassian right to return in the twenty-first century.

Jordan: The Double-Edged Sword of Prosperity

About fifty Shapsug families who survived the *Sphinx* disaster made it to the ruins that would become Amman by the end of 1878. A second group arrived in 1880 and settled at the neighboring village of Wadi Seer.[42] Oliph-ant reported in 1880 that 500 had arrived several months earlier but that the majority had left almost immediately, leaving a population of around 150.[43] In addition to adapting to a new climate and other conditions they had never encountered (such as impure water), the Circassians had the Bedouins to attend to. Circassian historian and statesman Shauket Mufti told Jane Hacker that the Bedouins would not only raid the settlement at Amman but would also try to intimidate the newcomers with "boasts and taunts." After all that the Circassians had been through, it is little wonder that this produced the opposite of its intended effect. Mufti told Hacker an amusing story about his grandfather's confrontation with the Bani Sakhr. Their sheikh came on a "taunting raid" and the Circassians had had enough. Mufti's grandfather went out to meet the sheikh and shouted, "I have fought many men; I have the scars of seven wounds on my body; if you want to fight, then fight. But be sure to bring enough camels to carry away your corpses!" After a few of these exchanges the Bedouins realized that the Circassians were not to be trifled with. Most of the clans backed down, and eventually several concluded truces with their new neighbors.[44] By 1900 the Bani Sakhr were fighting alongside the Circassians in their war against the Balqawiyeh tribe.[45]

Other colonies were established in Transjordan as Kabardians and Bjedukhs migrated to the region: Jerash (1885) and Na'ur (1900) were two such communities that prospered alongside Amman.[46] Fruit trees and veg-etable gardens slowly filled the ruins of ancient Philadelphia. The Jerash and Na'ur kept some animals but never became large-scale herders as they had been in Circassia, most likely because the Arabs had this mar-ket already cornered. They also produced and sold iron implements and brought new technology to Transjordan.[47] Their introduction of the wicker cart apparently caused quite a stir. Fifteen feet long and drawn by oxen, these two-wheeled carts had never been seen by anyone in the region. Naturally, they quickly established themselves as fine horse breeders, crossing the few they managed to bring along with the local Arab breeds.[48]

When the Hejaz Railroad arrived in 1903 the Bedouins saw it as a threat to their business of charging for passage to Mecca, and by 1907 a two-hundred-man Circassian cavalry was created to guard the line.[49] The railroad gave Amman a real advantage over the neighboring town of Salt, and there was a large influx of merchants. By 1914 there were approximately three hundred families, primarily Circassian, but Amman's success as a trading center attracted Christians and Muslims alike.[50] When World War I began, the railroad made Amman a strategic center, and the settlement became a boom town. By 1918 Amman was an established commercial center with a growing population.[51] Like their compatriots to the north, the Circassians of Transjordan remained loyal to the Porte during the war, defending the rail lines and mobilizing wherever unrest threatened to destabilize the region.[52]

During the turmoil following the war the Circassian population continued to be the Turks' most loyal supporters, which made their position somewhat precarious when the British Mandate was established in Transjordan.[53] The British immediately showed preference to the Arab tribes when disputes arose. For the first time since their plight had come to the world's attention, the Circassians found themselves lacking even the illusion of protection of a major power.[54] Nationalism in the Arab lands after the fall of the Ottoman Empire took the form of pan-Arabism instead of pan-Islamism, so non-Arabs of Transjordan found themselves in danger of being excluded from the public and political spheres.[55] The Circassians saw the arrival of Emir Abdullah in Amman on February 9, 1921, as an opportunity to gain allies, so Circassian leaders Mirza Pasha and Othman Hikmat joined a large contingent of town representatives to welcome him. Shortly afterward brothers Muhammad and Said al-Mufti volunteered to join Abdullah in his campaign to liberate Syria. They also offered to form a personal bodyguard for him, thus creating the Circassian Royal Guard.[56] This new privileged position allowed them to demonstrate their loyalty to the Jordanian regime while simultaneously maintaining their language and culture.[57] A 750-man security team previously organized with British help was reformed in early 1923, and Circassians ended up composing perhaps 30 percent of the overall force.[58] In August 1922 Circassian leader Mirza Wasfi played an important role in repelling a Wahhabi attack, and Circassian leaders helped avert a war in August 1923.[59] Kabardian chieftain Said al-Mufti came in conflict with Abdullah over governmental appointments, but even this turned out to be a blessing in disguise. His "loyal opposition" made him a popular figure among the disaffected and helped his political career.[60] In 1929 he was elected to the Legislative Council, served in the legislature between 1931 and 1947, and was appointed prime minister in 1950 and again in 1955.[61]

A number of reforms in 1928 gave the Circassians even more influence in Jordanian political and economic life. They were excluded from tribal politics and made the "keepers of the capital," which established a direct link between them and the emir. Perhaps even more importantly, a new electoral law allowed for one Circassian representative for every five thousand constituents, as opposed to one for every twenty-seven thousand for the remainder of the population. As a result, Circassians were consistently overrepresented in the government. Land reforms that were concluded in 1933 gave the Circassians definitive title to their property. Now with legal rights to their valuable farms, they established a lucrative export business to Palestine and by the 1940s had gained the reputation of a wealthy, landed class. Although the Palestinian market ended with the war with Israel in 1948, property values skyrocketed in Amman as refugees flooded into the city. The Circassians owned much of the prime real estate: their original farms are now the suburbs of Amman. The next generation of Circassians was even wealthier and became active in the economic development of the country. The Mufti family helped establish the Jordanian National Bank, and wealthy Circassians began sending their children to England and the United States to study. Today they enjoy a political, economic, and social status that is disproportionate to the relatively small percentage of the population they represent in Jordan.[62]

Despite their contributions to the nation, Circassians are viewed as outsiders by at least part of the population of Jordan. One extreme element of the Jordanian nationalist movement excludes minorities such as the Circassians from their concept of the nation.[63] The Circassians themselves are aware that their true home lies elsewhere and have tried to maintain ties with their homeland through channels such as the Circassian Charity Organization, created in the early 1930s, which provides scholarships to the University of Nalchik and built a school in the mid-1970s where the Circassian language is taught. Nevertheless, by the 1960s the Circassians had become so well integrated into mainstream Jordanian life, using Arabic as their primary language, that now many no longer speak Circassian.[64] Success had its price.

The Republic of Turkey: "Speaking Circassian Is Forbidden"

While the Syrian and Jordanian settlers faced new challenges with the fall of the Ottoman Empire, the Circassians who lived in Anatolia saw a change in their status so complete that it could even be said that they underwent yet another deportation. They went from being equal subjects based upon Islamic solidarity to being an unwanted minority that was targeted for assimilation in the new state ideology of Turkish nationalism.

Things began to go badly shortly after the Revolution of 1908 brought the Young Turks to power. Through their political apparatus, the Committee of Union and Progress, the Young Turks quickly removed ethnic minorities from positions of authority. More than ten thousand officers were purged from the army between 1908 and 1913, and minorities were the primary target.[65] Promotion through the ranks, a favorite method of all ethnic minorities, was discontinued. Clubs and organizations designed for minorities were shut down. Stripped of their protected status and under assault once again by a regime determined to destroy them, the Circassians petitioned the Entente Powers during World War I to establish an independent Circassian state in western Anatolia under the protection of Europe.[66] The Turks themselves were in no mood to hear of Circassian independence. Beginning in 1910 revolts broke out among the Albanians, Montenegrins, and Yemenis, so the idea of a minority seeking political or cultural autonomy in Anatolia never had a chance. In the chaos following the Russian Revolution, pan-Turkists such as Enver Pasha were looking to incorporate the Turkic lands of Central Asia into a pan-Turkic state stretching to China, not to accommodate their own ethnic minorities. Nevertheless, some Circassians saw the establishment of the constitutional monarchy as an opportunity to organize on their own. In August 1908 a group of Circassian intellectuals formed the Circassian Union and Mutual Assistance Society.[67] The first Circassian newspaper, *Ğuaze* (*The Guide*), appeared as well. In 1919 the Circassian Women's Assistance Committee opened the Circassian Model Academy, which was devoted to preserving the Circassian language and providing general education. Unfortunately, this proved to be a brief experiment, for in 1923 the new government in Ankara closed nearly all minority organizations.[68]

After the Bolshevik Revolution, Circassians under the leadership of Marshall Fuad Pasha asked Great Britain for help to return to the Caucasus and establish an independent state there. Their appeal fell on deaf ears, since in British eyes an independent Circassia was no longer a geopolitical asset:

> The moment when Turks are endeavouring to create an Islamic movement in the Caucasus seems ill-chosen for favoring return to that country of an unknown number of perhaps the most warlike of all Ottoman subjects, whose original immigration into Turkey is believed here to have been due rather to reluctance to remain under the rule of a Christian power than to alleged Russian oppression.
>
> At the same time we are not anxious to antagonize the Circassians who are a valuable asset in Turkey and might prove useful to us and you might tell Fuad, if he pressed you for an answer, that this is a matter which cannot be taken up until some general settlement of the Caucasus question has been reached but that His Majesty's Government will bear the wish of the Circassians in mind.[69]

The British were attempting to establish their control of Christian Georgia in the South Caucasus when this telegram was sent in 1918. The Circassians were now a possible threat to their newly defined interests (the British would abandon the Georgians to the Bolsheviks the following year). Instead, they were seen as a potential force to control the Turks. The Circassians, apparently believing British assurances that "His Majesty's Government" had not already made up their minds, continued with this project until 1920, when something akin to a zafes was held. Unfortunately, by now the Circassians had broken up into pro- and anti-Ottoman factions, and they had taken up arms against each other when the Turkish War of Independence began.[70] Those who were loyal to the nationalists, such as Ethem Bey, quickly realized their mistake. After his left wing Yeşil Ordu (Green Army) played a pivotal role in fighting the Greeks, Mustafa Kemal disbanded them, and in January 1921 he told Ethem Bey to disband the rest of his army. Bey refused, so Kemal sent his forces in and crushed Bey's army.[71]

By the time the 1923 Treaty of Lausanne created the Republic of Turkey, Anatolia was in dire straits. The nation had been at war for nearly ten years, much of it taking place on Turkish soil. The land was in ruins and Anatolia had lost perhaps 30 percent of its prewar population.[72] In addition to the 1 million or more Armenians who died in the genocide, 300,000 Greeks and 2.5 million Muslim Anatolians perished during the war. Refugees from eastern Anatolia flooded into the west, and the disruption in labor and agriculture led to famine and epidemics of cholera and typhus. Demographic shifts had their effect on the new state as well. More than 400,000 Muslim refugees came from Greece while more than 1 million Greeks left Anatolia. By the end of the migrations, Anatolia was far less ethnically diverse. There were two main groups—Turks and Kurds—and several much smaller minorities, including Greeks, Armenians, Syrians, Jews, and Circassians. These peoples quickly became targets of Turkification policies and worse as the Young Turks' nationalist policy was put into action. It resembled Imperial Russia's policies to some degree: rather than a racial notion of "Turkishness," the Young Turks promoted assimilation of the non-Turkish speaking Muslims (and, if they chose to convert, Christians) of Anatolia through the elimination of their languages and cultural institutions.[73] Circassian clans were broken up and deported in small groups. One typical example happened in May 1923 when the Turks accused Circassians living south of the Sea of Marmara of supporting the Greeks and deported fourteen Circassians from villages. Just as in the Caucasus, the Circassians were surrounded by troops, forced to sell their possessions, broken into small groups, and scattered throughout Anatolia. Settlements were arranged so that no more than 20 percent of any town would be populated by non-Turkish speakers.[74] In July the Treaty of Lausanne granted them permission to return to their villages, but many stayed where they were. Those who did return often found their homes occupied. Circassian leaders were targeted for repression. In 1927 Ankara expelled eighty-six leading figures from the country.[75]

Such measures were only a prelude to the 1934 Law of Settlement, however.[76] The law codified the assimilation tactics of the 1920s, openly stating that the establishment of "Turkishness" was the goal. Those who had been resettled were restricted from changing location for five years. The Turks hoped that the delay would allow the Circassians to become sufficiently settled to remain where they'd been sent and subsequently be assimilated into the larger Turkish community.[77] Also in 1934 the government passed a law making it compulsory for every Turkish citizen to have a surname (previously, Anatolian Turks didn't use surnames), so lists of acceptable names were produced by the government and sent to the village chiefs, who allocated one to each family, sometimes without the consent of the family in question. Of course, the Circassians (as well as many other minorities) already had surnames, but the law also stated that non-Turkish words couldn't be used. Circassian families often Turkified their surname or translated its meaning into Turkish, but others just changed them completely. Only the Circassians living in Hatay Province, at the time part of Syria, escaped the surname law and continued to live in Turkey under their original names.[78]

Pressure was kept on the Circassians to abandon their native language. There were "Citizen Speak Turkish!" campaigns, and signs were hung in Circassian villages announcing "Speaking Circassian Is Forbidden." Circassian children's given names were Turkified and Circassian villages' names were changed.[79] However, just as in Jordan, natural processes were more powerful than government policies in erasing Circassian identity. As Turkey's industrial base grew, many people from the provinces naturally gravitated toward urban centers looking for a better life. Forced to rely upon Turkish in the cities, they began to forget their own language. On the other hand, those who left the countryside developed into a new intellectual class that took advantage of the growing power of the media to create new organizations. In 1951 the North Caucasus Turkish Association for Culture and Assistance (later the United Caucasus Association) was formed in Istanbul, and in 1952 the Caucasus Cultural Association was created.[80] By the 1960s different political perspectives developed into competing organizations that had divergent ideas about how to deal with the diaspora. The Socialist Caucasus Association of Ankara developed ties with Moscow and promoted the idea of establishing links with the Caucasus without any plans for repatriation. Some Circassians migrated to Germany at the beginning of the 1960s, along with large numbers of Turks seeking seasonal work, and ended up staying there or in Holland.[81] Approximately thirty thousand Circassians currently live in Germany.[82] Today there are perhaps five million Circassians in Turkey, although only two million still consider themselves Circassian (rather than "of Circassian descent"), and less than one million can still speak the Circassian language. The last native speaker of Ubykh, Tevfik Esenç, passed away in 1992, although a handful of linguists still can communicate in Ubykh.

A Circassian revival began in the 1970s with the creation of two political platforms. The Devrimci (revolutionaries) believed a socialist revolution in Turkey would be the best route for securing Circassian rights, while the Dönüşçü (returnists) favored repatriation to the North Caucasus. The Devrimci understandably met resistance and ultimately lost support, but the Dönüşçü are still active. The coup of September 1980 resulted in a new wave of repression against Circassian societies in Turkey, and it was at this time that repatriation became a widely discussed topic.[83] As it turned out, events in the Soviet Union would soon make repatriation a real possibility for the first time since 1864.

7

Those Who Stayed Behind

Can a nation be free if it oppresses other nations? It cannot.
—Vladimir Lenin

In 1863 military consul to the Russian Embassy in Istanbul F. A. Frankini submitted several proposals for "the establishment of peace" in the western Caucasus to War Minister Milyutin. To Frankini's suggestion that the Circassians be given hereditary rights to their land as Alexander had promised, Milyutin replied, "Nonsense! Does the author want an enemy that hates Russia to have more rights than the Russian people?" The war minister likewise dismissed Frankini's warning that Russian actions were instilling hatred in the Circassians, claiming that "the experience of many years has proven that we will never make them our friends." Finally, to Frankini's assessment that Russian policy had "turned [the Circassians] into something resembling prisoners of war," Milyutin responded, "they are prisoners of war."[1]

Milyutin was right: the Russians considered the remaining Circassians an enemy population. Milyutin and his successors kept the North Caucasus in a state of military occupation for decades after the end of the war. Circassians were artificially divided into four separate administrative regions that threatened their ethnic unity and were surrounded by Cossacks who exploited and abused them. They were pressured to convert to Christianity and give up their native tongue, and by 1900 were being conscripted into the army. Many more chose exile in the Ottoman Empire during these years. The ones who remained hoped the advent of Soviet power would restore some of their rights. As it turned out, the Soviets codified some of tsarist Russia's worst policies and continued the process of Russification.

"Lands That Will Permanently Be in Their Possession"

It is unclear exactly how many Circassians remained in the North Cauca-sus. Russian records claim 106,798 while Adolph Berzhe estimates 50,000.[2] Rostislav Fadeev put the figure at 60,000 while Russian historian Galina Malakhova estimates only 40,400.[3] The first postdeportation census was conducted only in 1882; it put the Circassian population of Kuban Oblast at 65,900.[4] By then only a few thousand more had emigrated, so either the official Russian figure of more than 100,000 is an exaggeration or many thousands died during their migration to the Kuban region. Since that deportation also took place during the winter of 1863–1864, the lat-ter is a very likely possibility. If we assume that Berzhe's middle figure of 50,000 was close to the number who survived to settle in the lowlands, then between 95 percent and 97 percent of all Circassians were killed out-right, died during Evdokimov's campaign, or were deported. Those who remained were unofficially placed in a special category, neither subjects nor free tribesmen. They were kept under strict observation by the same the military command that brought so much destruction to their society. Cossacks were prioritized in every area of life and were given free rein to treat the Circassians however they wished. All of Alexander's promises made to the Circassians who remained were then systematically broken over the next twenty years.

The first dismemberment of what remained of Circassia came before the deportations had begun, when in 1860 Kabardia was assigned to the left wing of the Caucasus Line (future Tersk Oblast), administratively isolating it from the rest of Circassia. Instead, the Kabardians were lumped together with the Ossetians, Ingush, Chechens, and Dagestani peoples, who had little in common with them. Subsequently, Lesser Kabardia was assigned to the Ossetia Okrug region, dividing the tribe between two administrative units until 1905.[5] The right wing, which would become Kuban Oblast, was overwhelmingly populated by Cossack immigrants along with Karachays, Nogays, Armenians, Greeks, and the remnants of the Abazas and western Circassians. The few Abzakhs who were left were resettled in Maikop Uezd (district) between the Pshish and Laba Rivers along with other tribal rem-nants. Together they formed the core population of the current Republic of Adygeia. The rest were assigned to Batalpashinsk Uezd along the Kuban and Zelenchuk Rivers.[6] In both areas, the Circassians found themselves outnumbered approximately twenty to one by Slavic colonists.[7]

One last group was the Khakuchi, a Shapsug clan who continued to evade capture well into the late 1860s. Their fate was interesting. Toward 1870 they began coming down from the mountains and for some reason were allowed to settle among Cossacks living along the Black Sea coast. Most likely the Cossack settlers realized how valuable the Khakuchis' knowledge of the region would be. They readily accepted them into their communities, and the two peoples lived side by side as good neighbors. The Khakuchi who remained in the mountains continued to commit low-level attacks, however, and in June 1870 Grand Prince Mikhail proposed deporting the Khakuchi villagers north of the Kuban. Major General Dzhe-mardzhidze replied that the Khakuchi were "a hardworking and patient people" who were valued by the local administrators and Cossack settlers alike, and they were allowed to remain.[8]

The most valuable land went to the Russian officers and soldiers who conducted the campaign against the Circassians. Almost 20 percent of Lesser Kabardia, a total of 74,000 acres, was given to military figures.[9] In Batalpashinsk Okrug, one of the two areas supposedly reserved for Circassians, Cossacks were given nearly half of the available land.[10] Evdokimov proved Venyukov's charge of "passion for personal gain" true, awarding himself 28,782 acres. His top generals were given 16,200 acres each, and other officers were given smaller estates.[11] In addition, the military frequently appropriated land long after the war had concluded. In a report to Milyutin, Orbeliani testifies to the bad faith of the Russian administration:

> Societies, individual auls, and even individual families that have submitted to Russian rule have either been abandoned in their former places of residence or, more frequently, resettled in new lands assigned to them, but in either case they have been assigned land only approximately and temporarily. Then, because of the demands of the military situation, we frequently take part of the land we had given them for Cossack settlements, and once settled in their new lands, because of these demands we once again resettle them, sometimes repeatedly from place to place.[12]

To make room for the Cossacks and to ensure they received fertile land, the indigenous peoples were assigned the least valuable territory. In the words of I. A. Gavrilov, a witness to the process, "The best lands in terms of natural wealth and beauty in the lands on the left bank of the Kuban were not assigned to the region of the mountaineers' okrugs and were assigned for the most part to the Cossacks. The lands that were assigned to the mountaineers' okrugs, particularly Urup and Zelenchuk regions, had been deforested and for the most part were subject to undesirable conditions."[13] Land confiscations led to disputes among the indigenous peoples, particularly between Ossetians and Kabardians.[14] The Circassians were supposed to receive approximately sixteen acres per adult, barely enough to build a self-sufficient farm.[15] Ultimately, they were granted between thirty-two and forty-eight acres per household while the Cossacks were allotted eighty acres per person.[16] The land given to the Circassians was extremely poor: Malakhova estimates that two-thirds of the land granted to the Circassians was unsuitable for cultivation.[17]

The marginalization of the Circassians to the advantage of the Cossacks was part of a policy aimed at eliminating the native population. Where they couldn't physically annihilate them, the Russians did all they could to destroy their way of life. As the Cossack settlements expanded in 1863, the Hatukays were divided into small groups and resettled into large auls that had been created for the remaining Bjedukhs, and the Hatukay tribe quickly disappeared. In 1865 the Kabardians were forbidden from traveling to the other Circassian areas without permission, and by 1866 their traditional auls had been abolished and the people were resettled in larger communities and surrounded by Cossack stanitsy.[18] The Russians gave away large sections of Kabardia to Cossack settlers as well as to neighboring Balkaria and Ossetia, sowing animosity between peoples who formerly lived in relative harmony.[19] The Kabardians, whose territory once stretched nearly two hundred miles east to west, found themselves restricted to less than a quarter of their original homeland.

Seeing that the Russians were reneging on all their promises, many Circassians decided to immigrate to Turkey.[20] Now, however, the Russians needed the Circassians' experience in the region to help the struggling settlers. In December 1873 Kartsov informed Milyutin of this and recommended taking steps to discourage further emigration. However, he warned that the Cossacks' continued brigandage would eventually drive all Circassians to Turkey:

> [The Circassians] are surrounded for 250 miles on all sides by Cossack settlements, [and] half of them are people who were expelled from the mountains and have been driven by the war to desperation and think only about how they will feed themselves. . . . If we continue to show the population that we care about the property rights that they have been given and that we will defend them from their Cossack neighbors (which we frequently have to do) they will remain. But if on the other hand we ignore the needs of the people . . . by the end of next year ninety-nine percent of them will leave for Turkey.[21]

No action was taken on Kartsov's recommendations, and Cossack raids on the Circassians continued until the 1880s.[22] One could even argue that the Russo-Circassian War hadn't ended at all but had just moved to the lowlands. Not only were the Cossacks still attacking them with total impunity as they had since the days of Emperor Paul, the swamplands that they were given were taking their toll. In September 1865 General Ignatiev reported that "sickness in the region is incredibly widespread, due to a malignant fever caused by a rainy autumn . . . the mountaineers' main source of nourishment is sour milk and dried meat."[23] As many as 2,500 families, representing about 25 percent of the remaining Circassians, petitioned to emigrate and continued to press the government for nearly a decade, even going so far as to take up arms in 1873.[24]

While Kartsov and others in the military command recognized the value of the Circassians who remained, Evdokimov continued to "encourage" the Circassians to emigrate. He was appointed civil commander of Kuban Oblast in 1861 after his own officers demanded that he be removed as Tersk Oblast commander. He immediately targeted the Karachays, a tiny Turkic nation of sheepherders (seventeen thousand in 1867) living in the high Caucasus Mountains who had never seriously opposed Russian rule.[25] In 1862 he deprived them of their traditional pasturing lands and forced them to migrate east to the very highest elevations, where the half the fields were under a permanent layer of snow.[26] This also cut the Karachays off from other pastures they needed, so they were left with the choice of poaching on Kabardian land or starving.[27] After Evdokimov was forced into retirement in 1865, the appropriation of the lands Alexander had promised the Circassians would be "permanently be in their possession" continued apace. More and more territory was taken from them and given to Cossack immigrants and, later, to large-scale horse breeders and speculators. The speculators often left the land undeveloped or rented it back to the Circassians it had been taken from in the first place.[28] Circassian auls were also eliminated and their inhabitants resettled into large villages, where their distinct dialects disappeared.[29]

Ironically, the attempts to settle the mountains where the majority of the Circassians had lived met with total failure. Ya. Abramov described the situation during his visit to the North Caucasus in the 1870s:

> The lands formerly inhabited by the numerous mountain peoples are still abandoned. Only an insignificant portion of the area is occupied by Cossack stanitsy. The rest has been distributed among various officers. The Cossacks, however, are completely incapable of living in the places where they built their stanitsy. In 1868 alone twelve entire stanitsy in Kuban Oblast were abandoned "due to extreme unsuitability for agriculture, creation of communication lines and climate," as the official report stated. The lands given to private owners are completely undeveloped and empty to this day. Finally, no one has even tried to take possession of the huge expanses formerly occupied by the mountaineers because they're so unsuitable for agriculture. However, these lands had previously been occupied by large numbers of people and well cultivated.[30]

While the high mountains weren't exactly "well cultivated," the Circassians had been able to build a viable society there with the minimal resources available. The Cossacks were unaccustomed to the conditions there and were quickly forced to abandon the many stanitsy Evdokimov had established. Still, by the 1870s, Slavs represented 70 percent of the population of Kuban Oblast.[31] In Nalchik Okrug (created in 1882) the population increased from less than 50,000 in 1860 to nearly 181,000 in 1916, due almost exclusively to immigration. In Kuban Oblast, immigration was responsible for an increase in population to more than 3 million in 1916.[32]

During Russia's attempts to subjugate them, several Circassians who had been educated in St. Petersburg and Moscow did what they could to help their countrymen receive fair treatment. Two major figures were Khan Girey and Shora Nogmov, who used ethnography and history as their tools to try to enlighten the Tsarist government about the Circassians and their world. A third statesman of the same generation, Dmitry Kodzokov, took a more hands-on approach and tried to influence the post-deportation land reforms throughout the North Caucasus, particularly in Kabardia. In addition, he was a patron of numerous endeavors aimed at improving the Circassians' lot. Born Lukman Bek-Murzin Kodzokov around 1818, he was sent to Moscow at a very early age by his father, a low-level Kabardian aristocrat. He was taken in by the family of Aleksei Khomyakov, one of the future leaders of the Slavophile movement. The Slavophiles were a reaction to the dominant notion among Russian intellectuals that Russia needed to copy Western Europe in order to progress. The Slavophiles felt that only traditional Russian culture could save the country. While the Slavophiles eventually descended into the pan-Slavist ideology that engendered the Russian ethnic cleansing of Rumelia, their early leaders were quite enlightened. Men such as Khomyakov concerned themselves with questions of equality and justice for all Russians, hoping to find the solution in native institutions. While in Moscow Kodzokov learned not only Khomyakov's ideas but also a wide variety of academic subjects: in addition to modern and classical languages, he studied history, statistics, physics, and logic. In a sense, he was the first Circassian "renaissance man."

After graduating from Moscow State University in 1838, Kodzokov worked briefly in the Moscow law court, but by summer 1839 he was back in the Caucasus. He went to Tbilisi, where Caucasus commander in chief Mikhail Vorontsov assigned him the herculean task of resolving border disputes in the North Caucasus. During his first trip back to Kabardia he attempted to recover some lands that Ermolov had appropriated and succeeded in removing a particularly corrupt line commander. He also established an elementary school in his home village and drew up a plan for the creation of schools throughout Kabardia. With Khomyakov paying his expenses, he traveled throughout the region and gathered information about land distribution as well as ethnographical material. He was called back to Tbilisi in 1845 and only returned to the North Caucasus in 1863, but once there he continued to contribute to bettering the lot of his compatriots. In 1866 he successfully lobbied to keep a Circassian secondary school in Nalchik open, and in 1870 he established a horse breeding ranch for the benefit of the Kabardian people. However, it was in his work on the Land Reform Commission for Tersk Oblast that he made his greatest impact. He argued vigorously for the rights of the peasantry, and it is largely due to his efforts that the indigenous peasants received as much as they did. As a result, he earned the hatred of all the powerful parties in the North Caucasus; at one point the pro-Russian aristocrats actually plotted to assassinate him. He gained more enemies when he stated his opinion of the "voluntary emigration" of Kabardians to Turkey in 1865, openly accusing the Russian government of planting agents to deceive the Chechens and Ossetians as well as the Kabardians in a plot to reduce the numbers of all the indigenous peoples.[33]

Like Kodzokov, other Circassians did what they could within the Imperial system to preserve their nation's heritage. Sultan Adil-Girey gathered materials on Circassian customary law and wrote some of the first analytical pieces on the causes of the Russo-Circassian War. Adil-Girey Keshev, editor of Terskie Vedomosti (The Terek Gazette), promoted the education of all the peoples of the Caucasus and facilitated discussions of crucial issues. Kazi Atakhukin wrote the first grammars of the Circassian dialects and developed courses for primary education. At times, however, all the efforts of the rising Circassian intelligentsia weren't enough to satisfy their people's demands, and violence erupted. In April 1868 several hundred Circassians staged an armed uprising in response to land redistribution and an attempt to disarm them.[34] In 1904 and 1913 St. Petersburg had to send artillery into Kabardia to put down revolts, and in December 1905 rebels captured Nalchik and held it for most of the month.[35] Others voted with their feet, leaving for the Ottoman Empire. Between 1870 and 1881 at least two thousand Kabardians abandoned their homeland, and judging from census figures, thousands more western Circassians left as well.[36] Additional waves of emigration continued right up until the First World War.[37]

Despite Alexander's promises to the contrary, land taxes were imposed on the Circassians, but not the Cossacks, in 1866.[38] Although the money was purportedly for promoting economic development, by 1900 there had been no changes to the infrastructure or technological advancements: farming was the primary industry, practiced as it had been for centuries.[39] Unable to pay their taxes, poorer peasants were forced to abandon their land and migrate to Cossack stanitsy and cities to provide seasonal labor. No improvements in social services were made either: in 1913 there was only one hospital in Batalpashinsk Okrug.[40] In 1882, when Emperor Alexander III ordered that the North Caucasus be fully integrated into the Empire, more taxes were imposed on Circassian peasants for the maintenance of the nonexistent public services. Additionally, peasants were now subject to conscription for road construction and other projects. Once again the aristocracy, wealthy landowners, and Cossacks were exempted from these obligations.[41] Users' fees were also imposed on the Circassians and Balkars for access to their traditional grazing lands.[42]

One irony in all this was the fact that Alexander II was earning himself the title of "Tsar Liberator" at the same time that he was wiping out Circassia and stripping the survivors of their liberties. Even his greatest achievement, the liberation of the serfs in 1861, didn't reach the North Caucasus. Kodzokov's commission wasn't even allowed to begin examining the problem in Tersk Oblast until May 1863, and then only because peasant uprisings threatened to drag the entire North Caucasus back into war.[43] As Kodzokov's commission sorted out the problem, the Kabardian aristocrats threatened to rebel: a group of more than four hundred assembled on the outskirts of Nalchik, requiring military intervention.[44] Grand Prince Mikhail ultimately convinced the aristocrats that their interests would be protected, and he worked out a scheme whereby slaves would be required to purchase their own freedom.[45] Those who couldn't afford this "liberation" had to continue to serve their owners until they "worked off" their debt. In Kuban Oblast liberation didn't even begin until 1868 and, as in Tersk Oblast, only then in response to violent uprisings.[46] There a four- to five-year term of labor was the standard assignment for "working off" debt. Upon liberation, peasants were required to hand over half of their personal property to their former masters, right down to their kitchen utensils.[47]

A campaign of Russification and Christianization had begun as early as 1843, when the Caucasus Spiritual Consistory was created in Stavropol. The Orthodox Church quickly became St. Petersburg's primary tool to sever the Circassians' cultural ties with the Islamic world. In 1863 the Society for the Establishment of Orthodox Christianity began its activities, and by 1889 there were 572 Christian schools throughout the North Caucasus.[48] The secular educational system worked to assimilate the Circassians as well. In March 1870 the Ministry of Public Education identified three categories of "mountaineers" that each required different methods for assimilation: "not at all russified," "living in areas where there are large numbers of Russians," and "sufficiently russified."[49] At the same time, St. Petersburg moved quickly to destroy the legal system that Alexander had promised would be preserved as well. In 1858 the Russians had already eliminated the traditional court structure of the Kabardians, transforming it into a puppet court under control of the Russian military, which frequently ignored even its own rules and treated the region as if it were under martial law.[50] Then, in August 1864, Evdokimov wrote Grand Prince Mikhail that it was essential "to immediately impose a new legal system on the natives."[51] In October Mikhail ordered Evdokimov to proceed, noting that allowing the Circassians to preserve their own legal system was a "temporary" measure intended only until the end of the war.[52] The same system as in Kabardia was imposed, with Russian officers deciding cases unilaterally. Although the Circassians were allowed to petition abuses in Nalchik, delegations were frequently arrested when they arrived. Collective punishment became official policy, as the punitive expedition was recast as the *ekzekutsiia*: a Russian squadron would occupy a village where a fugitive was suspected to be hiding and would help themselves to whatever goods the villagers possessed, sometimes for months on end. The hase was renamed the *pristavstvo*, deprived of its legislative power and limited to the discussion of economic questions. Other traditional methods of mutual consultation were also co-opted and placed in the hands of the Russian administration.[53]

As Kartsov mentioned in his letter to Milyutin, the Cossack settlers treated the natives with general contempt. Of course, any rational person could have easily predicted that placing people who had recently been at war with each other side by side couldn't possibly lead to any other outcome, but the Russian administration seemed to be oblivious to this conclusion. The unfair land distribution gave the clear impression that the Circassians were second-class citizens, and the Cossacks took advantage of their superior legal position as well as the fact that they, unlike the Circassians, were permitted to carry weapons. Circassians and Chechens alike were subjected to verbal harassment and physical abuse by Cossacks as well as murder.[54] The administration often exacerbated the situation, razing auls and forcing the Circassians onto even less-fertile lands after they complained of Cossack abuse.[55]

In every way, St. Petersburg treated the Circassians as a conquered enemy. No attempts were made to improve the lot of the natives, and in fact right up to the First World War steps continued to be taken to further restrict their ability to live freely. In the 1890s a series of regulations severely restricted the movement of the indigenous peoples and even their ability to live in communities outside the lands in which they had been settled, effectively ghettoizing them. It was also at this time that the beginning of systematic xenophobia against the Caucasus peoples was first promoted by the State Duma and the Russian press. Right-wing publications regularly printed articles that described the Circassians and Chechens as bandits, thieves, and brigands.[56] The legacy of this propaganda campaign continues today and is one of the main sources of the misery Russia faces as a result of its policies in the Caucasus.

Slow Death under the Soviets

One must admit that the Soviets were egalitarian concerning ethnic minorities: during the seventy-three years of their rule, they treated them all with contempt. In the gross and universal violation of human rights that characterized Soviet rule, the Circassians' plight became just one among hundreds of tragedies. Nevertheless, the Soviets not only continued Tsarist policies concerning the Circassians but also escalated the tactics to wipe out every vestige of their national character. They were spared the horrific catastrophe that struck the Karachay-Balkars, but this only escalated tensions between these formerly good neighbors and complicated the Circassian struggle for survival.

Initially Bolshevik rule promised to improve the lot of the Caucasus peoples but only because Moscow's violence was directed against the Cossacks. Tens of thousands of Cossacks were deported to Siberia for being "collaborators" with the White Army, although the real reason was to clear an overpopulated region of its least reliable element.[57] In 1925 the Soviets realized they needed Russian-speakers in the Caucasus, so they stopped their deportation of the Cossacks and turned their wrath upon the indigenous peoples. Once it began, the Soviet assault on the Circassians was even more fundamental than Tsarist efforts. It was in fact a comprehensive attempt to destroy every vestige of tradition that remained. The first victim was Kabardia, which was put on the chopping block once again. The Kabardians tried to outmaneuver Moscow and declared autonomy in May 1921, but they lost it the following January when the Kabardino-Balkar Oblast was created. Much of Kabardia's remaining pasture land was given to the Balkars, Karachays, Ossetians, and Ingush.[58] The Kabardians were now left with only a tiny fraction of their original territory, and they shared it with more than forty other ethnic groups.[59] Also in January the Karachaevo-Cherkess United Oblast was created; there seventy thousand Slavs, fifty-one thousand Karachays, fourteen thousand Abazas, six thousand Nogays, and several other smaller ethnic groups lived alongside fourteen thousand Circassians.[60] The Circassians there were officially labeled Cherkes and identified as a subethnic group distinct from the Kabardians. The oblast didn't last long. A dispute between the Karachays and Circassians quickly escalated, and in 1926 the oblast had to be divided into the Karachay Autonomous Oblast and the Cherkess National Okrug to avoid violence.[61]

There is little information about the Karachay–Circassian conflict, but it most likely arose from the land distribution issue. Russian Imperial documents never mention any hostilities between the two nations, who appear to have been good neighbors since the Karachays arrived sometime between the tenth and thirteenth centuries. A reclusive people, the Karachays possessed no arable land and existed exclusively on their herds. Residing in the highest habitable areas of the Caucasus Mountains, they were vulnerable to the slightest vagaries of nature. An early winter or late spring meant the deaths of thousands of animals and starvation throughout the land.[62] Devastating floods from melting snow and glaciers continue to destroy entire communities to this day. When Evdokimov seized their most valuable pastures in 1862 and cut them off from other essential lands, the Karachays faced near-total annihilation, and many immigrated to the Ottoman Empire. Unfortunately, this didn't bring any relief to the Karachays who remained, since the land the émigrés abandoned was confiscated by the Russian government and given to Cossacks.[63] When the Bolsheviks took over, the Kabardians successfully evicted the Karachays from pastures they had appropriated out of desperation in the 1860s and permanently assigned them to Kuban Oblast, despite their pleas to be united with their close relatives, the Balkars.[64]

The two other groups were the Circassians of former Maikop Uezd and the Khakuchi Shapsugs living along the coast. The former were united in the Cherkess (Adygei) Autonomous Oblast in July 1922.[65] To avoid confusion with the Karachaevo-Cherkess National Oblast, it was renamed Adygei Autonomous Oblast in August, and another fictional "subethnic" group was created.[66] The "Adygeis," as they were now known, were encircled by Kuban Oblast, outnumbered 100 to 1 by Cossacks.[67] The Shapsugs were granted limited autonomy in November 1924 when the Bolsheviks created the Shapsug National Raion (region), but they felt this was unsatisfactory and continued to petition for full autonomy.[68]

Once the Soviets dismembered the Circassian community, they launched a campaign to destroy every vestige of Circassian national identity. While the Imperial government used proselytization and economic pressure to convert the Circassians to Christianity, the Soviets used brute force to wipe Islam out completely while offering nothing in its place. Like many of their practices during their early days when they were unsure of their power, the Bolsheviks' approach to religion was rather devious. They established Sharia courts in the North Caucasus in an apparent concession to the people there. However, it was a sham. Party officials were in charge of proceedings, and members of the local Islamic leadership were forbidden to participate.[69] As the Bolsheviks grew more confident, they restricted the scope of the Sharia courts' jurisdiction, and in 1925 they abolished them altogether. The official anti-Islamic campaign began the following year. Islamic scholars found themselves banned from all public affairs, Arabic-language schools were closed, mullahs were arrested, and pilgrimages to Mecca were forbidden.[70] In 1928 thousands of religious manuscripts were burned.[71] By the 1940s there were only seven working mosques in Kabardino-Balkaria and none in Cherkess Okrug or Adygei Oblast. Out of the 10,000 mullahs and religious scholars active in the North Caucasus in 1921, only 150 remained in 1940.[72] Without their mullahs, religious texts, or even a place to gather, Circassians and other Muslim peoples of the North Caucasus found an important part of their communal life destroyed. Islam was preserved as a small set of rituals, divorced from their religious significance.

The Soviets also sought to destroy the Circassians' code of adyge habze. The resulting campaign has been described as "a medieval carnival" in which innocuous traditions were labeled counterrevolutionary and stamped out with brutal efficiency.[73] Family solidarity, the very essence of village life in the Caucasus, was seen as an impediment to the campaigns to wipe out the so-called *kulaks* (successful farmers) of the late 1920s and 1930s, when the Soviets shot or deported any farmers who had succeeded in pulling themselves out of poverty. The Bolsheviks tried to replace it, along with the customs of blood-brotherhood and hospitality, with their own version of "mutual assistance." Naturally, this effort failed miserably. Most bizarre, and tragic, was the Soviet campaign against the elderly in the Northwest Caucasus. Articles appeared decrying the gerontocracy of the Circassian and Karachay-Balkar peoples: "The elderly were the guardians and zealots of tradition, and therefore we cannot break with the past without destroying the prestige the elderly enjoy."[74] Older villagers were first forbidden to participate in village councils and then stripped of the right to vote. By the 1930s the absurd neologism *starikovstvo* (elderism) was coined and the elders of Circassia were labeled class enemies. The final chapter of this travesty was the deportation of the elderly to Siberia. One can only imagine the surreal scene of trainloads of elderly Circassians, Karachays, and Balkars being shipped off to the gulags to die.[75]

The Soviets adopted two other Tsarist practices aimed at erasing Circassian culture from the Caucasus. The unofficial policy of eliminating Circassian toponyms, which began as soon as the Russo-Circassian War ended, continued throughout the Soviet period. Two examples stand out as particularly offensive to the memory of the war. First, in 1945 the Shapsug National Raion was renamed Lazarevsky Raion in honor of the Russian admiral whose fleet bombarded the Shapsugs in the final stages of the war. Second, the settlement of Psezuapse was renamed Arkhipo-Osipovka in honor of a Russian soldier who blew himself up along with a group of Circassians there.[76] The Tsarist policy of eliminating the traditional Circassian aul was also taken to extremes during the collectivization campaign of the 1930s, when nearly all auls were abolished and their inhabitants moved to large villages where they were integrated with other ethnic groups.[77] Naturally, they had to use Russian to communicate with one another. Not only the Circassians but all the peoples of the North Caucasus would find their languages under assault for the rest of the Soviet period.

There was a brief respite from Soviet efforts to eradicate the individuality of the Circassians and other Caucasus peoples in 1935 when a new policy called *korenizatsiia* (rootification) encouraged the non-Russian peoples to express their cultural heritages. For a short time, indigenous languages were promoted in schools, national histories were written, and folk cultures were represented on the stage. But only for a short time. When korenizatsiia fell out of favor during the Great Terror of 1937–1939, the teachers, historians, and artists who took part in the cultural revival were arrested and murdered.

The Circassians, Balkars, and Karachays had been pushed to the limit, and many young men fled to Karachay to mount a rebellion. The nearly inaccessible region had already become a refuge for anti-Soviet groups as well as deserters, draft dodgers, and common criminals of all ethnicities, and had been the base for a major uprising in 1930. In that instance, the rebels had laid down their arms after the government dropped leaflets from airplanes promising them amnesty. After they surrendered, the Soviets slaughtered them.[78] When the Nazis arrived in the Caucasus in 1941, this new batch of anti-Soviet refugees, who knew nothing about Nazi ideology, saw them as liberators. Caucasian émigrés had already parachuted into the region with promises of independence if the indigenous peoples would support the Nazis. After all the Soviets had done to them, many naively thought this was a chance for freedom.[79] The major collaborators in the North Caucasus were the Cossacks, although some Circassians and Karachays fought on the German side.[80] However, far more North Caucasians joined the Red Army and fought against the Germans until the end of the war, and pro-Soviet partisan bands in the Caucasus caused the Nazis no end of trouble.[81] Thanks in part to partisan efforts, the Red Army was able to drive the invaders out of the Caucasus by January 1943. The region had sustained huge losses in agricultural equipment, livestock, and manpower but was well on the way to recovery by summer.[82] What happened next was truly extraordinary.

In September 1943 more than sixty thousand NKVD (People's Commissariat for Internal Affairs) troops appeared throughout Karachay posing as Soviet soldiers on leave from combat.[83] On the morning of November 2 the troops surrounded the Karachay villages and forced all the residents—mostly women, children, and the elderly—into trucks at machine-gun point. They were told that due to their collaboration with the White Army forces during the Civil War (they had refused to hand over Cossacks who were hiding in their villages), the uprising of 1930, and their supposed collaboration with the Nazis, the Karachays had been declared a "traitor nation" and were to be deported. They were given one hour to gather a maximum of one hundred kilograms of possessions; according to some witnesses, not even that much time was allowed.[84] They were packed into cattle cars and sent to camps in Central Asia where they spent the next fourteen years as slave laborers. Their animals were left to die.[85] Nation after nation met the same fate over the next two months: the Chechens, Ingush, Kalmyks, and others were each surrounded and shipped to "special camps" throughout Central Asia. In March 1944 the Balkars, quite possibly the most inoffensive people of all time, were likewise rounded up and shipped off to Kazakhstan and Kyrgyzstan.[86]

The Circassians were untouched by the Soviets during the deportations. In the correspondence between Soviet dictator Joseph Stalin and NKVD chief Lavrenty Beria, there isn't even any discussion of deporting them.[87] It wasn't a matter of numbers: in 1939 there were nearly four hundred thousand Chechens and only three hundred thousand Circassians in the Soviet Union. Furthermore, Chechnya was never occupied by the Nazis, so they couldn't have collaborated, whereas an entire Circassian division fought on the German side.[88] Yet the Chechens were deported. One possible explanation is logistics. In each of the deportations, the Soviets relied on surprise to catch their victims unaware. The Circassians had been scattered into four separate administrative units, and there were another seventeen thousand Circassians living in Stavropol Krai, north of the Caucasus. A simultaneous operation would have been impossible, and if the Soviets had moved against a single Circassian oblast, the other communities would have certainly prepared to defend themselves. If this were the case, then at least in one instance the fragmentation of the Circassian people worked to their advantage.

On November 24, 1956, the Balkars were granted to right to return home; 80 percent were back in the mountains within one year.[89] It wasn't a pleasant homecoming. There had been no serious attempt to repopulate their lands, and less than a quarter of their homes were still standing.[90] They were promised money to rebuild, but little came, and the infrastructure there remains primitive to this day.[91] Perhaps more importantly, the administrative division of Kabardino-Balkaria that existed prior to the deportation and that gave the Balkars some degree of autonomy was not reestablished. As a result, Balkars found themselves a minority in all spheres of public life. The Balkars' sense of injustice at their deportation, coupled with the difficulties they faced upon their return, led to tensions between them and the Kabardians that persist today.

The return of the Karachays was even more problematic. First and foremost, their autonomous oblast was not restored to them as the order concerning their return had promised. Instead, the failed Karachay-Cherkess Autonomous Oblast was resurrected. No public announcement of the Karachays' innocence was ever made either. While this was true of all the deported peoples, the Karachays represented about 35 percent of a highly multiethnic society. When they returned, many of the Russians, Cossacks, Circassians, and others believed they had been "pardoned," that is, that the entire nation had been somehow guilty of something.[92] Unlike Balkaria, their lands had been colonized by Georgians, but rather than wait for the Georgians to be deported, many of the Karachays settled in the lowlands alongside Russian, Circassian, and Abaza villages. Their presence diluted the political voices of the other ethnic groups, and this caused resentment on top of suspicion. They were also angered by what they believed to be the Soviets' continued discrimination against them.[93] The Karachays remain a deeply aggrieved people who have little sympathy for the Circassians' plight.

The leaders of the Brezhnev era found these tensions a useful tool to divert the Karachays' and Circassians' anger away from Moscow and toward each other. The primary agent in this effort was Mikhail Gorbachev, who was made First Secretary of Stavropol Krai in 1971. In 1974 he began a scapegoat campaign against the Karachays, blaming them for "displays of nationalism and nationalist narrow-mindedness."[94] He also accused the Karachays of "traitorous behavior" during World War II, resurrecting Stalin's false charges against them.[95] Hostilities intensified after Gorbachev's campaign to the point that the entire oblast nearly descended into civil war over a motorcycle accident. A Karachay boy was killed by a Cossack motorcyclist, who was found hanged shortly afterward. The confrontation soon engulfed much of the republic, with the Karachays on one side and the Cossacks and Circassians on the other. The Soviets sent in a military unit. The Karachays panicked, thinking they were going to be deported again. A Ministry of Internal Affairs commission came from Moscow and defused the situation, but nothing was done to address the ethnic tensions that had caused it.[96] Relations between the Circassians and Karachays have remained hostile ever since, and the two formerly good neighbors have come close to civil war on more than one occasion since 1991.

By 1990 there were 650,000 Circassians in the North Caucasus, approximately half their 1860 population. They had been deceived, abused, bullied, and terrorized; their traditions had been wiped out or driven underground; what remained of their nation had been hacked to pieces; and their identity as a single people had been subverted by a perverse Soviet nationality policy. When the Soviet Union collapsed at the end of 1991, the Circassians began to gather the pieces to try to build a new future for themselves and their compatriots in exile. A new era opened up opportunities for the Circassians never seen before. While not without challenges and frustrations, the process of reclaiming their history and heritage could at least begin.

8

The Road to Sochi

> Violence can only be concealed by a lie, and the lie can only be maintained by violence.
>
> —Aleksandr Solzhenitsyn

> The ancient Greeks lived around Sochi lots of centuries ago. I also saw the rock near Sochi to which, so legend has it, Prometheus was chained. It was Prometheus who gave people fire, fire which is ultimately the Olympic flame.[1]

With these words Russian president Vladimir Putin unwittingly declared war on the Circassian people. His implication that the ancient Greeks were the first inhabitants at Sochi struck Circassians worldwide as the most blatant and public attempt yet to erase their history. Most likely, Putin believed linking the Prometheus legend to the Olympic flame was a clever way to accept the nomination and nothing more. What it did, however, was galvanize the Circassian community in a way perhaps nothing else could.

This was the worst in a series of missteps the Moscow government made in the first decade of the twenty-first century. First, Moscow not only rejected repeated Circassian appeals to recognize the genocide but it went out of its way to try to discredit the proponents of genocide recognition and to distort the Russian conquest of the Caucasus. Second, Moscow infiltrated the leadership of the early Circassian nationalist movements in an attempt to control them, but this only led to the creation of new organizations that were more assertive and less amenable to cooperation. These movements are now well organized and have begun to pursue their goals. Third, Russia has sponsored a series of "anniversaries" to rewrite the relationship between Russia and Circassia all the way back to the sixteenth century, outraging Circassians around the globe. Finally, Russia's military and political assistance to Abkhazia in its fight for independence from Georgia further emboldened the proponents of Circassian reunification. Circassians both in Russia and abroad began actively to campaign for the creation of a united Circassian homeland and the right to repatriation. But before they were able to start, the Circassians had to deal with an entirely new political situation that threatened to balkanize the Northwest Caucasus and drag it into civil war.

The Chaos of Freedom

A Circassian national renaissance actually began in the late 1980s with the advent of Mikhail Gorbachev's policy of glasnost, when groups aiming to revive the cultures of each of the North Caucasus peoples emerged. Initially interested in promoting native languages and cultures, the leaders of these movements quickly realized that cultural preservation was ultimately dependent on political autonomy. The first organization to address the Circassians' concerns was Adyge Hase, which was created at the Conference of the Assembly of the Mountain Peoples of the Caucasus at Sukhumi, Georgia, in August 1989. In addition to the goals of most other ethnic organizations in the North Caucasus—agricultural and economic reform, cultural revival, ecological preservation—Adyge Hase's program included the unification of all Circassians in the Soviet Union into a single republic as well as the repatriation of Circassians living abroad.[2] These remain the Circassians' two central demands today.

In 1989 Karachaevo-Cherkessia was an autonomous oblast within Stavropol Krai (Province). The ethnic mix in the oblast was one of the most complex and contradictory in all the Soviet Union. In 1989 the population was 414,970, with Russians and Cossacks accounting for 42 percent and Karachays representing 31 percent. The Circassians were not only a tiny minority at 9 percent, they were scarcely more numerous than the Abazas, who had their own memories of war and deportation and their own agenda. The Nogays, a Turkic people distinct from the Karachay-Balkars, represented only 3 percent of the population but had strong organizational ties with a larger Nogay community north of Chechnya. There were also small populations of Greeks and Ossetians, and many Armenian refugees from the 1988 Spitak earthquake that devastated Armenia. Virtually no one was happy with the status quo, and conflicts would have been inevitable under the best of circumstances. However, other problems in the republic made things even worse. There had been no upgrading of infrastructure since the days of Stalin, and the majority of the native population lived in villages at subsistence level. Dumping of heavy metals and other toxins had polluted many of the rivers. Major disagreements over land distribution, particularly between the Karachays and the Cossacks, had been simmering since the 1950s. The Karachays themselves felt they had never been properly compensated for their suffering during the deportation and had become a disgruntled population. They lobbied throughout 1989 and 1990 with increasing vigor for autonomy within their regions of the oblast and, in contradiction to Soviet law, declared the creation of the Karachay Autonomous Oblast on June 9, 1990.[3]

Adyge Hase had its sights on more than autonomy for the Circassians of Karachaevo-Cherkessia. It quickly created chapters in all the Circassian-populated areas of the Russian Federation and worked to establish links with diaspora groups. Arguing (correctly) that the Kabardians, Cherkes, Adygeis, and Shapsugs were one nation, Circassian representatives at Adyge Hase's second congress voted to adopt the name Cherkes as their common appellation. After convincing several other organizations to merge into Adyge Hase, the group began to work up plans for the establishment of an autonomous republic encompassing all the Circassian regions. As part of this plan, a massive repatriation of the diaspora was proposed that would facilitate the re-creation of Circassia along the Black Sea coast. While many young people enthusiastically backed the idea, the reality was that repatriation would be a gradual process at best. Krasnodar Krai, which encompasses most of historical Circassia, is heavily populated with Cossacks. Large numbers of migrants from throughout the Soviet Union—Armenian refugees from the Spitak earthquake, Tajiks and Uzbeks fleeing war in Central Asia, Abkhazian and even Kurdish and Chinese refugees—have moved into the region.[4] Tremendous resistance would be met should the Circassians begin to return in large numbers.

Actually, breaking Karachaevo-Cherkess Oblast up would have made a lot of sense, but, thanks to Soviet mismanagement and the Tsarist legacy, the logistics were insurmountable. Rather than deal with the problem directly, Russian president Boris Yeltsin let oblast strongman Vladimir Khubiev manipulate the situation. Khubiev was a Karachay but had loyalty to no one but himself. He was almost universally detested but had developed a powerful coterie during the Brezhnev years and had powerful allies in Moscow. After Karachay's declaration of autonomy, the Cossacks and Abazas countered by proposing the establishment of Karachaevo-Cherkessia as an autonomous republic. For Khubiev, this was the best way to ensure his continued role as head of the oblast, and soon July 3, 1991, he withdrew the oblast from Stavropol Krai and declared its autonomy. In response, a joint congress of Peoples of Karachaevo-Cherkessia proposed the creation of a Circassian autonomous region, but because it would include Nogay villages, their delegation boycotted the congress and the resolution failed. At this point the "Cossack" organization Rus declared the creation of the Batalpashinsk and Zelenchuk-Urup Republics in November and December, respectively. In fact, Rus was primarily Russian. In 1989 Cossacks represented perhaps only 5 percent of the population of the oblast. Rus opened its membership to both Russians and Cossacks but presented itself as a Cossack society. This allowed it to operate in tandem with much larger Cossack circles throughout the North Caucasus that were determined to strip all the autonomous republics of their Cossack-populated regions. Rus claimed its goals were "peace, friendship, and mutual understanding between the peoples of the republic," but its central goal was the creation of a separate Cossack republic with Cherkessk, to be renamed Batalpashinsk (the city's original name), as its capital. It also planned to appropriate large amounts of land from the Karachays, create its own paramilitary militia that would be outside the control of the Russian armed forces, and start military and "patriotic" training of youth in schools. By 1992 armed bands of Cossacks were acting as vigilante police forces in several stanitsy, and it began to look like the old Tsarist days again. The looming crisis caught Yeltsin's attention, and in February he recommended partitioning Karachaevo-Cherkessia into three autonomous regions. Khubiev called upon his Moscow allies and defeated the plan, proposing instead that a referendum be held on Karachay autonomy, to be voted on only by the Karachays. Through some very skillful manipulation, he managed to change the referendum into a question concerning the unity of the republic so that everyone could vote. The new proposal was approved by nearly 80 percent of the voters on March 5, and this allowed Khubiev to remain in power until 1999, much to the chagrin of nearly everyone.[5]

This complex situation came to a head that year when Karachaevo-Cherkessia finally held its first election for republic *glava* (chief). In the first round of voting on April 25 Circassian mineral-water magnate Stanislav Derev and retired general Vladimir Semyonov, who was half-Karachay and half-Cossack, received 40 percent and 18 percent of the vote, respectively, while Khubiev received less than 7 percent. Immediately after the election an apparently well-orchestrated wave of terrorism struck the republic: two assassination attempts were made on Derev and houses of supporters of both finalists were set on fire. Khubiev traveled to Moscow and tried to persuade authorities there that the violence proved the republic was not ready for open elections. While it was fairly clear that Khubiev was the organizer of the terrorism, the effective result was intensified suspicion between the Karachays and Circassians. The second round took place on May 16, with more than 76 percent of the voters choosing Semyonov. That evening, thousands of Circassians and Abazas began a protest in Cherkessk and issued an ultimatum to Moscow demanding that the Circassians be allowed to secede from the republic. On July 30 virtually the entire Karachay nation arrived in Cherkessk—estimates range between 150,000 and 175,000 people—and faced off against the Circassian and Abaza protestors. Special operations troops were sent in, but the situation was chaotic. To their credit, the troops just kept the two sides apart.[6] Semyonov went ahead with his inauguration on September 15, but since it was still unsafe for him in Cherkessk the ceremony was held in his native village. Two days later the Circassians announced the creation of the Cherkess Autonomous Oblast. The Slavs likewise threatened secession, the Abazas and Nogays organized protests, and terrorist acts continued unabated. Boris Akbashev, the Republican leader of Adyge Hase, organized a new rally of several thousand Circassians and Abazas in Cherkessk, again demanding the creation of a Cherkess Autonomous Oblast. The protest dwindled, but animosity between Circassians and Karachays escalated, and by October there was talk of a "second Chechnya" brewing. By late October a tenuous compromise was reached, and the republic narrowly avoided civil war.

In contrast to their compatriots in Karachaevo-Cherkessia, the Circassians of Adygeia found themselves in a uniquely advantageous political position. They accounted for just over 20 percent of the population while Cossacks represented 68 percent. However, their status as "titular" ethnic group, coupled with Adyge Hase's organizational abilities, allowed them to gain control of the republic.[7] A new curriculum was set up almost entirely in Circassian and laws were passed that made it difficult, and in some cases impossible, for Cossacks to participate in political life.[8] Throughout the 1990s the Adygei government established a series of acts, orders, and regulations aimed at promoting the repatriation of Circassians living abroad and even declared August 1 "Repatriation Day." The Cossacks were less than enthused. In 1992 the Union of Slavs of Adygeia was created by Nina Konovalova and Vladimir Karataev, and the group actively opposed all actions of the Adygei government that prioritized the rights of Circassians. Their public stance—that the rights of the Slavic majority should be respected—was really a device to achieve their ultimate goal: the dissolution of the republic altogether. Their position was that by simply being born on the wrong side of the border they were deprived of numerous rights enjoyed by their compatriots in Krasnodar Krai, and they felt like unwelcome guests in their own homes.

The full story was more complicated. After the fall of the Soviet Union, the Cossacks were granted many of the same rights they had under the tsars. They were allowed to carry weapons, a criminal offense for the Circassians and one of the most blatant symbols of the disgrace of their defeat. Cossack youths were prioritized for admission into military academies and were allowed to fulfill their service responsibilities in Cossack militias. The Cossacks of Adygeia enjoyed all these privileges. Konovalova's group wanted other special privileges for themselves—a special budget, special accommodations for local rule, for example—that their compatriots in Krasnodar and Stavropol Krais enjoyed but which they did not. At the same time they campaigned to eliminate the "indigenous rights" of the Circassians.[9] A compromise never materialized and the Slavs of Adygeia have continued their efforts unabated. At the same time, Adygeia's Adyge Hase leadership composition changed dramatically. Originally run by college-educated activists, it was taken over during the second half of the 1990s by the business elite with connections to Moscow. By the early twenty-first century the organization had transformed into a vehicle to advance one's career and had lost legitimacy in the eyes of many Circassians, particularly the younger generation.[10] To fill the gap, activists organized the Circassian Congress, which in 2005 took Adyge Hase's place as the premier Circassian organization in Adygeia, adopting a much more aggressive stance concerning Circassian rights. Konovalova's group has responded by becoming even more belligerent, holding marches that have been accused of promoting "xenophobia and radical nationalism."[11]

One event in Adygeia that drew a lot of attention was Moscow's granting permission for 165 Circassians to immigrate to the republic in 1998 from war-torn Kosovo. The repatriates had high hopes when they returned to their historical homeland, but—not surprisingly—there were significant challenges and disappointments for many of them. As a result of their contact with the Ottoman Empire, they practiced a traditional form of Islam that conflicted with the far more syncretic traditions of the Circassians who stayed behind. They all spoke Circassian as their first language but had little or no knowledge of Russian, so they were isolated from the majority of the republic's population. Also, the circumstances under which they migrated were extreme: they had witnessed heavy bombing and ground battles between Kosovars and Serbs, and had lost all their property. The pressures were too much for some, who either returned to Kosovo or immigrated to Turkey. Still, most remain in Adygeia and have gradually adapted to a new life there.[12] Despite the small number involved, the episode has become something of a rallying cry for the proponents of repatriation and has taken center stage again now that Syrian Circassians are petitioning to repatriate for very similar reasons.

The third republic, Kabardino-Balkaria, was the only place in the North Caucasus where Circassians weren't a small fraction of the population, but they still weren't a majority. In the 1960s and 1970s there had been a large Slavic migration to the republic, and in 1989 the Kabardians represented only 48 percent of the population. They were also losing their unique dialect as more young people migrated to the cities. This, of course, was a result of the artificial nature of both of the "dual-titled" republics. Since Circassian and Balkar are completely unrelated languages, Russian has become the lingua franca of the cities. By the 1990s the Russian language had taken over all the public and industrial spheres, and the native languages were relegated to service industries, journalism, and education.[13] Under these circumstances it's no wonder that Kabardian intellectuals began campaigning to preserve their language and culture from the very first days of glasnost.

The Kabardians and Balkars, who had traditionally enjoyed extremely good relations, had their share of conflicts as well. As a result of Soviet blundering when they returned from exile, the Balkars' political voice was drowned out by the Russians and Kabardians. In the 1990 elections for representatives to the Russian Federal Supreme Council, only one Balkar was chosen, and then only after an appeal by the Kabardian regional director. Like the Karachays, the Balkars felt they had not been properly compensated for their suffering under Stalin and weren't particularly sympathetic to the Kabardians' concerns. In a symbolic act of cooperation, the republic's supreme council passed a joint declaration demanding reparations for the Balkars and recognizing the Russo-Circassian War as genocide against the Circassians. Unfortunately, things became tense soon afterward as both groups struggled to preserve their own distinct cultures and stake their claims on the small amounts of pasture land that remained.[14] The National Kabardian Movement, which united several political parties and civil groups, took the lead in fighting for the Circassian agenda. Its early goals were to unite the Circassians into a single political unit and facilitate the repatriation of Circassians in diaspora. Meanwhile, the Slavic population mobilized to undermine what autonomy the Kabardians and Balkars enjoyed in their own homeland. The Congress of Russian Speakers was particularly adamant that the special privileges the native peoples enjoyed in their titular republics should be revoked. Essentially, the congress was proposing a return to the Tsarist system where the indigenous peoples would be politically silenced by the overwhelming Slavic majority in the region. However, much like Khubiev in Karachaevo-Cherkessia, Republican president Valery Kokov was able to consolidate his rule. The republic remained deceptively quiet until his retirement in 2005, when militants attempted to seize Nalchik.

The reasons for the assault on the capital are complicated, but in essence the ill-planned attempt to take over the Republican capital was an extreme reaction to the oppressive measures of the Russian security forces, known as the *siloviki*, particularly against practicing Muslims. In the late 1990s the local government began interfering in the selection of imams in mosques in Nalchik, and this drove many Muslims underground. A massive anti-Wahhabi campaign that had been ongoing since 1998 began to target these underground groups in 2001, and a conflict became inevitable.[15] On August 24, 2003, there was a shootout between police and suspected militants north of Nalchik, and that September officials closed mosques throughout the republic and arrested more than one hundred people.[16] Reports of abuse of practicing Muslims likewise increased.[17] In September 2005 more than four hundred Kabardians and Balkars submitted a petition to Russian president Vladimir Putin requesting permission to leave the country because of religious discrimination, echoing the Tsarist days of "voluntary" emigration.[18] On September 16 Kokov retired, and on the twenty-seventh Putin appointed Arsen Kanokov president of Kabardino-Balkaria.[19] A power struggle immediately emerged between Kanokov and Khachim Shogenov, Republican interior minister and longtime Kokov ally. It was then that the militants decided to make their move.

The assault on Nalchik began on the morning of October 13 and continued until mid-afternoon, although two hostage situations dragged out until the next day.[20] Fewer than six hundred "militants" were involved, and many were just random youths who spontaneously joined in.[21] The assault seemed to be poorly coordinated and intended merely as a show of strength, but speculations as to the rebels' intents assumed an alarmist character. Waves of arrests swept across Kabardino-Balkaria, and numerous accusations of torture were leveled against the siloviki.[22] There were similar police actions in the other autonomous republics in the Northwest. In Karachaevo-Cherkessia the siloviki began to harass suspected militants and opposition politicians alike.[23] In Adygeia there was a rumor of an impending terrorist attack, and nervous police in Maikop began to threaten the residents for spreading it.[24] People attending mosques were arbitrarily arrested, and the most important imam in the republic was beaten twice by police.[25] All this accomplished was to drive pious Muslims underground, where they became more susceptible to radical ideas. Kabardino-Balkaria has since been particularly plagued by factionalism that in some ways resembles the conflict between Muhammad Amin and Sefer-Bey Zanoko in the nineteenth century. Like Amin, the underground Islamists are determined to establish a pan-Caucasian Islamic state. They have even assassinated cultural figures who have studied and popularized Circassian pre-Islamic culture. In response, a group of Kabardians calling themselves the Black Hawks have vowed to destroy the Islamists and reestablish Circassian traditions. The republic has been descending further and further into chaos ever since.

With the fall of the Soviet Union, the Circassians in the Caucasus established closer contacts with their compatriots across the Black Sea than had ever been possible before. Radio broadcasts from Adygeia had always been available in Turkey, but now their frequency has increased. An office called Rodina (Motherland) was opened to establish links between Circassians in the Caucasus and those in diaspora. *Dernekler* (ethnic associations) promoting language courses, cultural evenings, and trips to the Caucasus appeared in every Turkish village and town where Circassians live. Ferry boats across the sea and regular flights between Istanbul and Maikop allowed easy access to the homeland. As a result, vacations to Russia and attendance in universities in the North Caucasus have increased dramatically and have instilled an even greater sense of national unity in the new generation of Circassians in Turkey. Exchanges of scholars and political figures also began in the early 1990s, and publications featured joint contributions by Russian and Turkish authors. International organizations with ties to the Caucasus began to appear beyond Turkey as well. The Circassian International Academy of Sciences, founded in 1993 in Nalchik, has opened branches in Israel and Jordan. The International Circassian Association, created by diaspora and Russian representatives in Nalchik in 1991, now has chapters as far away as Orange County, California, and has actively campaigned for Circassian rights in Russia and Europe. Folk dancers and musicians from the North Caucasus have toured the Middle East, sparking new interest in Circassian history and culture. In the case of the Turks, however, this new accessibility to their homeland has allowed them to "live on both banks of the river," as Ahyan Kaya has put it. Rather than militantly demand complete right of return, many have found the status quo an acceptable compromise.[26]

Circassians in Israel and the Arab states had different challenges to their aspirations for return. Jordan's dominant tribal politics led the Circassians and Chechens to form their own tribal council in 1980. To present themselves as an authentic Jordanian tribe, the proponents of the tribal approach have embraced the *hijra* narrative that describes their ancestors' departure from Circassia as a religiously motivated decision.[27] Many Jordanian Circassians have accepted this narrative and are more acquiescent about their current situation, although those who have studied Circassian history realize this interpretation is incorrect. Their political and economic success has also made them more reluctant to risk immigration to the Caucasus, where the economy is in a state of near-total collapse. Instead of Nalchik, many Jordanian Circassians send their children to Europe and America for college. The economic issue is a central concern for the Israeli Circassians as well. The few who returned to the Caucasus were shocked by the low standard of living in Russia and quickly returned to Israel. In addition, many Israeli Jews are dismayed that their Circassian co-nationals wish to leave, and this has had a psychological effect on them. Those who might consider emigrating don't want to upset the good relations their compatriots enjoy with their Israeli neighbors.[28] The one hundred thousand Syrian Circassians were well-integrated into public life because of their longtime support of the Ba'ath Party, so there had been no strong impetus to repatriate. The events of the Arab Spring have changed that situation.

Despite all the hurdles, the Circassian diaspora began to consider seriously the possibility of return. Of course, many had never completely given up hope, but the Abkhaz-Georgian War of 1992 pushed them into action. The majority of the Abkhazians were driven out of their homeland by the Russians in 1865, and by the mid-twentieth century they were outnumbered by Georgians. During glasnost Abkhazians in Turkey embarked on a mass immigration project that would shift the numbers in their favor. With the help of Russian military intervention, Abkhazia established de facto independence and almost immediately created a department to facilitate the repatriation of the diaspora. The Circassians were watching and began seriously to consider the possibility of their mass repatriation as well. Demonstrations in Turkey concerning Russian acts in the Caucasus became commonplace and demands for repatriation started.[29] By 1993 nearly four thousand Circassians had returned to their homeland and another three thousand were in line. While these are seemingly insignificant numbers, Chen Bram notes that the first wave of Jewish migration to Palestine in 1882 was fewer than three thousand.[30]

While the Circassians of the Caucasus focused their efforts on political unification and repatriation during the 1990s, by the beginning of the twenty-first century they had turned their attention to the issue of the genocide. In April 2005 an online petition asked the United Nations, the U.S. Congress, and the European Union to recognize the Circassian genocide.[31]

On May 21 and 22, scholars, journalists, and political figures from Russia, Turkey, England, France, and other nations held a conference in Istanbul entitled "The Tragedy of the Caucasus," at which the delegates called upon the Russian Federation to recognize it as well.[32] On September 26 the Caucasus Forum of Turkey sent a letter supported by the Circassian Congress to the Russian Duma requesting that the Russian government formally recognize the Circassian genocide.[33] On January 27, 2006, the Duma rejected the request, arguing that the events occurred prior to the Soviet period (although no explanation was provided as to why that was relevant).[34] Undeterred, on October 11 Circassian representatives from nine countries asked European Parliament president Josep Borell to recognize the genocide.[35] Such efforts continue. The Circassians have also become more aggressive concerning repatriation. At a congress in Nalchik in March 2003 the International Circassian Association announced that its fundamental task was to facilitate the repatriation of Circassians in diaspora. Subsequent conferences in May in Maikop and in June in Cherkessk addressed repatriation issues and strategies to preserve the Circassian language.[36]

"The Falsification of History for the Benefit of Russia's Interests"

Russia's first response to all these activities, particularly the calls for recognition for the genocide, was to rewrite history. One novel move was the declaration of the 450th anniversary of the "voluntary unification of Circassia with Russia" in 2007, which was to be marked by a series of events in September and October. The reference was to a 1557 military alliance between Ivan the Terrible and a delegation of Kabardian and Besleney pshis.[37] The first written treaty actually dates from 1588 and consists of formulas typical of treaties Moscow drew up with other sovereign states, clearly indicating that Moscow considered Kabardia an independent political entity. Moreover, the 1588 treaty was signed by the Kabardians only, so there is no way to construe it as a unification of all of Circassia with Russia.[38] In addition to implying Russia controlled part of the North Caucasus far earlier than it really did, the celebration also subtly redefined the Russo-Circassian War. If Circassia was annexed by Russia in 1557, then the Russo-Circassian conflict was not really a war between two nations but a rebellion by disloyal subjects. Circassians worldwide interpreted these

events as a ploy by Moscow to thwart Circassian efforts to have the genocide recognized and were outraged.[39]

In February 2007 Adyge Hase announced its opposition to both the
450th anniversary and another politically motivated celebration, the 150th
anniversary of the founding of Maikop. It wasn't recognition of the city that
the Circassians objected to but rather the date chosen. As assistant chairman Mamet Edidzhi noted: "One could mark the occasion when the first
villages appeared in the area. That would be one date. One could talk about
the settlement's incorporation as a city—that would be another date. 1857,
the date selected as the year of Maikop's foundation, is the year when Tsarist soldiers fortified the region."[40] Choosing the year that Maikop became
the base of operations for Evdokimov's ethnic cleansing campaign seemed
to be a direct slap in the face of the Circassians. Edidzhi questioned the
need for a celebration at all and warned that Circassians would not participate in the event. He proposed 1870, the year of Maikop's incorporation,
as a compromise date, but this idea was rejected. Edidzhi also pointed out
that a special commission made up of historians concluded in 1997 that
there is no way that the treaty of 1557 could be construed as a "voluntary
union" between Kabardia and Russia, much less all of Circassia. Circassian
groups in the United States and Turkey launched coordinated protests at
the United Nations and the Russian consulate in Istanbul on October 4,
2007, the day before a concert connected to the 450th anniversary celebration called "Forever with Russia" was to take place in Moscow.[41]

The final straw for many Circassians was the International Olympic
Committee's (IOC) selection on July 4, 2007, of Sochi as the location for
the 2014 Winter Olympic Games. The city of Sochi stands as a particularly painful reminder for the Circassians. The location of their first and
only parliament, it became a site of suffering and death as their ancestors waited to be deported from their homeland while Russians celebrated
in Qbaada Meadow. Shortly after the deportation, Russians, Cossacks,
Ukrainians, and many other peoples began to settle Sochi. The Soviets saw
the potential of the area, with its warm shores and snow-covered mountains, and turned Sochi into a resort city for the Party elite. Initially the
shoreline was the primary focus of development, although recently the
mountains have become a destination for wealthy ski enthusiasts such as
Putin himself. During Soviet times, it was a city with two quite different

sets of residents: the descendants of the original colonists were primarily poor, while the seasonal visitors were from the highest levels of the Soviet political machine. The purported plan for the Sochi Olympics was to fully develop its winter sport capabilities and make it a year-round resort rather than just a summer beach city. Initially most Russians overwhelmingly supported the Sochi nomination, and so when Circassian organizations from around the world petitioned the IOC in December 2006 asking that Sochi be excluded from consideration, they had little support in the country.[42] The diaspora Circassians explained that the submission of Sochi for consideration was particularly offensive for several reasons. First, the site of the main complex was to be Krasnaya Polyana, which was the location of the final battle of the Russo-Circassian War and the place where the Russians held a victory parade and banquet. The notion of medals symbolizing peaceful competition between nations being awarded on the very ground where military decorations were handed out for the annihilation of the Circassian nation exactly 150 years earlier filled many with indignation. Second, the Sochi region was the home of the Ubykhs, one tribe completely driven out of the Caucasus by the Russians. Their civilization and culture have been completely eradicated, and their language is extinct. Third, multiple sites of archeological significance concerning Circassian history were located in the area and were in danger of being destroyed during the construction. While other concerns, particularly ecological damage, initially kept the Circassian issue in the background, by 2011 activism by the diaspora community, Russian mishandling of the situation, and completely unforeseen events have threatened to tarnish the Sochi Olympics in the international arena.

The terrible reality is that Moscow wasted a unique opportunity to facilitate "a conclusive reconciliation between [the Russian and Circassian] peoples," as Circassian athlete Aramby Khapay put it.[43] In 1999 the IOC provided the vehicle for such a reconciliation with *Agenda 21*, which among other things endorsed the "recognition and strengthening of [indigenous peoples'] role" in organizing and conducting the Games.[44] The following year the Australian government worked with the aboriginal community to implement the IOC's mandate, and in 2010 the Canadian government involved the Native Canadian peoples on multiple organizational levels not only to raise awareness of their role in the history of the country but also to create a long-term economic development plan. At the Vancouver 2010 Winter Olympic Games, Native Canadians were given seats of honor.[45] Rather than follow this lead, however, Moscow seemed to go out of its way to demonstrate its contempt for the Circassians' concerns. Even before the winner of the competition was to be announced, the news program *Vesti* featured a publicity spot that chronicled the "history" of Sochi but included no reference to the Circassians at all.[46] The IOC seemed to be complicit in the disregard of Circassian sensibilities, selecting Sochi as the site for the 2014 Olympics without ever having responded to Circassian petitions concerning the issue. From the very beginning, many Circassians both in Russia and abroad saw the Games as an attempt to obliterate the last memory of their presence in the Caucasus.

For the first few years after Sochi was chosen, the Circassians' concerns were drowned out by the multitude of other problems the Games faced. International attention was focused first and foremost on the environmental destruction that was under way: large numbers of old-growth trees felled, massive dumping into area rivers, and other serious violations that made Greenpeace Russia throw its hands up and walk out for a short time. Other problems appeared in the Russian press: massive embezzlement, endemic corruption, judicial abuse, and total disregard for the rights of the current residents of Krasnaya Polyana. Meanwhile, rather than protest the Sochi issue, the Russian Circassians were becoming more aggressive in their efforts to create a unified republic and facilitate repatriation. On November 23, 2008, an Extraordinary Conference of the Circassian People took place in Cherkessk. At this meeting, the youth organization Hase issued a declaration:

> The Federal authorities need to understand that the Circassians can no longer endure the current situation and consider this to be an opportune moment for the lawful resolution of the question of a single entity within the Russian Federation—Circassia. Without a doubt, silence and negligence do not solve problems, but rather lead to a worsening of a situation. . . . The Circassian youth of the North Caucasus who have come to this forum have decided to ask the Federal government about the resolution of the question of unification of the Circassians of the Caucasus into one republic in the Russian Federation.[47]

On September 12, 2009, a "Forum of the Circassian Youth" was held in Cherkessk to address the same issues. At this meeting, speakers decried the failure of Circassian organizations to adequately address the question of Circassian unity and issued an eight-point declaration that included recognition of the Adygeis, Cherkes, Kabardians, and Shapsugs as a single Circassian ethnic group.[48] Moscow's response was predictable. On January 19, 2010, Russian president Dmitry Medvedev announced the division of the Southern Federal District, which had included all three Circassian republics and the Shapsug Raion, into two districts: six of the seven North Caucasus republics and Stavropol Krai would be united in the North Caucasus Federal District while Adygeia and Shapsug Raion would remain in the Southern Federal District.[49] Although there was some speculation that this move was made to remove Sochi from the same district as the North Caucasus and give the illusion that a terrorist attack during the Games was less likely, the Circassian leadership both in Russia and abroad saw it as an attempt to thwart efforts to unify the Circassian community in Russia.

On the repatriation issue, the Forum of Kabardian (Circassian) Organizations was held in Nalchik on April 4, 2009, and was attended by more than four hundred delegates from across the north Caucasus regions where Circassians reside, representing Adyge Hase, the Circassian Congress, the Kabardian Congress, the Union of Abkhazian Volunteers of Kabardino-Balkaria, and other groups. A resolution was forwarded to President Medvedev requesting a simplification of the procedure for Circassian émigrés to obtain permission to return to one of the current Circassian enclaves in Russia. The resolution pointed out that there was no possibility of a massive repatriation of Circassians, but that such a simplification would be an act of "historical justice." A major obstacle to repatriation, as codified in a 2006 Russian order concerning repatriation of émigré Circassians, is the requirement that the applicant speak Russian. The forum suggested that the requirement for any person living abroad who belongs to a minority group in the Russian Federation be that the person speak the language of his or her nationality, with the stipulation that upon repatriation the applicant immediately undertake the study of Russian.[50] While none of these efforts were in any way threatening, on December 22 federal representative Vladimir Ustinov made comments in his annual speech on security in the North Caucasus in Moscow that tied Circassian national organizations to the rise of terrorism in the North Caucasus, stating that "Circassian nationalists" were one of the greatest threats in the region.[51] Moscow also began to intimidate Circassian diaspora investment in the North Caucasus. In just one incident, three Circassian businessmen on their way to an economic summit in Rostov-na-Donu were detained at the airport and deported.[52]

Despite all these efforts and despite Moscow's disregard for Circassian concerns, many groups in Russia including Adyge Hase announced that they would not officially oppose the Sochi Olympics.[53] There was even the suggestion of a "Circassiada," that is, an international athletic competition featuring Circassians from Russia and the diaspora to be held in 2012 in several cities and towns in the historical Circassian homeland. Originally conceived by Circassians in Russia, members of the diaspora joined the project. Throughout 2009 presentations about the Circassiada were made in Turkey, the United States, and several cities in Russia.

Many of the Circassians abroad felt this response was inadequate and adopted a more confrontational approach, and it is their movement that has gained international attention. The No Sochi 2014 Committee, founded in 2010, engendered a series of protests in Canada, the United States, Europe, and Turkey. Members traveled to Vancouver in February 2010 to protest at the Winter Games there and gained some modest news coverage. On May 21, 2011, Circassians protested at the Russian embassies and consulates in the United States, Turkey, Germany, Israel, and Jordan. Since then the Circassian anti-Sochi movement has gradually gained attention, including an article by Reuters in October 2011 and a mention in *Time* magazine.[54] Using social media tools such as Facebook and Twitter, Circassians have also created a network of anti-Sochi activists numbering in the thousands who continue to hold and plan protests, meetings, and discussions on a regular basis. Websites in English, Turkish, Arabic, Russian, German, and other languages publicize the Circassian campaign to stop, or at least discredit, the Sochi Games.

The Russian reaction has been a combination of hard-line policies to silence opposition in Russia and a multifaceted propaganda campaign. One part of this effort is designed to portray the opponents of the Sochi Games, and indeed all Circassian activists who have adopted a confrontational attitude toward Moscow, as part of a U.S.-driven effort to increase instability in the North Caucasus and perhaps even wrest it away from Russia altogether.[55] The Russian government itself continues to portray Circassian activists as extremists, and has gone as far as to file criminal charges against people who discuss the genocide of 1864.[56] On September 23 the Russian Ministry of Justice made the policy official, issuing a warning to the Circassian Congress in Adygeia that discussion of the "Russo-Circassian War" or "genocide" against the Circassians by the Russian Empire would be considered an extremist act.[57] At this same time, assassinations of Circassian activists began. Well-known Circassian activist Suadin Pshukov was murdered in Nalchik less than two weeks after the Ministry of Justice's announcement.[58] In addition to its efforts to silence Circassian activism, the Russian government began a campaign to undermine claims that the genocide of 1864 was in fact genocide. Much of this was predictable and has been going on since 2001, when the Russian Institute of Sciences published Fasikh Baderkhan's *Severokavkazskaya Diaspora v Turtsii, Siriii Iordanii* (*The North Caucasus Diaspora in Turkey, Syria, and Jordan*). Baderkhan conflates the genocide into the entire process of Muslim out-migration from Russia and omits the details of the 1864 campaign to portray it as voluntary. A more comprehensive effort was Mark Bliev's 2004 publication, *Rossiia i Gortsy Bol'shogo Kavkaza: Na Puti k Tsivilizatsii* (*Russia and the Mountaineers of the Great Caucasus: On the Road to Civilization*). Bliev repeats nearly every justification used for the genocide since the time of the Caucasus wars, from the myth of the Circassian "raiding culture" as the cause of the war to the claim that the Circassians were hostile to Russian aggression only because of British and Ottoman agents. Multiple television programs, conferences, and roundtables have echoed the claims of Baderkhan and Bliev, inciting public opinion against the Circassians. Moscow couldn't even leave a good deed unsullied while conducting this campaign. On November 16, 2011, Russian journalist Sergei Kholoshevsky reported on the nationally televised "Today's Results" that the Kosovo Circassians who immigrated to Adygeia in 1998 were "the descendants of soldiers and officers in the Tsarist army who were based in Yugoslavia after the revolution."[59] Of course this was utter nonsense: the Circassians in Kosovo were the remnants of the diaspora population in the Balkans that the Russians failed to kill or chase out in 1878. Not only was Kholoshevsky's fabrication viewed by the Circassian community as another attempt to conceal the results of Russia's genocide against the Circassians, it was seen as an attempt to distort Russia's role in the Balkans during the Russo-Turkish War of 1877–1878.

In the midst of all this rewriting of history, Russia and Georgia fought a brief war that had unexpected and profound consequences for the Circassian issue. At the beginning of August 2008 a conflict between the Georgian military and South Ossetian irregulars led to heavy shelling of South Ossetia and the killing of several Russian troops assigned there. Using this as a pretext, the Russian military invaded Georgia through North Ossetia and, using heavy air support, quickly moved toward Tbilisi. For a short time it appeared as though the Russians planned to occupy the Georgian capital, but they withdrew to South Ossetia, which they continue to occupy.

Of course, this wasn't the first time the Russian Federation intervened in the South Caucasus: it was primarily due to Russian support that Abkhazia gained de facto independence from Georgia in the early 1990s. Not only did Tbilisi lose valuable coastline, but the Georgian population of Abkhazia was driven out in an act of ethnic cleansing that outraged the Georgian people. Now South Ossetia was lost as well and the Georgians had apparently had enough. The government of Mikheil Saakashvili had few weapons at its disposal, but one was the Georgian State Archive. The entire history of the Caucasus wars is chronicled there in the form of field notes and official reports. Duplicates are located in Moscow, but the Soviet and Russian federal governments have denied access to much of the material. Apparently Tbilisi felt that opening the archive to international scrutiny would sufficiently embarrass Moscow, so scholars were allowed in.

The Circassians had been gaining little traction in their efforts to publicize what many in the diaspora now called "the Genocide Olympics," and Tbilisi stepped in to assist them. It was an interesting political move. Russia had been consolidating its control of Abkhazia and making the case that the Abkhazia/Georgia issue was essentially the same as the Kosovo/Serbia conflict that resulted in the independence of Kosovo. The Russians argued that the Abkhazians had been subjected to a genocidal campaign by the Georgians in August 1992 and faced further threats if they remained as Georgian citizens, just as the American government had argued concerning the Kosovars' push for independence. Tbilisi apparently saw the Circassian genocide as a powerful case against Russia and drew a parallel between Kosovo/Serbia and Circassia/Russia. This would allow Georgia to highlight the Circassian genocide and embarrass Russia as it prepared for the Sochi Olympics.

To more fully publicize the archival material, the Tbilisi government organized a conference on March 20–21, 2010, in cooperation with the Jamestown Foundation, an American analytical institute with strong ties to the U.S. government and a decidedly anti-Russian editorial stance. The conference was widely attended by both Circassian and non-Circassian scholars, although Moscow put considerable effort into preventing its citizens from going. While it was presented as a scholarly conference and in fact numerous internationally respected scholars did attend, the ultimate purpose was to have the participants issue a proposal to the Georgian government to recognize the Circassian genocide. This they did. Of course, Moscow had no trouble painting the entire event as politically motivated, especially since a follow-up conference was sponsored by Jamestown and held in Washington, D.C. However, it was impossible to dismiss the revelations of the Georgian State Archive.

The Russian response was again predictable. Russian nongovernmental organizations speaking for the Kremlin used every excuse from denying there ever was a genocide to arguing that because Georgians served in the Russian Imperial Army during the genocide the Georgian government had no right to talk about it. Moscow held its own roundtable on the Caucasus wars on February 14, 2011. After concluding that the Russo-Caucasus War wasn't a war after all but rather a "clash," roundtable organizer Ruslan Kurbanov tried to dismiss the entire movement to expose the Circassian genocide as an attempt to create chaos in the North Caucasus:

> Recently tough questions concerning the history of the peoples of the North Caucasus have become instruments of political manipulation, and they are being used to justify ethnic separatism and to inflame interethnic hostility in the region. . . . Unfortunately, since there is an absence of scholarly works, pseudo-historical works are being thrown into the field of information, inflaming interethnic hostility and delineating the peoples of the North Caucasus into indigenous and newcomers, dividing them into so-called possessors of high culture and barbarians, incapable of self-rule.[60]

Russian historian Alexei Malashenko went even further, claiming that Circassian efforts to recognize the genocide were directly tied to plans for a

terrorist attack on Sochi.[61] Moscow continued to portray the activists working to have the genocide recognized, as well as scholars interested in the
subject, as either extremists or agents of the CIA. The Russian government
tried to claim the high ground through the absurdly titled "Presidential
Commission of the Russian Federation to Counter Attempts to Falsify History to the Detriment of Russia's Interests" that had been created in 2009.[62]
One of the commission's projects was the publication of nineteenth-
century documents at the website runivers.ru in order to counter the supposed falsification efforts of Circassian and Western scholars. Ironically, it
was this website that provided me with much of the evidence of Ermolov's
genocide against the Kabardians as well as material that supported the
archival documents concerning the genocide of 1864. Apparently, no one
on the commission had bothered to read the documents they were making
available to the public.

The Georgian parliament chose May 20, 2011, the day before the 147th
anniversary of the final defeat of the Circassians at Qbaada, to vote on
recognizing the genocide. Not surprisingly, the measure passed unanimously. However, this was not the final salvo in the confrontation. The
Georgian government announced a competition to design a monument to
the Circassian genocide to be erected in Anaklia, just south of the border
with Abkhazia. On December 2, 2011, the Georgian government declared
Nalchik resident Kushen Kocheskov the winner of the competition. His
design—a mother and daughter embracing, with her son standing to their
right, hand on his dagger—was dedicated on May 21, 2012.

Today, the battle over Sochi continues. On November 19, 2011, Adyge
Hase/Circassian Parliament chairman Khapay called for 2014 to be declared
a year of "memory and mourning" in remembrance of the 150th anniversary of the genocide.[63] Protests and plans to publicize the event continue
apace. The issue was even discussed on the pages of *Time* magazine on
November 28, 2011:

> Before this region became part of the Russian empire, an indige-
> nous group known as the Circassians had lived there for millennia.
> Defeated by the Czar in 1864, they were herded to the same Sochi
> shore where the Games will be held and waited there for death or
> exile. In all, some 300,000 died, victims of disease, war and famine.

Many fled to the U.S., Turkey and the Middle East. Now a large Circassian community in New Jersey has organized the No Sochi 2014 campaign, which included protests at the 2010 Vancouver Games. YOU'LL BE SKIING ON MASS GRAVES is one of the more pungent warnings in its literature.[64]

Even with such publicity, the Circassian issue isn't very well known. What impact it will ultimately have on the 2014 Winter Games remains to be seen. Even if it has no international repercussions, Moscow's reaction to the activists' objections has poisoned Russo-Circassian relations for many years to come.

Yet another issue has arisen in the last few months that is challenging Moscow to face the consequences of Tsarist actions. In December 2011 dozens of Circassian families living in Syria requested repatriation because of the Assad's government's brutal response to protests against his regime. On January 22 leaders of Adyge Hase met in Maikop and resolved to fight for the repatriation of the Syrians. Longtime supporters of the Ba'ath Party in Syria, the Circassians began openly abandoning Assad as the regime's methods became increasingly murderous. This places Moscow in a difficult position. On the one hand, Medvedev's government has been a supporter of Assad and has even shipped him military supplies to aid in his attacks on his own citizens. On the other, the Circassian genocide has already entered the international arena because of the Sochi Olympics, and if Moscow were to reject the Syrians' request, this would bring even more attention to Russia's neglect of the Circassians' plight. The Syrians' situation is very similar to that of the Kosovars, so there is logically no reason why Moscow should refuse the request. However, logic has rarely had anything to do with Russia's policies in the Caucasus.

Epilogue

The Cherkesov Affair

In the early morning of December 6, 2010, a group of young Russian men got into a fight with a few young men from the Caucasus. During the clash Yegor Sviridov, a Russian, was shot and killed. An investigation identified Aslan Cherkesov, a twenty-six-year-old Circassian, as the trigger man. A drunken brawl ending in a homicide was really nothing unusual in Moscow and shouldn't have attracted any particular attention, but on December 11 several thousand protesters marched from the site of the shooting to Manezh Square across from the Kremlin, shouting nationalist slogans and making Nazi salutes. A race riot ensued, with the protestors smashing windows, attacking passersby who appeared to be non-Slavic, and flooding into the subways to look for victims. Special OMON forces were slow to arrive, and observers claimed that they were notably restrained in comparison with how they normally dealt with civil disturbances.[1] As it turned out, Sviridov was the leader of the Union Association, one of many ultra-nationalist gangs that pose as football fan clubs. Immediately after the shooting, Sviridov was canonized by right-wing forums and blogs that gave their own version of events. The riot was the result of this propaganda campaign. Afterward, the "football clubs" promised more violence if the government didn't crack down on Caucasians in Moscow. Russian president Dmitry Medvedev condemned the nationalists' actions and tried to patch up the quickly deteriorating relations between ethnic Russians and Caucasians. Prime Minister Vladimir Putin, on the other hand, visited Sviridov's grave and placed a bouquet of flowers there, an act that was widely viewed as a defense of the ultranationalists.[2]

The subsequent investigation was conducted like a celebrity trial. Politicians and journalists alike turned Sviridov into a martyr, murdered in cold blood by a Circassian criminal—most conveniently named Cherkesov—who had come to Moscow to terrorize the citizens there. The Kabardino-Balkaria Human Rights Center issued a statement on December 15 that summarized the Circassian perception of the event:

> We cannot but be disturbed and indignant at the anti-Caucasian hysteria fomented by some Russian media outlets and certain politicians in connection with the murder of Yegor Sviridov and the events on Manege Square.
>
> Over the past two years we have registered at least five cases of murder of people from our republic in large Russian cities for reasons of racial and ethnic hatred. No significant publications on any of these cases have appeared in the Russian press. In none of these cases has an objective investigation been conducted or charges been brought against the murderers.[3]

Their concerns fell on deaf ears. The ultranationalist narrative of the event was accepted by the court, and in a case where the maximum sentence should have been ten years, Cherkesov was sentenced to twenty. Since then, ultranationalists have used the murder to flood the Internet with their interpretation of the event and its significance. From racist blogs to Wikipedia, Sviridov is portrayed as an innocent "football fan" while Cherkesov and Caucasians in general are described as Islamic extremists who prey on innocent Russians.

Shortly after the Cherkesov affair the nationalists began a new campaign called "Stop Feeding the Caucasus." All the North Caucasus republics receive cash subsidies from Moscow, purportedly to help economic development. The nationalists argue that Moscow should stop sending money to support the Caucasus republics' economies as long as they continue to migrate to Russian cities.[4] Of course, there is an inherent contradiction in this proposal: the nationalists want to confine the Caucasians to their "reservations" by cutting off the funds that should be creating an infrastructure that would encourage them to stay there. In fact, the subsidies go straight into the pockets of the republican leaders and particularly the siloviki: it was estimated that eighteen million rubles disappeared in this manner in 2011 alone.[5] Prime Minister Putin argued for more "skillfully" planned investments to allow the region to develop while echoing the xenophobic sentiments of the nationalists. Putin claimed that the presence of peoples from the Caucasus in Russian cities "causes justified irritation among the local residents."[6] Putin has yet to reveal what these investments might consist of. The only current plan for the Caucasus is the development of a series of elite ski resorts, certainly a potential money-making venture but not one that will significantly increase employment. Actually, the Russian government is closer to starving the Caucasus than feeding it through the use of counterterrorism operations, known as KTOs. In Kabardino-Balkaria the continued application of a KTO regime has destroyed all tourism at the one ski resort that was actually functioning, creating wide-scale unemployment and the threat of starvation among the local population.[7] Of course, the idea of "quarantining" the Caucasus peoples and starving them should be familiar to the reader at this point.

As in the past, Russians hold an irreconcilable view of the Caucasus: the region is part of Russia, yet the people who have lived there for centuries are not. The territory can be exploited as Moscow sees fit, hence the disregard for Circassian sensibilities when planning the Sochi Olympics. The two Russo-Chechen wars of the last twenty years stand as proof that Moscow has no other strategies for dealing with the region other than repression, propaganda campaigns, and mass slaughter—the same methods used by the tsarist regime. As far as Circassian activism is concerned, the policy is to repress national sentiments through heavy-handed use of the siloviki, KTO regimes, killing and imprisoning activists, or driving them into exile. To keep the activists from creating a united front, Moscow has maintained the Soviet fiction of four "subethnic" groups and has divided them even further by splitting the Southern Federal District in two. By keeping the Circassians broken up in small communities and surrounding them with a Slavic population, Moscow is creating conditions in which the Circassian language will disappear and along with it the idea of Circassian nationality. Thanks to Russification policies of the Soviet and Imperial governments, the language is already gravely threatened. By the 1990s almost all business in Adygeia was conducted in Russian, even in towns that were nearly all Circassian.[8] To accelerate the process, Moscow recently downgraded the study of the Circassian language from a mandatory to an elective subject in primary schools in the Circassian republics. Meanwhile, politicians and academics have been successful in persuading the Russian public that Circassian activism is part of a separatist movement tied to the United States that seeks to wrest the Caucasus away from Russia.

Moscow's policy toward the diaspora seems to be to allow token immigration while placing insurmountable barriers to a genuine repatriation program. As time passes, Moscow seems to hope that the diaspora will give up their dreams of returning home and will ultimately be assimilated into their host societies. Because the current generation has become particularly susceptible to assimilation due to urbanization, the Russians have every reason to believe this strategy will be successful. Perhaps this is why so many Circassians I've talked to repeat the phrase, "the genocide continues."

By refusing the Circassians the right to repatriation, the current Russian government is in fact condemning the nation to a slow death. However, two factors make this unlikely. First, the ease of contact between Circassians in the Caucasus and those abroad will continue to be a powerful motivating force. In the twenty years since the fall of the Soviet Union, such extensive business and personal connections have been established that it is hard to imagine the Circassians in exile simply walking way. The Internet has proven to be a powerful tool in this regard. Young people talk nearly every day with their compatriots around the world, and although there is a lot of disagreement and some frustration, most agree that they "tend to be on the same page" when discussing issues such as repatriation, assimilation, and the Sochi Olympics. Many websites are devoted to Circassian issues and attract a large audience, in addition to general sites such as *Jamestown* and the *Institute for War and Peace Reporting*. Through these forums and websites young Circassians stay abreast of the major issues of the day and relate them to their parents and grandparents who are less comfortable with the Internet.

Second, the activist ideology that has motivated the younger generation of Circassians in New Jersey is infecting young people in the Middle East and elsewhere, and the potential energy that would be released in the case of broad, international activism is formidable. The No Sochi movement has already made a small impact on the international community, and it was organized by a handful of young people. This activism is already influencing the Turkish Circassians, who just recently began to challenge Ankara to address the Kemalist attack on Circassian cultural rights. "We demand non-mandatory education of our native tongue and 24/7 broad-casts in our language," the activists announced in their "Initiative for Circassian Rights" in February 2012. "We want our original surnames and the names of our towns restored. We want cultural centers for Circassians. We want the reputations of our forefathers restored and an end to the demonization."[9] If this assertiveness spreads throughout the Circassian diaspora and is directed toward Russia, it will be difficult for Moscow to ignore.

Activism may also increase since the Circassians abroad feel time is running out. Young people from Jordan to the United States have told me that the sense of community is disappearing. Living in diaspora for 150 years has placed tremendous pressure on them to adopt the host nation as their own despite their general feeling "of not belonging to the country I was born in." As one person told me, "it's not like we are being oppressed in the countries that we are currently living in, quite the opposite, I think most of my people built a stable existence and live a comfortable life, but we are not where we belong." Another said living in exile is "like being caught in the middle. [We're] losing identity year after year." A Turkish Circassian expressed this ambivalence more directly, noting that although "I love Turkey and am proud to be a Turkish citizen. . . . I couldn't learn my language at school, because of the lack of full democratic rights in Turkey." The absence of a body of literature or historical scholarship to preserve the memory of their ancestors was also a major concern of everyone I spoke with. When I asked about heroes or statesmen their families look up to, many were hard pressed to name more than one or two. Without such historical foundations, the diaspora Circassians have only adyge habze to look to as the force holding them together. Unfortunately, the younger generation seems to be losing this as well. "Fifty years from now there will be no habze, there will be no language, there will be no Circassians," one person from the Middle East lamented, touching upon the other major concern, preservation of the Circassian language. Adygebze (Circassian) is a relatively difficult language to learn, and despite the efforts of organizations throughout the world to teach young Circassians their native tongue, it's nearly impossible to preserve a language in diaspora.

Another issue that raises concerns among Circassians is that young people are frequently marrying outside their communities. One of the primary reasons Circassians have survived as long as they have in diaspora, many have told me, is because "we have always been a closed community in every country we live in." This was possible before Turkey and the Arab states became heavily urbanized, but now the pressures of integration and the natural tendency of urban youths to overlook ethnic differences when choosing friends and spouses is taking its toll on Circassian identity. With all of these challenges, some are close to giving up. As one person told me, "I feel the need to serve my people, and at the same time it feels like a lost cause." Another was a bit more optimistic but still cautious: "Not losing the motivation and the hope is still a very difficult task to accomplish, but we try."

As in the past, the Circassians lack unified leadership. Each community has its own issues and its own perspective, so the agenda of one group doesn't necessarily make sense to a community in a different country. Those who are farther away, particularly in the United States, have more difficulty establishing and maintaining regular contact with the Caucasus, so some of them have adopted an agenda that's more aggressive than that of the Turkish Circassians, who have to a great degree established permanent connections with their homeland. Some in Turkey see the gains they have made as being at risk if they were to press Russia any harder, which results in frustration on the part of those in the United States. Still, there is some optimism. As one Turkish Circassian put it, "Our differences do not have to prevent us from solidarity. There is still a strong tie between our people, enough to lead us looking for a common future." The genocide has played a central role in this regard. "Every Circassian is affected by the genocide in some way" is a comment I heard many times. It is often used as a starting point for discussions, debates, and plans for action, and perhaps most importantly as a bridge for mutual respect. Also, despite the lack of consensus on how to proceed, almost all Circassians agree that the recovery of their homeland is the ultimate goal. As John Haghor, an American Circassian, told the European Parliament on November 7, 2011, "Among the Circassians there is a growing understanding that returning to the homeland is not simply a call of the heart, but an absolute necessity for the survival of our people."[10] Haghor called on the parliament to support the Circassian right to return to their homeland and to establish a channel of communication with the region to monitor the worsening trend of attacks on Circassian activists.

Unfortunately, in the same way that Russia's behavior toward the Caucasus hasn't changed since the nineteenth century, the response of the international community is not likely to be much different than that of

Great Britain and the Ottoman Empire during the Russo-Circassian War. Russia has historically been a nation that other powers are extremely reluctant to provoke, and at the very best the Western powers will only verbally and tentatively support Circassian national aspirations. Russia's extreme reaction to Western scholars' study of the genocide shows that any direct challenge to their way of dealing with the Circassian issue will be met with uncompromising hostility. Ultimately the West will leave Moscow to its own devices, and this in turn will only lead to more misery for both the Russian and Circassian peoples. Even if Moscow's pretences of being concerned with the economic development of the Caucasus were true, such efforts would not address the fundamental issues: recognition of the genocide, free repatriation, and unification of the Circassian republics into a single political entity. Any sort of economic or political concessions short of this will not end the problem. Unfortunately, Russia is not going to address these issues in a meaningful way anytime soon.

The Cherkesov affair stands as stark evidence that the Russian people and government are not prepared even to treat the Circassians as equal citizens, much less discuss the crimes of their ancestors against them. The "Stop Feeding the Caucasus" campaign is not, as some have suggested, a step toward relinquishing control over the Caucasus but rather an old strategy aimed at reducing the population to absolute destitution. A lack of real investment coupled with extended KTO regimes will ensure that the region remains poverty-stricken for decades. Prime Minister Putin's suggestion that the Caucasus peoples must be quarantined so that ethnic Russians won't be "irritated" by their presence is likewise a revival of the ghettoization policies of the late Imperial period. In many ways, the Caucasus War is still going on.

Even though the status quo in the Caucasus can't possibly continue, a sincere effort by the current Russian government to address the problems there is outside the realm of possibility. It's also highly unlikely that the misery brought by the continuing conflict will make Russia abandon the region once and for all. As the 2008 invasion of Georgia has demonstrated, Russia needs the North Caucasus as a springboard for further military actions. The most probable scenario is that Moscow will become even more oppressive and violent in its efforts hold onto the North Caucasus as long as it possibly can despite the economic, social, and psychological damage it will cause all parties involved. Since neither the seven hundred thousand Circassians in the Caucasus nor the three to five million abroad are likely to be silenced any time soon, this policy will only perpetuate the misery begun two hundred years ago. As with so many cases of genocide, the victims who survived are left to fight for a future in the face of denial by governments afraid to face their past.

NOTES

INTRODUCTION

1. "Komissiia po Protivodeistviiu Popytkam Falsifikatsii Istorii."
2. My thanks go to Nawriz Pshidatok and Bozii Astemir for this information.
3. By the mid-nineteenth century the Russian calendar was twelve days behind the Gregorian calendar. When referring to Russian archival documents in the notes, I've preserved the old dates and annotated them with "(OS)." In the main text I've converted dates given in Russian documents to the Gregorian calendar.
4. Drozdov, "Posledniaia Bor'ba s Gortsami na Zapadnom Kavkaze," 456–457.
5. Betrozov, *Adygi—Vozniknovenie i Razvitie Etnosa*, 80–105.
6. The Adyge-Abkhaz language group has no known relatives among modern languages.
7. Betrozov, *Adygi—Vozniknoveniei Razvitie Etnosa*, 173; and T. V. Polovinkina, *Cherkesiia—Bol' Moia*, 18–22.
8. Romaskevich and Volin, *Sbornik Materialov*, 2:62, 248.
9. Dzamikhov, *Adygi v Politike Rossii*, 76–80.
10. "Inal" was a royal title of the Oguz Turks, who raided the Caucasus in the ninth and tenth centuries, so the possibility exists that the Circassian term "Inal" may have originally referred to a leader who adopted this title.
11. For a discussion of the problem of the split in Kabardia, see Kokiev, "Raspad Kabardy," 198–206.
12. Khan-Girey, *Zapiski o Cherkesii*, 162–185.
13. Chirg, *Razvitie*, 53–54.
14. Khan-Girey, *Zapiski o Cherkesii*, 298–305.
15. Ibid., 300–301.
16. Taitbout de Marigny, *Three Voyages*, 72–73.
17. Ibid., 76.
18. Liausheva, *Evoliutsiia Religioznykh*, 17.
19. Khanakhu, *Traditsionnaia Kul'tura*, 65.
20. Khan-Girey. *Zapiski o Cherkesii*, 268–270; and Chirg, *Razvitie*, 30–34.
21. Atkin, *Russia and Iran*, 46.

1. "THE PLAGUE WAS OUR ALLY"

1. Mal'bakhov, *Kabarda v Period ot Petra I do Ermolova*, 175.

2. Berzhe and Kobiakov, eds., *Akty*, 2:1128.

3. Tuganov, *Izmail-Bei*, 51–52.

4. Berzhe and Kobiakov, eds., *Akty*, 2:957–958.

5. Ibid., 2:960–961.

6. Tuganov, *Izmail-Bei*, 67.

7. Berzhe and Kobiakov, *Akty*, 2:977.

8. LeDonne, *Russian Empire and the World*, 98–99; B. K. Mal'bakhov, *Kabarda v Period ot Petra I do Ermolova*, 29.

9. Khodarkovsky, *Where Two Worlds Met*, 163.

10. LeDonne, *Russian Empire and the World*, 93.

11. Ibid., 94; Bukalova, *Kabardino-Russkie otnosheniia*, 2:33–34.

12. Potto, *Kavkazskaya Voina*, 1:169.

13. Baddeley, *Russian Conquest of the Caucasus*, 61.

14. Atkin, *Russia and Iran*, 73; and Lang, *A Modern History of Soviet Georgia*, 51.

15. Potto, *Kavkazskaya Voina*, 1:171.

16. Gordin, *Kavkaz*, 68–79.

17. Ibid., 78.

18. Tuganov, *Izmail-Bei*, 90–91.

19. Bukalova, *Kabardino-Russkie otnosheniia*, 2:237, 240–241, 251–252; and Kokiev, "Pereselenie Kabardinskikh Kholopov," 224.

20. Barrett, "Crossing Boundaries," 232.

21. Berzhe and Kobiakov, *Akty*, 4:882–883.

22. Ibid., 3:655.

23. Tuganov, *Izmail-Bei*, 94.

24. Berzhe and Kobiakov, *Akty*, 4:847–849.

25. Tuganov, *Izmail-Bei*, 96–97.

26. Mal'bakhov, *Kabarda v Period ot Petra I do Ermolova*, 98; and Berzhe and Kobiakov, *Akty*, 4:847.

27. Potto, *Kavkazskaya Voina*, 1:361.

28. Berzhe and Kobiakov, *Akty*, 3:635–641.

29. Mal'bakhov, *Kabarda v Period ot Petra I do Ermolova*, 184–185.

30. Kumykov, *Ekonomicheskoe i Kul'turnoe Razvitie*, 57.

31. Berzhe and Kobiakov, *Akty*, 4:823–825, 828–831.

32. Mal'bakhov, *Kabarda v Period ot Petra I do Ermolova*, 186.

33. Kazharov, *Traditsionnye obshchestvennye instituty kabardintsev*, 294–295.

34. Mal'bakhov, *Kabarda v Period ot Petra I do Ermolova*, 188–189.

35. Ibid., 208–209.

36. Berzhe and Kobiakov, *Akty*, 5:520–525.

37. Begeulov, *Tsentral'nyi Kavkaz*, 216–217.

38. Baddeley, *Russian Conquest of the Caucasus*, 96–97.

39. Ibid., 99.

40. Gordin, *Kavkaz*, 114–115.

41. Baddeley, *Russian Conquest of the Caucasus*, 97.
42. Ibid., 98.
43. Lapin, "K Obrazu A. P. Ermolova," 33.
44. Gordin, "O Roli Kostromskoi Ssylki," 3.
45. Baddeley, *Russian Conquest of the Caucasus*, 125.
46. Potto, *Kavkazskaya Voina*, 2:10.
47. Baddeley, *Russian Conquest of the Caucasus*, 99–100.
48. Potto, *Kavkazskaya Voina*, 11.
49. Gammer, *Muslim Resistance to the Tsar*, 35.
50. Gammer, *Lone Wolf and the Bear*, 35.
51. Potto, *Kavkazskaya Voina*, 2:210.
52. Berzhe and Kobiakov, *Akty*, 6.2:466.
53. Ibid.
54. Ibid., 6.2:466–467.
55. Fedorov, *Zapiski A. P. Ermolova*, 311.
56. Kokiev, "Raspad Kabardy," 200–201; and Berzhe and Kobiakov, *Akty*, 91.
57. Mal'bakhov, *Kabarda v Period ot Petra I do Ermolova*, 222–224.
58. Fedorov, *Zapiski A. P. Ermolova*, 283.
59. Ibid., 336–354.
60. Potto, *Kavkazskaya Voina*, 2:208–214.
61. Berzhe and Kobiakov, *Akty*, 6.2:468–469.
62. Ibid., 469–470.
63. Beituganov, *Kabarda i Ermolov*, 80; and Potto, *Kavkazskaya Voina*, 2:219.
64. Berzhe and Kobiakov, *Akty*, 6.2:468–469.
65. Mal'bakhov, *Kabarda v Period ot Petra I do Ermolova*, 227–231; Beituganov, *Kabarda i Ermolov*, 76–82; and Kudashev, *Istoricheskie Svedeniia*, 16.
66. Mal'bakhov, *Kabarda v Period ot Petra I do Ermolova*, 237.
67. Potto, *Kavkazskaya Voina*, 2:219–220.
68. Mal'bakhov, *Kabarda v Period ot Petra I do Ermolova*, 233–234.
69. Fedorov, *Zapiski A. P. Ermolova*, 377–379.
70. Mal'bakhov, *Kabarda v Period ot Petra I do Ermolova*, 240; and Fedorov, *Zapiski A. P. Ermolova*, 379.
71. Beituganov, *Kabarda i Ermolov*, 89–90.
72. Convention on the Prevention and Punishment of the Crime of Genocide, Resolution 260 (III)A, December 9, 1948, U.N.T.S. I-1021, Article 2.
73. Kudashev, *Istoricheskie Svedeniia*, 114.
74. Kasumov and Kasumov, *Genotsid Adygov*, 14; and Dzamikhov, *Adygi v Politike Rossii*, 75.
75. Beituganov, *Kabarda i Ermolov*, 90.
76. Ibid.
77. Berzhe and Kobiakov, *Akty*, 6.2:471–472.
78. Potto, *Kavkazskaya Voina*, 1:226; and Kudashev, *Istoricheskie Svedeniia*, 107.
79. Berzhe and Kobiakov, *Akty*, 6.2:471–472.
80. Potto, *Kavkazskaya Voina*, 2:246–276, passim.

81. Ibid., 278.

82. Ibid., 279.

83. Ibid., 282–291.

84. Lapinskii, *Gortsy Kavkaza*, 209–210.

85. Gammer, *Muslim Resistance to the Tsar*, 37.

2. A PAWN IN THE GREAT GAME

1. Solov'ev, *Istoriia Rossii*, 28:560.

2. "Adrianopol'skii Mir."

3. Tornau, *Vospominaniia Kavkazskogo Ofitsera*, 33.

4. Ibid.

5. Berzhe, *Vyselenie Gortsev*, 13–14.

6. Khan-Girey, "Besl'nii Abat"; and Chirg, *Razvitie*, 52.

7. Chirg, *Razvitie*, 52.

8. Khan-Girey, *Zapiski o Cherkesii*, 191; and Khan-Girey, "Besl'nii Abat."

9. Chirg, *Razvitie*, 53; and Khan-Girey, *Zapiski o Cherkesii*, 191–192.

10. Chirg, *Razvitie*, 53.

11. Shcherbina, *Istoriia Kubanskiago Kazach'iago Voiska*, 2:152.

12. Potto, *Kavkazskaya Voina*, 1:317; and Polovinkina, *Cherkesiia—Bol' Moia*, 107.

13. Potto, *Kavkazskaya Voina*, 1:317; and Kasumov and Kasumov, *Genotsid Adygov*, 60–61.

14. Shcherbina and Felitsyn, *Kubanskoe Kazachestvo*, 95.

15. Ibid., 18.

16. Potto, *Kavkazskaya Voina*, 1:296.

17. Ibid., 1:54.

18. Shcherbina and Felitsyn, *Kubanskoe Kazachestvo*, 27–38.

19. Kabuzan, *Naselenie Severnogo Kavkaza*, 144.

20. Barrett, *At the Edge of Empire*, 180.

21. Shcherbina, *Istoriia Kubanskiago Kazach'iago Voiska*, 2:152.

22. Shcherbina and Felitsyn, *Kubanskoe Kazachestvo*, 77.

23. Potto, *Kavkazskaya Voina*, 2: 204.

24. Berzhe and Kobiakov, *Akty*, 3:627–628.

25. The Navruz were a clan, not a separate tribe. Berzhe and Kobiakov, *Akty*, 3:654.

26. Shcherbina, *Istoriia Kubanskiago Kazach'iago Voiska*, 164–165.

27. Potto, *Kavkazskaya Voina*, 1:320.

28. Khan-Girey, *Zapiski o Cherkesii*, 85.

29. Berzhe and Kobiakov, *Akty*, 4:928–929; Chirg, *Razvitie*, 35–36; and Chirg, "Iz Istorii Russko-Adyskhikh Torgovykh Sviazei," 5.

30. Chirg, "IzIstorii Russko-Adygskhikh Torgovykh Sviazei," 5–7.

31. Chirg, *Razvitie*, 35–36.

32. Barrett, *At the Edge of Empire*, 113–114. See also Berzhe and Kobiakov, *Akty*, 7:887–891.

33. Taitbout de Marigny, *Three Voyages*, 45.

34. Kumykov, *Ekonomicheskoe i Kul'turnoe Razvitie*, 74–86.

35. Berzhe and Kobiakov, *Akty*, 6.2:451.

36. Ibid., 6.2:485.

37. Chirg, "Iz Istorii Russko-Adyskhikh Torgovykh Sviazei," 12.

38. Shcherbina, *Istoriia Kubanskiago Kazach'iago Voiska*, 2:244.

39. Ibid., 2:238–239.

40. Kasumov and Kasumov, *Genotsid Adygov*, 65; and Berzhe and Kobiakov, *Akty*, 7:373.

41. Shcherbina, *Istoriia Kubanskiago Kazach'iago Voiska*, 2:244–245.

42. Potto, *Kavkazskaya Voina*, 2:329–330.

43. Shcherbina, *Istoriia Kubanskiago Kazach'iago Voiska*, 2:244.

44. Ibid., 2:245.

45. Kodinets to Paskevich, May 22 (OS) 1827, Georgian State Archive (Tbilisi), f. 2, op. 1, doc. 2000, 8–12.

46. Berzhe and Kobiakov, *Akty*, 7:873–874; and Chirg, "Iz Istorii Russko-Adyskhikh Torgovykh Sviazei," 13.

47. Kodinets to Paskevich, May 22 (OS) 1837, Georgian State Archive (Tbilisi), f. 2, op. 1, doc. 2000, 9–11.

48. Berzhe and Kobiakov, *Akty*, 7:882.

49. Ibid.

50. Filipson, "Vospominaniia Grigoriia Ivanovicha Filipsona," 242.

51. Berzhe and Kobiakov, *Akty*, 7:887–891.

52. Potto, *Kavkazskaya Voina*, 2:278.

53. Berzhe and Kobiakov, *Akty*, 7:902.

54. Ibid., 7:902–907.

55. Gardanov and Mambetov, "Vedenie," 3–8.

56. Gordin. *Kavkaz: Zemlia i Krov'*, 150.

57. Ibid., 207–216.

58. This final section included the following chapters:

    1. Observations on the Importance of the Circassian People among the Peoples of the North Caucasus
    2. Observations on the Reasons for the Circassian People's Lack of Goodwill toward Russia
    3. General Observations on the Value of Enlightenment of the Mountaineers
    4. Observation: Some Opinions Concerning the Means and Methods for the Incorporation of the Circassian People into Civil Society by Peaceful Means with the Possibility of Avoiding Bloodshed.

59. Gardanov and Mambetov, "Vedenie," 19.

60. Kumykov, *Obshchestvennaia Mysl'*, 51.

61. Gardanov and Mambetov, "Vedenie," 28–29.

62. Gordin, *Kavkaz*, 155.

63. Ibid., 163.

64. LeDonne, *Russian Empire and the World*, 97–98, 117.

65. Ibid., 118.

66. Gleason, *Genesis of Russophobia*, 16–135, passim.

67. LeDonne, *Russian Empire and the World*, 123–124.

68. Gardanov, *Adygi, Balkartsy i Karachaevsty.*

69. "For the Ladies," *Times*, August 1, 1794, 6.

70. King, "Imagining Circassia," 243.

71. Bolsover, "David Urquhart and the Eastern Question," 445–446.

72. Urquhart, *Turkey and Its Resources*, 218–236.

73. Temperley, *England and the Near East*, 75–76.

74. The version of the story popular among Circassians today is that the Circassians themselves designed the flag and Urquhart merely provided the materials. The overwhelming evidence in his published works demonstrates that Urquhart was a propagandist with little concern for the truth. For a good overview of Urquhart's political career, see Gleason, *Genesis of Russophobia*, 164–204. For an insightful study of his character and personal life, see King, "Imagining Circassia."

75. Bolsover, "David Urquhart," 464.

76. Gleason, *Genesis of Russophobia*, 164–204; and King, "Imagining Circassia," 193.

77. Urquhart, *British Diplomacy.*

78. Spencer, *Travels in Circassia*, 1:iii, v.

79. Ibid., 1:329, 335.

80. Ibid., 1:330–331.

81. Bell, *Residence in Circassia*, ix.

82. Ibid., 1:450.

83. Ibid., 1:172.

84. Henze, "Circassian Resistance to Russia," 80–81.

85. Ibid.

86. Berzhe and Kobiakov, *Akty*, 8:766.

87. Kasumov and Kasumov, *Genotsid Adygov*, 88–91.

88. Berzhe and Kobiakov, *Akty*, 8:739–769.

3. FROM WAR TO GENOCIDE

1. Drozdov, "Posledniaia Bor'ba," 457.

2. Nemzera, *Memuary Dekabristov*, 518.

3. Ibid.

4. Ibid., 517–518.

5. Gordin, *Kavkaz*, 166.

6. Rubenstein, *Cunning of History*, 49.

7. Gordin, *Kavkaz*, 248.

8. Ibid., 73.

9. Barrett, "Crossing Boundaries," 242; and Ol'shevskii, *Kavkaz c 1841 po 1866 god*, 477.

10. Velyaminov to Malinovsky, March 5 (OS), 1836, Georgian State Archive (Tbilisi), f. 416, op. 2, doc. 24, 3–4.

11. Journals of Generals Malinkovsky and Velyaminov for June 1836, Georgian State Archive (Tbilisi), f. 416, op. 2, 17–18, 41–50.

12. Unsigned staff report for May, 1838, Georgian State Archive (Tbilisi), f. 416, op. 2, doc. 24, 164–178.

13. Unsigned journal of military operations for July, 1838, Georgian State Archive (Tbilisi), f. 416, op. 2, doc. 24, 186–188, 192; and Paskevich and Velyaminov to Staff Headquarters, 1839(?), Georgian State Archive (Tbilisi), f. 416, op. 2, doc. 24, 231–232.

14. Spencer, *Travels in Circassia*, 1:285–86; and Polovinkina, *Cherkesiia—Bol' Moia*, 128.

15. Ibid., 123.

16. Gordin, *Kavkaz*, 250.

17. Ibid.

18. Velyaminov to Company Commander, October 31 (OS), 1836; Journal of Velyaminov for September 24–October 19, 1836, Georgian State Archive (Tbilisi), f. 416, op. 2, doc. 24, 112–126.

19. See, for example, Georgian State Archive (Tbilisi), f. 416, op. 2, docs. 24, 17, 48, 117 passim.

20. Journal of Velyaminov for September 24–October 19, 1836, Georgian State Archive (Tbilisi), f. 416, op. 2, doc. 24, 117–118.

21. Chernyshev to Korpusky, January 15 (OS), 1839, Georgian State Archive (Tbilisi), f. 416, op. 2, doc. 24, 233–239.

22. Ibid., 235.

23. "K." "Obzor Sobytii na Kavkaze v 1846 Godu," 322–23; and Gordin, *Kavkaz*, 270.

24. Berzhe and Kobiakov, *Akty*, 9:889–891; and Chirg, *Razvitie*, 101.

25. Stal,' "Etnograficheskii Ocherk," 159–160; and Pershits, *Abaziny*, 26.

26. Richmond, *Northwest Caucasus*, 69–71; Polovinkina, *Cherkesiia—Bol' Moia*, 134; and Chirg, *Razvitie*, 109.

27. Chirg, *Razvitie*, 128–151.

28. Spencer, *Turkey, Russia, and the Black Sea*, 229–230.

29. Ibid.

30. Dzhakhiev, "Severnyi Kavkaz," 114.

31. King, "Imagining Circassia," 242.

32. Goldfrank, *Origins of the Crimean War*, passim; and Curtiss, *Russia's Crimean War*, 167–237.

33. Varle, *Krymskaia Voina*, 2:517.

34. Curtiss, *Russia's Crimean War*, 415.

35. Gadzhiev and Ramazanov, *Dvizhenie Gortsev*, 652; and Allen, *Caucasian Battle-fields*, 68.

36. Esadze, *Pokorenie*, 342–343; and Polovinkina, *Cherkesiia—Bol' Moia*, 141.

37. Chirg, *Razvitie*, 154.

38. Curtiss, *Russia's Crimean War*, 190–191, 207–208, 236–237, 293–294, 308–309.

39. Berzhe and Kobiakov, *Akty*, 11:69–73.

40. Chirg, *Razvitie*, 155.

41. Varle, *Krymskaia Voina*, 519; and Chirg, *Razvitie*, 155.

42. Baumgart, *Peace of Paris*, 25–37.

43. Varle, *Krymskaia Voina*, 546–550.

44. Baumgart, *Peace of Paris*, 111–112; and Conacher, *Britain and the Crimea*, 195–196.

45. Conacher, *Britain and the Crimea*, 203, 215–217.

46. Curtiss, *Russia's Crimean War*, 522.

47. Conacher, *Britain and the Crimea*, 220.

48. Kasumov and Kasumov, *Genotsid Adygov*, 134–135, 138.

49. Ol'shevskii, *Kavkaz c 1841 po 1866 god*, 482.

50. Ibid., 596; and Veniukov, *Iz Vospominanii*, 291.

51. Berzhe, *Vyselenie Gortsev*, 17.

52. Ol'shevskii, *Kavkaz c 1841 po 1866 god*, 599; and Baumgart, *Peace of Paris*, 113–116, 158–164, 191–195.

53. Ol'shevskii, *Kavkaz c 1841 po 1866 god*, 513; and Fonvill', *Poslednii God*, 10–11.

54. Ol'shevskii, *Kavkaz c 1841 po 1866 god*, 516.

55. Fonvill', *Poslednii God*, 3.

56. Ol'shevskii, *Kavkaz c 1841 po 1866 god*, 476.

57. Ol'shevskii, "Kavkaz i Pokorenie," 302–303.

58. Veniukov, *Iz Vospominanii*, 319.

59. Esadze, *Pokorenie*, 351.

60. Ibid., 351; Kumykov, ed., *Arkhivnye Materialy*, 60–61, 66; and Ol'shevskii, *Kavkaz c 1841 po 1866 god*, 518.

61. Ol'shevskii, *Kavkaz c 1841 po 1866 god*, 488.

62. Ibid., 518; and Tuganov, *Tragicheskie Posledvstviia*, 87.

63. Drozdov, "Posledniaia Bor'ba,"417.

64. Ibid., 415.

65. Ol'shevskii, *Kavkaz c 1841 po 1866 god*, 502.

66. Tuganov, *Tragicheskie Posledvstviia*, 13–18, 21.

67. Ibid., 27.

68. Ibid., 32–36.

69. Ibid., 38.

70. Valuev to Mikhail Nikolaevich, February 20 (OS), 1863, Georgian State Archive (Tbilisi), f. 416, op. 3, doc. 140, 1; and Tuganov, *Tragicheskie Posledvstviia*, 42–48.

71. Valuev to Mikhail Nikolaevich, February 20 (OS), 1863, Georgian State Archive (Tbilisi), f. 416, op. 3, doc. 140, 3.

72. Berzhe, *Vyselenie Gortsev*, 21–22; Ol'shevskii, *Kavkaz c 1841 po 1866 god*, 510; and Drozdov, "Posledniaia Bor'ba," 457.

73. Kreiten, "Colonial Experiment," 222.

74. Tuganov, *Tragicheskie Posledvstviia*, 48–49.

75. Ibid., 53–54.

76. Ol'shevskii, *Kavkaz c 1841 po 1866 god*, 516–517.

77. Tuganov, *Tragicheskie Posledvstviia*, 29.

78. Ibid.

79. Ibid., 29–30.

80. Kreiten, "Colonial Experiment," 217.

81. Ibid., 216–217.

82. Berzhe, *Vyselenie Gortsev*, 19–20.

83. Kreiten, "Colonial Experiment," 217.

84. Tuganov, *Tragicheskie Posledvstviia*, 81.

85. Veniukov, *Iz Vospominanii*, 297.

86. Drozdov, "Posledniaia Bor'ba," 402–406, 415.

87. Ibid., 395.

88. Ibid., 394–395.

89. Ol'shevskii, *Kavkaz c 1841 po 1866 god*, 508–509.

90. Berzhe, *Vyselenie Gortsev*, 27.

91. Drozdov, "Posledniaia Bor'ba," 418–419.

92. Kasumov and Kasumov, *Genotsid Adygov*, 140.

93. Esadze, *Pokorenie*, 352.

94. Ol'shevskii, *Kavkaz c 1841 po 1866 god*, 517.

95. Berzhe and Kobiakov, *Akty*, 12:933.

96. Esadze, *Pokorenie*, 352–353.

97. Ibid., 354–355.

98. Ol'shevskii, *Kavkaz c 1841 po 1866 god*, 524.

99. Veniukov, *Iz Vospominanii*, 298.

100. Berzhe and Kobiakov, *Akty*, 926.

101. Veniukov, *Iz Vospominanii*, 356–357.

102. Ibid., 298.

103. Evdokimov to Kartsov, September 19 (OS), 1863, Georgian State Archive (Tbilisi), f. 416, op. 3, doc. 139, 2.

104. Ol'shevskii, *Kavkaz c 1841 po 1866 god*, 532.

105. Ibid., 533.

4. 1864

1. Ol'shevskii, *Kavkaz c 1841 po 1866 god*, 533.

2. Drozdov, "Posledniaia Bor'ba,"417.

3. Ol'shevskii, *Kavkaz c 1841 po 1866 god*, 539.

4. Ibid., 535, 537–539.

5. Ibid., 540–541; and Field notes of Evdokimov, June–December 1863, Georgian State Archives (Tbilisi), f. 416, op. 3, doc. 1177, 100–199, passim.

6. Evdokimov was so hated by the Circassians that at one point they attempted to organize a "hit team" to assassinate him. See Tuganov, *Tragicheskie Posledvstviia*, 56.

7. Drozdov, "Posledniaia Bor'ba," 433. See also 425–425, 430–431.

8. Ibid., 434. See also 434–435, 441–442.

9. Ibid., 437, 442–444.

10. Esadze, *Pokorenie*, 370.

11. Drozdov, "Posledniaia Bor'ba," 447–448.

12. Ol'shevskii, *Kavkaz c 1841 po 1866 god*, 542–543.

13. Berzhe, *Vyselenie Gortsev*, 27.

14. Ibid., 22.

15. Kartsov to Novikov, August 23 (OS), 1863, Georgian State Archive (Tbilisi), f. 416, op. 3, doc. 1103, 1.

16. Ibid., 2.

17. Evdokimov to Kartsov, September 19 (OS), 1863, Georgian State Archive (Tbilisi), f. 416, op.3, doc. 139, 2–3.

18. Evdokimov to Kartsov, January 7 (OS), 1863, Georgian State Archive (Tbilisi), f. 416, op. 3, doc. 139, 1.

19. Ol'shevskii, *Kavkaz c 1841 po 1866 god*, 543.

20. Drozdov, "Posledniaia Bor'ba," 452–453.

21. Veniukov, "K Istorii Zaseleniia Zapadnogo Kavkaza," 249–250.

22. Zabudsky to Kartsov, August 10 (OS), 1864, Georgian State Archive (Tbilisi), f. 416, op. 3, doc. 149, 12.

23. Field notes of Evdokimov for June–December 1863, Georgian State Archive (Tbilisi), f. 416, op. 3, doc. 1177, 100–199 passim.

24. Ibid., 111.

25. Kartsov to Novikov, August 23 (OS), 1863, Georgian State Archive (Tbilisi), f. 416, op. 3, doc. 1103, 2.

26. Field notes of Evdokimov for June–December 1863, Georgian State Archive (Tbilisi), f. 416, op. 3, doc. 1177, 111–112.

27. Ibid., 135–136.

28. Ibid., 101.

29. Ibid., 116.

30. Ibid., 142.

31. Ibid., 100–199, passim.

32. Ibid., 123–124.

33. Ibid., 123.

34. Ibid., 116; Mikhail Nikolaevich to Miliutin, December 10 (OS), 1863, Georgian State Archive (Tbilisi), f. 416, op. 3, doc. 216; Kartsov to Evdokimov, November 26 (OS), 1863, Georgian State Archive (Tbilisi), f. 416, op. 3, doc. 220; Mikhail Nikolaevich to Miliutin, January 5 (OS), 1864, Georgian State Archive (Tbilisi), f. 416, op. 3,doc. 221.

35. Ol'shevskii, *Kavkaz c 1841 po 1866 god*, 490.

36. Field notes of Evdokimov for June–December 1863, Georgian State Archive (Tbilisi), f. 416, op. 3, doc. 1177, 138, 158–159, 161–163, 164–168, 191–192.

37. Fonvill', *Poslednii God*, 11, 18.

38. Kasumov and Kasumov, *Genotsid Adygov*, 152.

39. Fonvill', *Poslednii God*, 19–20.

40. Berzhe, *Vyselenie Gortsev*, 31.

41. Drozdov, "Posledniaia Bor'ba," 455.

42. Berzhe, *Vyselenie Gortsev*,31.

43. Fadeev, *Kavkazskaia Voina*, 187.

44. Kartsov to Black Sea Fleet Commander, May 13 (OS), 1864, Georgian State Archive (Tbilisi), f. 416, op. 3, doc. 149, 5.

45. Berzhe, *Vyselenie Gortsev*, 31.

46. Report of Glazenap, April 17 (OS), 1864, Georgian State Archive (Tbilisi), f. 416. op. 3, doc. 149, 1.

47. Berzhe, *Vyselenie Gortsev*, 29; Unsigned report to Evdokimov, April 30 (OS), 1864, Georgian State Archive (Tbilisi), f. 416, op. 3, doc. 145; and Zabudsky to Cherkesov, January 13 (OS), 1864, Georgian State Archive (Tbilisi), f. 416, op. 3, doc. 148.

48. Ol'shevskii, *Kavkaz c 1841 po 1866 god*, 549.

49. Ibid., 549–550.

50. Saydam, *Kırım ve Kavkas Göçleri*, 88.

51. Ol'shevskii, *Kavkaz c 1841 po 1866 god*, 550.

52. Ibid., 551.

53. Ibid.

54. Kumykov, *Vyselenie Adygov*, 66.

55. Ibid., 66–67.

56. Berzhe, *Vyselenie Gortsev*, 31.

57. Kumykov, *Vyselenie Adygov*, 74.

58. May 21 on the old Russian calendar. Circassians worldwide recognize this date as their day of mourning.

59. Kumykov, *Vyselenie Adygov*, 74–75.

60. Kumykov, *Arkhivnye Materialy*, 166.

61. Drozdov, "Posledniaia Bor'ba," 455–457.

62. In a letter of September 1867, Grand Prince Mikhail admitted that the ethnic cleansing had to be conducted quickly "in light of a possible European coalition." See Mikhail Nikolaevich to Novikov, September 20 (OS), 1867, Georgian State Archive (Tbilisi), f. 416, op. 3, doc. 160, 2.

63. Kumykov, *Arkhivnye Materialy*, 284.

64. Mikhail Nikolaevich to Miliutin, Georgian State Archive (Tbilisi), f. 416, op. 3, document 145, 8.

65. Kartsov to Evdokimov, March 5 (OS), 1863, Georgian State Archive (Tbilisi), f. 416, op. 3, doc. 137, 2.

66. Berzhe, *Vyselenie Gortsev*, 28; and Kartsov to Evdokimov, September 27 (OS), 1863, Georgian State Archive (Tbilisi), f. 416, op. 3, doc. 136.

67. Zabudsky to Cherkesov, January 13 (OS), 1864, Georgian State Archive (Tbilisi), f. 416, op. 3, doc. 148, 1.

68. Evdokimov to Kartsov, April 8 (OS), 1864, Georgian State Archive (Tbilisi), f. 416, op. 3, doc. 148, 4.

69. Berzhe, *Vyselenie Gortsev*, 6–7.

70. There are one hundred kopeks in a ruble.

71. Kartsov to Evdokimov, March 1863, Georgian State Archive (Tbilisi), f. 416, op. 3, doc. 148, 2.

72. Tuganov, *Tragicheskie Posledvstviia*, 92.

73. Report of Commander Smekalov, December 10 (OS), 1864, Georgian State Archive (Tbilisi), f. 416, op. 3, doc. 151.

74. Unsigned report, May 17 (OS), 1864, Georgian State Archive (Tbilisi), f. 416, op. 3, doc. 146, 1–2.

75. Habiçoğlu, *Kafkasyadan Anadoluya Göçler*, 77.

76. Tuganov, *Tragicheskie Posledvstviia*, 92.

77. Kasumov and Kasumov, *Genotsid Adygov*, 160; Berzhe, *Vyselenie Gortsev*, 21–22; Ol'shevskii, *Kavkaz c 1841 po 1866 god*, 510; and Drozdov, "Posledniaia Bor'ba," 457.

78. Kasumov and Kasumov, *Genotsid Adygov*, 160; Tuganov, *Tragicheskie Posledvstviia*, 90; and Proclamation of the Turkish Government to the Circassians, June 1 (OS), 1864, Georgian State Archive (Tbilisi), f. 416,.Op. 3, doc. 1115, 1.

79. Tuganov, *Tragicheskie Posledvstviia*, 92.

80. Ibid., 91–92; Drozdov, "Posledniaia Bor'ba," 453; and Ol'shevskii, *Kavkaz c 1841 po 1866 god*, 549.

81. Kumykov, *Arkhivnye Materialy*, 214–215.

82. Evdokimov to Kartsov, September 19 (OS), 1863, Georgian State Archive (Tbilisi), f. 416, op. 3, doc. 139; Report of the Commander of the Dakhovsky Detachment, April 30 (OS), 1864, Georgian State Archive (Tbilisi), f. 416, op. 3, doc. 145; Zabudsky to Cherkesov, January 13 (OS), 1864, Georgian State Archive (Tbilisi), f. 416, op. 3, doc. 148; Unsigned report on the deportation of the mountaineers to Turkey, February 18 (OS), 1865, Georgian State Archive (Tbilisi), f. 416, op. 3, doc. 154; and Kumykov, *Arkhivnye Materialy*, 153–168.

83. Rosser-Owen, "First 'Circassian Exodus,'" 23–24.

84. Report of the Commander of Fort Nikolaevskaya, April 17 (OS), 1864, Georgian State Archive (Tbilisi), f. 416, op. 3, doc. 149, 1–2.

85. Report of Smekalov, November 18 (OS), 1864, Georgian State Archive (Tbilisi), f. 416, op. 3, doc. 149, 16.

86. Report of Zabudsky, August 10 (OS), 1864, Georgian State Archive (Tbilisi), f. 416. op. 3, doc. 149, 12.

87. Report of Mikhail Nikolaevich, August 14/19 (OS), 1864, Georgian State Archive (Tbilisi), f. 416, op. 3, doc. 141, 1.

88. Olshevsky to Kartsov, December 2 (OS), 1864, Georgian State Archive (Tbilisi), f. 416, op. 3, doc. 149, 18.

89. Kartsov to Olshevsky, December 14 (OS), 1864, Georgian State Archive (Tbilisi), f. 416, op. 3, doc. 149, 20.

90. Karpat, *Ottoman Population*, 68–69. For a discussion of the disparities in estimates, see Rosser-Owen, "First 'Circassian Exodus,'" 21–22.

91. "Circassian Exodus," *Times*, May 12, 1864, 10.

92. Gellately and Kiernan, *Specter of Genocide*, 15.

93. Rubenstein, *Age of Triage*, 124.

94. Ibid., 124–127.

95. Tuganov, *Tragicheskie Posledvstviia*, 27.

96. Sherry, "Social Alchemy," 17–18, is the most recent example of this argument.

97. Ol'shevskii, *Kavkaz c 1841 po 1866 god*, 507.

98. Ibid., 512.

99. Nemzera, *Memuary Dekabristov*, 459–461.

100. Valuev to Mikhail Nikolaevich, February 20 (OS), 1863, GSA, f. 416, op. 3, document 140.

101. Tuganov, *Tragicheskie Posledvstviia*, 92.

102. Berzhe, *Vyselenie Gortsev*, 20.

103. Drozdov, "Posledniaia Bor'ba," 457.

104. Fadeev, *Kavkazskaia Voina*, 152; and Berzhe, *Vyselenie Gortsev*, 20.

105. Kumykov, *Arkhivnye Materialy*, 80.

106. Weitz, "Modernity of Genocides," 58–59.

107. Fadeev, *Kavkazskaia Voina*, 152–153.

108. Weitz, "Modernity of Genocides," 59.

109. Field notes of Evdokimov, June–December 1863, Georgian State Archive (Tbilisi), f. 416, op. 3, doc. 1177, 131.

110. Ibid., 139.

111. Kumykov, *Vyselenie Adygov*, 62.

112. Ibid.

5. A HOMELESS NATION

1. Tuganov, *Tragicheskie Posledvstviia*, 83.

2. Mackey, "Circassians in Jordan," 21.

3. Saydam, *Kırım ve Kavkas Göçleri*, 97.

4. Karpat, *Ottoman Population*, 66. There is a great deal of disagreement over the number of Crimean Tatars to emigrate. For a brief summary of this debate, see McCarthy, *Death and Exile*, 21n27.

5. McCarthy, *Death and Exile*, 17.

6. Pinson, "Ottoman Colonization," 74, 79.

7. Karpat, *Ottoman Population*, 69.

8. Saydam, *Kırım ve Kavkas Göçleri*, 97–98.

9. Saydam, "Kavkaz Muhacileri," 17–18.

10. Berzhe, *Vyselenie Gortsev*, 36.

11. Saydam, *Kırım ve Kavkas Göçleri*, 89.

12. McCarthy, *Death and Exile*, 37.

13. Rosser-Owen, "First 'Circassian Exodus,'" 38–39.

14. Saydam, *Kırım ve Kavkas Göçleri*, 97.

15. Rosser-Owen, "First 'Circassian Exodus,'" 23, 36, 38.

16. Saydam, *Kırım ve Kavkas Göçleri*, 136.

17. Ibid., 88, 136–137.

18. Rosser-Owen, "First 'Circassian Exodus,'" 30; and McCarthy, *Death and Exile*, 38.

19. Tuganov, *Tragicheskie Posledvstviia*, 132.

20. Rosser-Owen, "First 'Circassian Exodus,'" 33.

21. McCarthy, *Death and Exile*, 38; and Rosser-Owen, "First 'Circassian Exodus,'" 32.

22. Rosser-Owen, "The First 'Circassian Exodus,'" 32.

23. Tuganov, *Tragicheskie Posledvstviia*, 84.

24. Berzhe, *Vyselenie Gortsev*, 37.

25. Chochiev, "Some Aspects," 5–6, 15.

26. Rosser-Owen, "First 'Circassian Exodus,'" 30.

27. Pinson, "Ottoman Colonization," 1.

28. Chochiev, "Some Aspects," 12, 13.

29. Kushkhabiev, *Cherkesy v Sirii*, 1.

30. Pinson, "Ottoman Colonization," 73.

31. Chochiev, "Some Aspects," 3–4.

32. Ibid., 4.

33. Ibid., 6; and Saydam, *Kırım ve Kavkas Göçleri*, 135–136.

34. Pinson, "Ottoman Colonization," 78, 79.

35. McCarthy, *Death and Exile*, 47–48.

36. Karganov to Kartsov, August 14 (OS), 1864, Georgian State Archive (Tbilisi), f. 416.op. 3, doc. 149, 7; and Pinson, "Ottoman Colonization," 77.

37. Pinson, "Ottoman Colonization," 73–74.

38. Saydam, *Kırım ve Kavkas Göçleri*, 138.

39. Pinson, "Ottoman Colonization," 75–76.

40. Ibid., 82.

41. Toumarkine, *Les Migrations*, 28.

42. Rosser-Owen, "First 'Circassian Exodus,'" 37.

43. Saydam, *Kırım ve Kavkas Göçleri*, 100.

44. Commander of the Gurian Military Line to the Governor of Kutais, Georgian State Archive (Tbilisi), f. 416, op. 3, doc. 149, 10.

45. Saydam, *Kırım ve Kavkas Göçleri*, 100.

46. Rosser-Owen, "First 'Circassian Exodus,'" 37.

47. Pinson, "Ottoman Colonization," 78.

48. Chochiev, "Some Aspects," 6, 13.

49. Pinson, "Ottoman Colonization," 81, 83.

50. Chochiev, "Some Aspects," 7, 8, 9, 13.

51. Layard to Derby, July 24, 1877, Records of the British Foreign Office. National Archives, Kew, Richmond, Surrey, F.O. 424/59, Confidential (3344), No. 19, 17.

52. Stavrianos, *Balkans*, 2:347.

53. Because Russian agents were active in Rumelia inciting ethnic tensions between the Bulgarians and Circassians, there is of course the possibility that the Russians also encouraged the Bulgarian partisans to burn Circassian villages. More research needs to be done to determine the answer to this question, but the evidence points to this as a distinct possibility. See Rosser-Owen, "First 'Circassian Exodus,'" 37.

54. McCarthy, *Death and Exile*, 59–61.

55. Reade to Derby, May 2, 1877, Records of the British Foreign Office. National Archives, Kew, Richmond, Surrey, F.O. 424/53, Confidential (3210), No. 79, 35; and Sankey to Layard, May 8, 1877, Records of the British Foreign Office. National Archives, Kew, Richmond, Surrey, F.O. 424/53, Confidential (3210), No. 600, 294–95.

56. Şimşir, *Rumeli'den Türk Göçleri*, 1:83, 141, 158, 162–163.

57. *Atrocités Russes*, 17–18, 51–52, 56.

58. Layard to Derby, May 1, 1877, Records of the British Foreign Office. National Archives, Kew, Richmond, Surrey, F.O. 424/53, Confidential (3210), No. 40,

22; and Siborne to Derby, May 12, 1877, Records of the British Foreign Office. National Archives, Kew, Richmond, Surrey, F.O. 424/53, Confidential (3210), No. 587, 284–285.

59. Toumarkine, *Les Migrations*, 34.
60. *Atrocités Russes*, 72.
61. Ibid., 77–78.
62. Ibid., 76–77.
63. Pacha, "A La Mission Ottomane a Paris," July 14, 1877, in Şimşir, *Rumeli'den Türk Göçleri*, 134.
64. Layard to Derby, August 1, 1877, Records of the British Foreign Office. National Archives, Kew, Richmond, Surrey, F.O. 424/59, Confidential (3344), No, 124, 88.
65. McCarthy, *Death and Exile*, 68.
66. Layard to Derby, undated, Records of the British Foreign Office. National Archives, Kew, Richmond, Surrey, F.O. 424/57, Confidential (3210), No. 248, 129.
67. Şimşir, *Rumeli'den Türk Göçleri*, 131.
68. "Mr. Blunt, British Consul at Adnrinople, to Mr. Layard, British Ambassador at Istanbul, July 14, 1877," in Şimşir, *Rumeli'den Türk Göçleri*, 136.
69. Walpole to Wolf, January 9, 1879, Records of the British Foreign Office. National Archives, Kew, Richmond, Surrey, F.O. 424/79, Confidential (3910), No. 352/1, 306–307.
70. Layard to Salisbury, June 20, 1879, Records of the British Foreign Office. National Archives, Kew, Richmond, Surrey, F.O. 424/84, Confidential (3965), No. 478, 379–380.
71. Ipek, *Rumeli'den Anadolu'ya*, 55, 85, 170–236, passim.
72. Allen, *Caucasian Battlefields*, 126–131, 171–172. Allen points out that desertion was spreading among the Kurds as well, and he blames the "mountaineers' instinctive dislike of winter operations" for their desertion. Certainly a combination of the weather and mishandling of military operations contributed to the desertions, but it would be difficult to imagine the Circassians deserting if they had been in sight of their homeland.

6. SURVIVAL IN DIASPORA

1. Mackey, "Circassians in Jordan," 39.
2. Conder, *Heth and Moab*, 167–168.
3. Freer, *In a Syrian Saddle*, 101–102.
4. Mufti, *Heroes and Emperors*, 273; and Lewis, *Nomads and Settlers*, 97.
5. Ipek, *Rumeli'den Anadolu'ya*, 213–214.
6. Sanger, *Where the Jordan Flows*, 264; and Lewis, *Nomads and Settlers*, 98.
7. Hacker, *Modern 'Amman*, 14, 15–16.
8. Ipek, *Rumeli'den Anadolu'ya*, 212–214.
9. Ruppin, *Syria*, 33.
10. Aydemir, *Göç*, 174–175; and Kaya, "Political Participation Strategies," 224.
11. Baderkhan, *Severokavkazskaia Diaspora*, 62.
12. Kushkhabiev, *Cherkesy v Sirii*, 63–64.

13. Aydemir, *Goç*, 171.

14. Kushkhabiev, *Cherkesy v Sirii*, 68.

15. Ipek, *Rumeli'den Anadolu'ya*, 212; and Lewis, *Nomads and Settlers*, 99.

16. Lewis, *Nomads and Settlers*, 99.

17. Baderkhan, *Severokavkazskaia Diaspora*, 64–65.

18. Oliphant, *Land of Gilead*, 44–45.

19. Ibid., 51.

20. Ibid., 50–51.

21. Kushkhabiev, *Cherkesy v Sirii*, 82–84.

22. Baderkhan, *Severokavkazskaia Diaspora*, 69.

23. Kushkhabiev, *Cherkesy v Sirii*, 89–91.

24. Ibid., 97–98.

25. Eliseev, *Po Belu Svetu*, 3:273.

26. Baderkhan, *Severokavkazskaia Diaspora*, 66.

27. Kushkhabiev, *Cherkesy v Sirii*, 72–75.

28. Dündar, *Ittihat*, 130–134.

29. White, *Emergence of Minorities*, 51–52.

30. Ibid., 53–54.

31. Kushkhabiev, *Cherkesy v Sirii*, 118–121.

32. White, *Emergence of Minorities*, 146–148.

33. Kushkhabiev, *Cherkesy v Sirii*, 121.

34. Ibid., 124–127.

35. Ibid., 130, 131.

36. Harris, "War and Settlement Change," 312.

37. Fakhr, "Voices from the Golan," 23.

38. Harris, "War and Settlement Change," 315; and Fakhr, "Voices from the Golan," 23.

39. Quoted in Fakhr, "Voices from the Golan," 22–23.

40. Ibid., 7, 23–24.

41. Ibid., 7, 25.

42. Hacker, *Modern 'Amman*, 10.

43. Oliphant, *Land of Gilead*, 252–253.

44. Hacker, *Modern 'Amman*, 15.

45. Mackey, "Circassians in Jordan," 57–58.

46. Peake, *History of Jordan*, 222.

47. Hacker, *Modern 'Amman*, 12.

48. Sanger, *Where the Jordan Flows*, 264–265.

49. Mackey, "Circassians in Jordan," 59.

50. Hacker, *Modern 'Amman*, 19.

51. Mackey, "Circassians in Jordan," 23.

52. Dündar, *Ittihat*, 133–134.

53. Alon, *Making of Jordan*, 19.

54. Mackey, "Circassians in Jordan," 66–67.

55. Assab, "Circassians in the Age of Nation-States."

56. Mackey, "Circassians in Jordan," 69–70.
57. Assab, "Circassians in the Age of Nation-States."
58. Mackey, "The Circassians in Jordan," 73–74.
59. Alon, *Making of Jordan*, 52, 54.
60. Mackey, "Circassians in Jordan," 72.
61. Ibid., 79, 81, 88, 97.
62. Ibid., 6, 72, 76–77, 86–87, 89, 96, 98–99.
63. Alon, *Making of Jordan*, 157.
64. Mackey, "Circassians in Jordan," 81, 102.
65. Zürker, *Turkey*, 105.
66. Kushkhabiev, *Cherkesy v Sirii*, 102.
67. Berzeg, *Gurbetteki Kavkasya'dan Belgeler*, 5–6.
68. Kuşba, "Türkiyedeki Çerkes."
69. Unsigned cipher telegram to Admiral Webb, 11/30/1918, Records of the British Foreign Office. National Archives, Kew, Richmond, Surrey, F.O. 608/196/482.
70. Kushkhabiev, *Cherkesy v Sirii*, 19.
71. Zürker, *Turkey*, 159, 164; and Kuşba, "Türkiyedeki Çerkes."
72. Tunçay et al., *Türkiye Tarihi*, 4: 171.
73. Kushner, *Rise of Turkish Nationalism*, 20–56.
74. Ülker, "Assimilation of the Muslim Communities," para. 26, 32.
75. Kuşba, "Türkiyedeki Çerkes."
76. Iskan Kanunu, No. 2510, 6/14/1934. *Türkiye Cumhuriyeti Adelet Bakanlığı*. http://www.mevzuat.adalet.gov.tr/html/554.html.
77. Ülker, "Assimilation of the Muslim Communities," para. 9, 33.
78. Personal correspondence with Metin Sönmez, January 14, 2012.
79. Kuşba, "Türkiyedeki Çerkes."
80. Ibid.
81. Shami, "Circassian Encounters," 623.
82. Bram, "Circassian Reimmigration to the Caucasus," 208.
83. Kaya, "Political Participation Strategies," 231, 232.

7. THOSE WHO STAYED BEHIND

1. Tuganov, *Tragicheskie Posledvstviia*, 97.
2. Berzhe, *Vyselenie Gortsev*, 20.
3. Fadeev, *Kavkazskaia Voina*, 201–202; and Malakhova, *Stanovlenie*, 218.
4. Kabuzan, *Neselenie Severnogo Kavkaza*, 202.
5. Kalmykov, *Ustanovlenie*, 12, 24.
6. Malakhova, *Stanovlenie*, 202–203.
7. Kabuzan, *Neselenie Severnogo Kavkaza*, 202.
8. Pimenko to Tsanni, July 18 (OS), 1869, Georgian State Archive (Tbilisi), f. 416, op. 3, doc. 158, 1–4; Tsanni to Staroslavsky, October 17 (OS), 1869, Georgian State Archive (Tbilisi), f. 416, op. 3, doc. 158, 5–6; and Mikhail Nikolaevich to Milyutin, November 5–12 (OS), 1869, Georgian State Archive (Tbilisi), f. 416, op. 3, doc. 158, 8–9.

9. Dzidzoev, *Natsional'nye Otnosheniia*, 90.

10. Malakhova, *Stanovlenie*, 230.

11. Nevskaia, "Karachay v XIX Veke," 269.

12. Dzidzoev and Mokhnacheva, *Narody*, 1:8–9.

13. Nevskaia, "Karachay v XIX Veke," 270–271.

14. Dzidzoev and Mokhnacheva, *Narody*, 1:128–150.

15. Olshevsky to Kartsov, December 5 (OS), 1864, Georgian State Archive (Tbilisi), f. 416, op. 3, doc. 145, 5.

16. Abramov, *Kavkazskie Gortsy*, 21.

17. Malakhova, *Stanovlenie*, 228.

18. Dukmasov to Staroselsky, November 9 (OS), 1865, Georgian State Archive (Tbilisi), f.416, op. 3, doc. 1116, 4; and Malakhova, *Stanovlenie*, 222–223.

19. Kazharov, "Etnoterritorial'nyi Aspekt," 9; and Kardanov, *Agrarnoe Dvizhenie*, 47.

20. Kumykov, *Arkhivnye Materialy*, 102–104.

21. Kartsov to Milyutin, December 14 (OS), 1865, Georgian State Archive (Tbilisi), f. 416, op. 3, doc. 156.

22. Abramov, *Kavkazskie Gortsy*, 21.

23. Dukmasov to Staroselsky, November 9 (OS), 1865, Georgian State Archive (Tbilisi), f. 416, op. 3, doc. 1116, 5.

24. Nikolaevich to Dzhemardzhidze, May 25 (OS), 1870, Georgian State Archive (Tbilisi), f. 416, op. 3, doc. 126; Caucasus Commander to Sviatapolk-Mirsky, March 6 (OS), 1872, Georgian State Archive (Tbilisi), f. 416, op. 3, doc. 159; Report of Commander of Kuban Oblast, September 9 (OS), 1872, Georgian State Archive (Tbilisi), f. 416, op. 3, doc. 160; Commander of Kuban Oblast to Caucasus Commander-in-Chief, March 13 (OS), 1864, doc. 162, 1–3; Dukmanov to Staroselsky, November 9 (OS), 1865, Report of Commander of Kuban Oblast, September 9 (OS), 1872, Georgian State Archive (Tbilisi), f. 416, op. 3, doc, 1116, 2–4; and Kokiev, *Krest'ianskaia Reforma*, 7.

25. Kabuzan, *Naselenie Severnogo Kavkaza*, 145.

26. Nevskaia, "Karachay v XIX Veke," 272.

27. Kardanov, *Agrarnoe Dvizhenie*, 47.

28. Dzidzoev, *Natsional'nye Otnosheniia*, 89.

29. Ibid., 80–81; and Malakhova, *Stanovlenie*, 222–223.

30. Abramov, *Kavkazskie Gortsy*, 9.

31. Malakhova, *Stanovlenie*, 215.

32. Kalmykov, *Ustanovlenie*, 27.

33. Maksimov, "Kabardintsy," 139–187.

34. Narochnitskii, *Istoriia Narodov Severnogo Kavkaza*, 261.

35. Richmond, *Northwest Caucasus*, 102–103.

36. Kokiev, *Krest'ianskaia Reforma*, 7.

37. Kalmykov, *Ustanovlenie*, 87.

38. Malakhova, *Stanovlenie*, 230–231.

39. Richmond, *Northwest Caucasus*, 92.

40. Maslov, *Severnyi Kavkaz*, 359.

41. Dzidzoev, *Natsional'nye Otnosheniia*, 86–88.

42. Kardanov, *Agrarnoe Dvizhenie*, 51.

43. Narochnitskii, *Istoriia Narodov Severnogo Kavkaza*, 269–270.

44. Kokiev, *Krest'ianskaia Reforma*, 12–13.

45. Nevskaia, "Karachay v XIX Veke," 282.

46. Narochnitskii, *Istoriia Narodov Severnogo Kavkaza*, 234, 273.

47. Malakhova, *Stanovlenie*, 234.

48. Ibid., 182–183, 186.

49. Ibid., 186.

50. Ibid., 236; and Kalmykov, *Ustanovlenie*, 16.

51. Evdokimov to Mikhail Nikolaevich, August 17 (OS), 1864, Georgian State Archive (Tbilisi), f. 416, op. 3, doc. 109, 1–2.

52. Directive to the Troops of Kuban Oblast, September 30 (OS), 1864, Georgian State Archive (Tbilisi), f. 416, op. 3, doc. 109, 5.

53. Kalmykov, *Ustanovlenie*, 34–35, 41–44, 61, 68–69.

54. Abramov, *Kavkazskie Gortsy*, 16–21.

55. Dzidzoev, *Natsional'nye Otnosheniia*, 100.

56. Ibid., 101, 104.

57. Richmond, *Northwest Caucasus*, 106–107.

58. Dzidzoev, *Natsional'nye Otnosheniia*, 154–155, 160.

59. Bugai and Gonov, *Kavkaz*, 64–65.

60. Pershits, *Abaziny*, 40.

61. Bugai and Gonov, *Severnyi Kavkaz*, 152.

62. Nevskaia, "Karachay v XIX Veke," 146–155.

63. Aslanbek, *Karaçay*, 12.

64. Kazharov, "Etnoterritorial'nyi Aspekt," 16–17.

65. Bugai ed., *Natsional'no-Gosudarstvennoe Stroitel'stvo*, 183–187.

66. Ibid., 188.

67. Pchelintseva and Samarina, *Sovremennaia Etnopoliticheskaia i Etnokul'turnaia Situatsiia*, 1.

68. Ter-Sarkisyants, *Sovremennaia Etnopoliticheskaia Situatsiia*, 10.

69. Babich, *Evoliutsiia*, 165.

70. Ibid., 165–166; Karcha, "Genocide in the Northern Caucasus," 76; Aslanbek, *Karaçay*, 29; and Richmond, *Northwest Caucasus*, 111.

71. Comins-Richmond, "Legal Pluralism," 61.

72. Babich, *Evoliutsiia*, 146; and Richmond, *Northwest Caucasus*, 111.

73. Dumanova and Pershits, "Narodnye Traditsii," 2:24.

74. Ibid., 28.

75. Ibid., 28–29.

76. Artiunov and Anchabadze, *Mezhnatsional'nye Otnosheniia*, 3, 5.

77. Mambetov, "Agrarnaia Politika," 43.

78. Pershits, *Abaziny*, 41; and Bugai and Gonov, *Kavkaz*, 124.

79. Bugai and Gonov, *Kavkaz*, 51, 164.

80. Richmond, *Northwest Caucasus*, 114.

81. Pohl, *Ethnic Cleansing*, 75.

82. Sabanchiev, "Vyselenie Balkarskogo Naroda."

83. Shamanov et al., *Karachaevtsy*, 15–16

84. Aliev, "Shleif," 19; and Baicharov, "Za Polnuiu Pravdu," 312.

85. Malyshev, "Izgnanniki," 286.

86. Richmond, *Northwest Caucasus*, 116–119.

87. Bugai, "Deportatsiia," 101–112.

88. Kovalev, *Natsistskaia Okkupatsiia*, 102.

89. Bugai and Gonov, *Kavkaz*, 286; and Belozerov, *Etnicheskaia Karta*, 100.

90. Bugai and Gonov, *Kavkaz*, 300.

91. Akkieva, *Etnopoliticheskaia Situatsiia*, 9.

92. I have spoken to educated Russians who still believe the Karachays all collaborated with the Nazis.

93. Comins-Richmond, "Karachay Struggle after the Deportation," 68–73.

94. Shamanov ed. *Karachaevtsy*, 149.

95. Ibid., 149–151.

96. Aliev, "Shleif," 28–29.

8. THE ROAD TO SOCHI

1. "Real Snow Guaranteed: Putin," *Russia Today*, July 5, 2007. http://rt.com/news/real-snow-guaranteed-putin/.

2. Smirnova, *Karachaevo-Cherkesiia*, 6–7.

3. Chervonnaia, "Etnicheskie Vyzovy."

4. Riazantsev, *Sovremennyi Demograficheskii i Migratsionnyi Portret*, 122–146.

5. Smirnova, *Karachaevo-Cherkesiia*, 6–7, 12–13, 20, 21–22.

6. Chervonnaia, *Karachaevo-Cherkesiia 1999*, 6, 8–9, 16–17.

7. Khadzhibiekov and Poliakova, *Etnopoliticheskaia Situatsiia v Adygee*, 7; Denisova, *Etnicheskii Faktor*, 165; and Pchelintseva and Samarina, *Sovremennaia Etnopoliticheskaia i Etnokul'turnaia Situatsiia*, 5.

8. Bram, "Circassian Reimmigration to the Caucasus," 210.

9. Tlisova, "Moscow's Favoritism Towards Cossacks."

10. Kazenin, "*Tikhie Konflikty*," 27.

11. "'Soiuz Slavian Adygei': 'Russkii Marsh' ne Byl Proiavleniem Natsizma," *Kavkazskii Uzel*, October 11, 2006. http://www.kavkaz-uzel.ru/articles/103346/.

12. Namitokova, *Kosovskie Adygi v Adygee*, 5–18.

13. Akkieva, *Etnopoliticheskaia Situatsiia*, 8.

14. Ibid, 10.

15. Yarlykapov, "Sovremennye Islamskie Dvizheniia," 122.

16. Katazhukov, "Kabardino-Balkaria Cracks Down on Islamists."

17. Tlisova, "Kabardino-Balkaria Fears."

18. "400 Musul'man Kabardino-Balkarii Namereny Pokinut' Rossiiu," *Kavkazskii Uzel*, September 24, 2005. http://www.kavkaz-uzel.ru/articles/82183/.

19. "Prezidentom Kabardino-Balkarii Stanet Arsen Kanokov," *IA REGNUM*, September 27, 2005. http://www.regnum.ru/news/kab-balk/519573.html.

20. "V Nal'chike Prodolzhaetsia Perestrelka," *IA REGNUM*, October 13, 2005. http://www.regnum.ru/news/kab-balk/528149.html

21. "Vse Ognevye Tochki v Nal'chike Podavleny," *Novosti Rossii*, October 15, 2005. http://newsru.com/arch/russia/14Oct2005/nalchik.html; and "MVD Kabardino-Balkarii Soobshchaet, Chto Ataka Boevikov na Nal'chik Otbita," *Kavkazskii Uzel*, October 13, 2005. http://www.kavkaz.memo.ru/newstext/news/id/870811.html."

22. "Former Nalchik Detainee Charges Torture," *North Caucus Analysis*, 6, no. 41 (December 31, 1969). http://www.jamestown.org/programs/nca/single/?tx_ttnews%5Btt_news%5D=3073&tx_ttnews%5BbackPid%5D=187&no_cache=1; and "Memorial Alleges Ongoing Repression in Kabardino-Balkaria," *North Caucus Analysis* 6, no. 42 (December 31, 1969). http://www.jamestown.org/programs/nca/single/?tx_ttnews%5Btt_news%5D=3065&tx_ttnews%5BbackPid%5D=187&no_cache=1.

23. Gukemukhov, "Fears and Arrests in Karachaevo-Cherkessia."

24. "Mnimaia Terroristicheskaia Ugroza v Stolitse Adygei Vyzvala Perepolokh," *IA REGNUM*, October 21, 2005. http://www.regnum.ru/news/adyg/532469.html.

25. "V Adygee Eshche ne Znaiut, Chto Slovo 'Vakhkhabism,' s Razresheniem Kozaka—Uzhe ne Rugatel'noe," *IA REGNUM*, November 30, 2005. http://www.regnum.ru/news/adyg/552438.html.

26. Kaya, "Political Participation Strategies," 226, 227.

27. Shami, "Circassian Encounters," 624–625.

28. Bram, "Circassian Reimmigration to the Caucasus," 215–216.

29. Kuşba, "Türkiyedeki Çerkes Varlığı."

30. Bram, "Circassian Reimmigration to the Caucasus," 211.

31. "Cherkesy Trebuiut Priznat' Genotsid," *IA REGNUM*, April 18, 2005. http://regnum.ru/news/440249.html.

32. "Simpozium 'Tragediia Kavkaza.' Prizyvaet Rossiu Priznat' Genotsid Cherkesov-Adygov," *Kavkazskii Uzel*, May 26, 2005. http://www.kavkaz-uzel.ru/articles/78060/.

33. "Kavkazskii Forum Turtsii Napravil Pis'mo v Gosdumu Rossiiskoi Federatsii o Priznanii Genotsida Adygskogo Naroda," *IA REGNUM*, September 27, 2005. http://regnum.ru/news/518853.html.

34. "Gosduma RF ne Priznala Fakta Genotsid Adygskogo (Cherkesskogo) Naroda," *IA REGNUM*, January 27, 2001. http://regnum.ru/news/580644.html.

35. "Cherkesskie Organizatsii Prosiat Evroparlament Priznat' Cherkesskii Genotsid," *Kavkazskii Uzel*, October 12, 2006. http://www.kavkaz-uzel.ru/articles/101702/.

36. "Osnovnoi Zadachei Mezhdunarodnoi Cherkesskoi Assotsiatsii Priznana Repatriatsiia Zarubezhnykh Adygov," *Kavkazskii Uzel*, March 23, 2003. http://www.kavkaz-uzel.ru/articles/35348/?print=true.

37. Koshelev, *Polnoe Sobranie Russkikh Letopisei*, 13.1:228, 259, 277, 283; "Karachaevo-Cherkesiia Otmechaet Prisoedinenie k Rossii," *IA REGNUM*, September 29, 2007. http://www.regnum.ru/news/fd-south/892184.html; and "450 Let c Rossiei," *Stavropol'skaia Pravda*, September 26, 2007, http://www.stapravda.ru/20070926/450_let_s_Rossiej_1718.html.

38. Dzamikhov, "Istoricheskii Opyt," 15–16.

39. Marshenkulov, "Outrage at 'Fake' Circassian Anniversary."

40. "'Adyge Khase' Adygei Vystupaet Protiv Prazdnovaniia Dvukh Iubileinykh Dat," *Kavkazskii Uzel*, February 27, 2007. http://www.kavkaz-uzel.ru/articles/110816/."

41. "Cherkesskaia Diaspora Provela v SshA i Turtsii Aktsii Protesta Protiv Politiki Rossii na Severnom Kavkaze," *Kavkazskii Uzel*, October 7, 2007. http://www .kavkaz-uzel.ru/articles/124903/.

42. "Cherkesskii Kongress Protiv Zimnei Olimpiady v Sochi," *IA REGNUM*, December 11, 2006. http://regnum.ru/news/753519.html.

43. Ibid.

44. *Olympic Movement's Agenda 21*: Sport for Sustainable Development. International Olympic Committee, 1999. http://www.olympic.org/Documents/Reports/ EN/en_report_300.pdf, 45.

45. Lew, "Vancouver Olympics."

46. "Cherkesskii Kongress Vystupil Protiv Olimiady v Sochi."

47. Epifantsev, "Velikaia Cherkesiia."

48. Shukhov, "Rezoliutsiia Foruma Cherkesskoi (Adygskoi) Molodezhi."

49. "Medvedev Creates New North Caucasus Federal District," *Radio Free Europe/ Radio Liberty*, January 20, 2010. http://www.rferl.org/content/Medvedev_Creates _New_North_Caucasus_Federal_District/1934705.html.

50. "V Nal'chike Proshel Forum."

51. "Cherkesy Pozhalovalis' Medvedu na Ustinova," *IA REGNUM*, December 29, 2009. http://www.regnum.ru/news/1238927.html; and Tlisova, "Moscow Continues Campaign."

52. "D. Dzhandemir: Zaderzhaniei Vysylka Turetskikh Biznesmenov B'et po Imizhu Rossii," *Kavkazskii Uzel*, October22, 2007. http://www.kavkaz-uzel.ru/ articles/125933/.

53. "'Adyge Khase' Adygei Vystupaet."

54. Grove, "Genocide Claims"; and Thornburgh, "Olympic Dreams."

55. Gulevich, "Circassian Theme of Syria's Tragedy."

56. A Circassian blogger in Russia who reproduced my interview with Voice of America concerning the Circassian genocide was subsequently charged with extremism in August 2011.

57. "AROD 'Cherkesskii Kongress' Vyneseno Preduprezhdenie," *Adyge Sait*, October 12, 2011. http://www.elot.ru/main/index.php?option=com_content&task=view &id=2590&Itemid=1.

58. "Ubit Suadin Pshukov," *Adyge Sait*, October 4, 2001. http://www.elot.ru/main/ index.php?option=com_content&task=view&id=2579&Itemid=1.

59. Kapaeva, "Cherkesskaia Obshchesvennost' Obzhalovalos.'"

60. "Kruglyi Stol 'Kavkaz: Problemy i Ponimaniia Istorii,'" *Kavkazskii Uzel*, February 12, 2011. http://www.kavkaz-uzel.ru/articles/180942/.

61. Zhemukhov, "Circassian Question."

62. "Komissiia po Protivodeistviiu Popytkam Falsifikatsii Istorii v Ushcherb Interesam Rossii," *Prezident Rossii*. http://state.kremlin.ru/commission/21/news.

63. "Zaiavlenie Chlenov Ispolkoma OD Adyge Khase—Cherkesskii Parlament,"
    Informatsionno-Analiticheskoe Agenstvo NatPress, November 19, 2011. http://www
    .natpress.ru/index.php?newsid=6989.
64. Thornburgh, "Olympic Dreams."

EPILOGUE

1. Artunian, "Race Riot on Manezhnaya"; and "Cherkesov Aslan Magomedovich,"
   Kavkazskii Uzel, June 21, 2011. http://www.kavkaz-uzel.ru/articles/187639/.
2. Levy, "Putin Makes Symbolic Visit."
3. Khatazhukov, "Zaiavlenie Kabardino-Balkarskovo Pravozashchitnogo Tsentra."
4. "Politics behind 'Stop Feeding the Caucasus," *PIK*, September 29, 2001. http://
   pik.tv/en/news/story/20170-politics-behind-stop-feeding-the-caucasus.
5. "Disappearing Funds in North Caucasus," *PIK*, November 11, 2011. http://pik.tv/
   en/news/story/23683-disappearing-funds-in-north-caucasus.
6. "Putin on 'Feeding the Caucasus,'" *PIK*, December 15, 2011. http://pik.tv/en/
   news/story/26011-putin-on-feeding-the-caucasus.
7. "Deviat' Mesiatsev KTO: Priel'brus'e na Grani Vyzhivaniia." *Memorial Human
   Rights Center*, October 27, 2011. http://www.memo.ru/2011/10/27/2710112.html.
8. Bram, "Circassian Reimmigration to the Caucasus," 217.
9. Baydar, "Circassians Speak Out."
10. "Vystuplenie Dzhona Khagora v Evroparlamente," *Adyge Sait*, November 11, 2011.
    http://www.elot.ru/main/index.php?option=com_content&task=view&id=2637
    &Itemid=1."

BIBLIOGRAPHY

SOURCES IN ENGLISH

Allen, E. D. *Caucasian Battlefields: A History of the Wars on the Turco-Caucasian Border, 1828–1921.* Cambridge: Cambridge University Press, 1953.

Alon, Yoav. *The Making of Jordan: Tribes, Colonialism and the Modern State.* London: I. B. Taurus, 2007.

Artunian, Anna. "Race Riot on Manezhnaya." *Moscow News*, December 13, 2010. http://themoscownews.com/politics/20101213/188276816.html.

Assab, Nour. "Circassians in the Age of Nation-States: Stateless Entities, Banal Nationalism in the Pan-Islamism, Pan-Arabism and Territorial Nationalism in the Middle East." *MERC Research Awards Cycle 3*, July 2007. http://www.mercprogram.org/pdf/merc_proposals/Nour.pdf.

Atkin, Muriel. *Russia and Iran, 1780–1828.* Minneapolis: University of Minnesota Press, 1980.

Baddeley, John F. *The Russian Conquest of the Caucasus.* New York: Longmans, Green and Company, 1908.

Barrett, Thomas M. "Crossing Boundaries: The Trading Frontiers of the Terek Cossacks." In *Russia's Orient: Imperial Borderlands and Peoples, 1700–1917*, edited by Daniel R. Brower and Edward J. Lazzerini, 227–248. Bloomington: University of Indiana Press, 1997.

———. *At the Edge of Empire: The Terek Cossacks and the North Caucasus Frontier, 1700–1860.* Boulder, Colo.: Westview Press, 1999.

Baumgart, Winfried. *The Peace of Paris 1856: Studies in War, Diplomacy, and Peacemaking.* Translated by Ann Pottinger Saab. Santa Barbara, Calif.: ABC-Clio, 1981.

Baydar, Yavuz. "Circassians Speak Out." *Today's Zaman*, February 26, 2012. http://www.todayszaman.com/columnistDetail_getNewsById.action?newsId=272580.

Bell, James Stanislaus. *Residence in Circassia during the Years 1837, 1838 and 1839*, vol. 1. London: Edward Moxon, 1840.

Bolsover, G. S. "David Urquhart and the Eastern Question, 1833–1837: A Study in Publicity and Diplomacy." *Journal of Modern History* 8, no. 4 (December 1936): 444–467.

Bram, Chen. "Circassian Reimmigration to the Caucasus." In *Roots and Routes: Ethnicity and Migration in Global Perspective*, edited by Shalva Weil, 205–222. Jerusalem: Magnes Press, 1999.

Chochiev, Georgy. "Some Aspects of Social Adaptation of the North Caucasian Immigrants in the Ottoman Empire in the Second Half of the XIXth Century (on the
Immigrants' Applications to Authorities)." Extended version of paper presented
at the XVth Turkish Congress of History, Ankara, Turkey, September 2006.

Cohn, Norman. *Warrant for Genocide: The Myth of the Jewish World Conspiracy and the
"Protocols of the Elders of Zion."* Chico, Calif.: Scholars Press, 1981.

Comins-Richmond, Walter. "The Karachay Struggle after the Deportation." *Journal of
Muslim Minority Affairs* 22, no. 1 (April 2002): 63–79.

———. "Legal Pluralism in the Northwest Caucasus: The Role of Sharia Courts." *Religion, State and Society* 32, no. 1 (2004): 59–73.

Conacher, J. B. *Britain and the Crimea, 1855–56: Problems of War and Peace.* New York:
St. Martin's Press, 1987.

Conder, Claude Reignier. *Heth and Moab: Explorations in Syria in 1881 and 1882.* London:
Richard Bentley and Son, 1885.

Fakhr, Sakr Abu. "Voices from the Golan." *Journal of Palestine Studies* 29, no. 4 (Autumn
2000): 5–36.

Freer, A. Goodrich. *In a Syrian Saddle.* London: Methuen & Co., 1905.

Gammer, Moshe. *The Lone Wolf and the Bear: Three Centuries of Chechen Defiance to Russian Rule.* Pittsburgh: University of Pittsburgh Press, 2006.

———. *Muslim Resistance to the Tsar: Shamil and the Conquest of Chechnia and Daghestan.*
London: Frank Cass, 1994.

Gellately, Robert, and Ben Keirnan, eds. *The Specter of Genocide: Mass Murder in Historical Perspective.* Cambridge: Cambridge University Press, 2003.

Gleason, John Howes. *The Genesis of Russophobia in Great Britain: A Study of the Interac-
tion of Policy and Opinion.* New York: Octagon Books, 1972.

Goldfrank, David M. *The Origins of the Crimean War.* London: Longman, 1994.

Grove, Thomas. "Genocide Claims Complicate Russian Olympics Plans." *Reuters*, October 13, 2011. http://af.reuters.com/article/worldNews/idAFTRE79C2XP20111013.

Gukemukhov, Murat. "Fears and Arrests in Karachaevo-Cherkessia." *Institute for
War and Peace Reporting*, December 17, 2005. http://iwpr.net/report-news/
fears-and-arrests-karachai-cherkessia.

Gulevich, Vladislav. "Circassian Theme of Syria's Tragedy." *Strategic Culture Foundation*,
February 16, 2012. http://www.strategic-culture.org/news/2012/02/16/circassian
-theme-of-syria-tragedy.html.

Hacker, Jane M. *Modern 'Amman: A Social Study.* Durham, U.K.: Department of Geog-
raphy, Durham College, 1960.

Harris, W. W. "War and Settlement Change: The Golan Heights and the Jordan Rift,
1967–77." *Transactions of the Institute of British Geographers* 3, no. 3 (1978):
309–330.

Henze, Paul B. "Circassian Resistance to Russia." In *The North Caucasus Barrier: The
Russian Advance towards the Muslim World*, edited by Marie Bennigsen Broxup,
62–111. New York: St. Martin's Press, 1992.

Karcha, Ramzan. "Genocide in the Northern Caucasus." *Caucasian Review* 2 (1956): 76.

Karpat, Kemal. *Ottoman Population 1830–1914: Demographic and Social Characteristics.* Madison: University of Wisconsin Press, 1985.

Katazhukov, Valery. "Kabardino-Balkaria Cracks Down on Islamists." *Institute for War and Peace Reporting,* February 21, 2005. http://www.iwpr.net/report-news/ kabardino-balkaria-crackdown-islamists.

Kaya, Ahyan. "Political Participation Strategies of the Circassian Diaspora in Turkey." *Mediterranean Politics* 9, no. 2 (Summer 2004): 221–239.

Khodarkovsky, Michael. *Where Two Worlds Met: The Russian State and the Kalmyk Nomads, 1600–1771.* Ithaca, N.Y.: Cornell University Press, 1992.

King, Charles. "Imagining Circassia: David Urquhart and the Making of North Caucasus Nationalism." *Russian Review* 66, no. 2 (2007): 238–255.

Kreiten, Irma. "A Colonial Experiment in Ethnic Cleansing: The Russian Conquest of the Western Caucasus, 1856–65." *Journal of Genocide Research* 11, no. 2–3 (June–September 2009): 213–241.

Kushner, David. *The Rise of Turkish Nationalism 1876–1908.* London: Frank Cass, 1977.

Lamb, Margaret. "Writing up the Eastern Question in 1835–1836." *International History Review* 15, no. 2 (May 1993): 239–268.

Lang, David Marshall. *A Modern History of Soviet Georgia.* New York: Grove Press, 1962.

LeDonne, John P. *The Russian Empire and the World, 1700–1917: The Geopolitics of Expansion and Containment.* New York: Oxford University Press, 1997.

Lemkin, Raphael. *Axis Rule in Occupied Europe: Laws of Occupation, Analysis of Government, Proposals for Redress.* Washington, D.C.: Carnegie Endowment for International Peace, 1944.

Levy, Clifford J. "Putin Makes Symbolic Visit in Ethnic Strife." *New York Times,* December 21, 2010. http://www.nytimes.com/2010/12/22/world/europe/22russia.html.

Lew, Josh. "Vancouver Olympics Bring Unprecedented Opportunities to Canada's Indigenous People." *Mother Nature Network,* February 8, 2010. http://www.mnn .com/lifestyle/eco-tourism/stories/vancouver-olympics-bring-unprecedented -opportunities-to-canadas-indige#.

Lewis, Norman N. *Nomads and Settlers in Syria and Jordan, 1800–1980.* London: Cambridge University Press, 1987.

Longworth, John August. *A Year among the Circassians.* London: Henry Colburn, 1840.

Mackey, Bruce Douglas. "The Circassians in Jordan." Unpublished master's thesis. Monterey, Calif.: Naval Postgraduate School, 1979.

Marshenkulov, Marina. "Outrage at 'Fake' Circassian Anniversary." *Institute for War and Peace Reporting,* October 5, 2007. http://iwpr.net/report-news/outrage-fake -circassian-anniversary.

McCarthy, Justin. *Death and Exile: The Ethnic Cleansing of the Ottoman Muslims, 1821–1922.* Princeton, N.J.: Darwin Press, 1995.

Mufti, Shauket. *Heroes and Emperors in Circassian History.* Beirut: Librairie du Liban, 1944.

Oliphant, Laurence. *The Land of Gilead.* Edinburgh: William Blackwood and Sons, 1880.

Peake, Frederick Gerard. *A History of Jordan and Its Tribes.* Coral Gables, Fla.: University of Miami Press, 1958.

Pinson, Mark. "Ottoman Colonization of the Circassians in Rumili after the Crimean War." *Etudes Balkaniques* 3 (1972): 1–85.

Pohl, J. Otto. *Ethnic Cleansing in the USSR, 1937–1949*. Westport, Conn.: Greenwood Press, 1999.

Richmond, Walter. *The Northwest Caucasus: Past, Present, Future*. London: Routledge Press, 2008.

Rosser-Owen, Sarah A. S. Isla. "The First 'Circassian Exodus' to the Ottoman Empire (1858–1867) and the Ottoman Response, Based on the Accounts of Contemporary British Observers." Unpublished Master's Thesis, School of Oriental and African Studies, University of London, 2007.

Rubenstein, Richard L. *The Age of Triage: Fear and Hope in an Overcrowded World*. Boston: Beacon Press, 1983.

———. *The Cunning of History: The Holocaust and the American Future*. New York: Harper and Row, 1975.

Ruppin, Arthur. *Syria: An Economic Survey*. Translated by Nellie Straus. New York: Provisional Zionist Committee, 1918.

Sabanchiev, Khadzhi-Murat. "Vyselenie Balkarskogo Naroda v Gody Velikoi Otechestvennoi Voiny: Prichiny i Posledstviia." In *Tsentral'naia Asiia i Kavkaz*, edited by Murad Esenov. http://www.ca-c.org/datarus/sabanch.shtml.

Sanger, Richard H. *Where the Jordan Flows*. Washington, D.C.: Middle East Institute, 1963.

Scott, H. M. "Russia as a European Great Power." In *Russia in the Age of the Enlightenment: Essays for Isabel de Madariaga*, edited by Roger Bartlett, 7–39. New York: St. Martin's Press, 1990.

Shami, Setenay. "Circassian Encounters: The Self as Other and the Production of the Homeland in the North Caucasus." *Development and Change* 29 (1998): 617–646.

Sherry, Dana. "Social Alchemy on the Black Sea Coast, 1860–65." *Kritika: Explorations in Russian and Eurasian History* 10, no. 1 (Winter 2009): 7–30.

Spencer, Edmund. *Travels in Circassia, Krim Tartary, Etc.* 2 vols. London: Henry Colburn, 1836.

———. *Turkey, Russia, and the Black Sea, and Circassia*. London: Routledge, 1855.

Stavrianos, L. F. *The Balkans since 1453*. New York: Rinehart, 1958.

Taitbout de Marigny, Édouard. *Three Voyages in the Black Sea to the Coast of Circassia: Including Descriptions of the Ports, and the Importance of Their Trade: With Sketches of the Manners, Customs, Religion, &c. &c., of the Circassians*. London: John Murray, 1837.

Temperley, Harold. *England and the Near East: The Crimea*. New York: Longmans, Green and Co., 1936.

Thornburgh, Nathan. "Olympic Dreams: Will Sochi Rehabilitate Russia's Image?" *Time*, November 18, 2011. http://www.time.com/time/magazine/article/0,9171,2099428,00.html#ixzz1e4fpiSx5.

Tlisova, Fatima. "Kabardino-Balkaria Fears Spread of Terror." *Institute for War and Peace Reporting*, February 21, 2005. http://iwpr.net/report-news/kabardino-balkaria-fears-spread-terror.

———. "Moscow Continues Campaign to Suppress Circassian National Aspirations." Eurasia Daily Monitor 7, no. 2 (January 5, 2010). http://www.jamestown.org/single/?no_cache=1&tx_ttnews%5Btt_news%5D=35870.

———. "Moscow's Favoritism Towards Cossacks Mocks Circassian History." North Caucus Analysis 9, no. 30 (August 1, 2008), http://www.jamestown.org/single/?no_cache=1&tx_ttnews%5Btt_news%5D=5093.

Ülker, Erol. "Assimilation of the Muslim Communities in the First Decade of the Turkish Republic (1923–1934)." European Journal of Turkish Studies, 2007. http://ejts.revues.org/index822.html.

Urquhart, David. British Diplomacy Illustrated in the Affair of the Vixen. Newcastle: Currie and Bowman, 1839.

———. Turkey and Its Resources. London: Saunders and Otley, 1833.

Weitz, Eric D. "The Modernity of Genocides: War, Race, and Revolution in the Twentieth Century." In The Specter of Genocide: Mass Murder in Historical Perspective, edited by Robert Gellately and Ben Kiernan, 53–74. Cambridge: Cambridge University Press, 2003.

White, Benjamin Thomas. The Emergence of Minorities in the Middle East: The Politics of Community in French Mandate Syria. Edinburgh: Edinburgh University Press, 2011.

Zhemukhov, Sufian. "The Circassian Question in Russian-Georgian Relations." PONARS Eurasia Policy Memo No. 188 (2010). http://www.gwu.edu/~ieresgwu/assets/docs/pepm_118.pdf.

Zürker, Erik J. Turkey: A Modern History. London: I. B. Tauris & Co., 1993.

SOURCES IN RUSSIAN

Abramov, Ya. Kavkazskie Gortsy. Krasnodar: Izdanie Obshchestva Izucheniia Adygeiskoi Avtonomnoi Oblasti, 1927.

"Adrianopol'skii Mirnyi Dogovor Mezhdu Rossiei i Turtsiei, Russia-Ottoman Empire September 14, 1829." In Pod Stiagom Rossii: Sbornik Arkhivnykh Dokumentov, edited by A. A. Sazonov, 102–116. Moscow: Russkaia Kniga, 1992.

Akkieva, S. I. Etnopoliticheskaia Situatsiia v Kabardino-Balkarskoi Respubliki. Moscow: Rossiiskaia Akademiia Nauk, 1994.

Aliev, Ismail. "Shleif bed i Stradanii: Zametki o 'Karachaevskom Voprose.'" In Tak Eto Bylo: Natsional'nye Repressii v SSSR 1919–1952 Gody, edited by Svetlana Alieva, 2:7–36. Moscow: Insan, 1993.

Artiunov, S. A., and Yu D. Anchabadze. Mezhnatsional'nye Otnosheniia v SSSR. Moscow: Rossiiskaia Akademiia Nauk, 1990.

Babich, Irina. Evoliutsiia Pravovoi Kul'tury Adygov (1860–1990-e gody). Moscow: Rossiiskaia Akademiia Nauk, 1999.

Baderkhan, Fasikh. Severokavkazskaia Diaspora v Turtsii, Sirii i Iordanii. Moscow: IV RAN, 2001.

Baicharov, Ismail. "Za Polnuiu Pravdu: Vospominaniia." In Tak Eto Bylo: Natsional'nye Repressii v SSSR 1919–1952 Gody, edited by Svetlana Alieva, 1:312–316. Moscow: Insan, 1993.

Begeulov, Rustam. *Tsentral'nyi Kavkaz v XVII-Pervoi Chetverti XIX Veka: Ocherki Etno-politicheskoi Istorii.* Karachaevsk: KChGU, 2005.

Beituganov, Safarbi. *Kabarda i Ermolov: Ocherki Istorii.* Nal'chik: El'brus, 1993.

Belozerov, Vitalii. *Etnicheskaia Karta Severnogo Kavkaza.* Moscow: OGI, 2005.

Berzhe, Adol'f. *Vyselenie Gortsev Kavkaza.* Nal'chik: Izdatel'stvo M. i V. Kotliarovykh, 2010.

Berzhe, Adol'f, and Dmitrii Kobiakov, eds. *Akty, Sobrannye Kavakzskoiu Arkheogra-ficheskoiu Kommissieiu.* 12 vols. Tiflis: Arkhiv Glavnago Upravleniia Namestnika Kavkaza, 1866–1904.

Betrozov, Ruslan. *Adygi—Vozniknovenie i Razvitie Etnosa.* Nal'chik: Elbrus, 1998.

Bliev, Mark. *Rossiia i Gortsy Bol'shogo Kavkaza: Na Puti k Tsivilizatsii.* Moscow: Mysl', 2004.

Bugai, Nikolai. "Deportatsiia: Beriia Dokladivaiet Stalinu." *Kommunist* 3 (1991), 101–112.

———, ed. *Natsional'no-Gosudarstvennoe Stroitel'stvo Rossiiskoi Federatsii: Severnyi Kavkaz (1917–1941 gg.).* Maikop: Adygeiskii Respublikanskii Institut Gumani-tranykh Issledovanii, 1995.

Bugai, Nikolai, and Askarbi Gonov. *Kavkaz: Narody v Eshelonakh (20–60-e Gody).* Moscow: Insan, 1998.

———. *Severnyi Kavkaz: Novye Orientiry Natsional'noi Politiki (90-e Gody XX Veka).* Moscow: Novyi Khronograf, 2004.

Bukalova, V. M., ed. *Kabardino-Russkie otnosheniia v XVI—XVIII vv: Dokumenty i Mate-rialy.* Moscow: Izdatel'stvo Akademii Nauk SSSR, 1957.

Chervonnaia, Svetlana. "Etnicheskie Vyzovy i Tupiki Federal'noi Politiki na Sever-nom Kavkaze." *Soros Conference "Etnicheskii Faktor v Federalizatsii Rossii."* Kazan, January 18, 2000. http://federalmcart.ksu.ru/conference/seminar3/chervonnaja .htm.

———. *Karachaevo-Cherkesiia 1999: Vybory Glavy Respubliki.* Moscow: Rossiiskaia Aka-demiia Nauk, 1999.

Chirg, Akhmad. "Iz Istorii Russko-Adygskikh Torgovykh Sviazei na Chernomor-skom Poberezh'e Kavkaza v Pervoi Chetverti XIX v." In *Nekotorye Voprosy Obshchestvenno-Politicheskikh Otnoshenii na Severo-Zapadnom Kavkaze v kontse XVIII-pervoi polovine XIX v.,* edited by V. P. Gromov, 5–13. Maikop: Adygeiskii Nauchno-Issledovatel'skii Institut Ekonomiki, Iazyka, Literatury i Istorii, 1987.

———. *Razvitie Obshchestvenno-Politicheskogo Stroia Adygov Severo-Zapadnogo Kavkaza (Konets XVIII-60-e gg. XIX v.* Maikop: Kabardino-Balkarskii Nauchnyi Tsentr Rossiiskoi Akademii Nauk/Agygeiskii Respublikanskii Institut Gumanitarnykh Issledovanii, 2002.

Denisova, G. S. *Etnicheskii Faktor v Politicheskoi Zhizni Rossii 90-x Godov.* Rostov na Donu: Rostovskii Gosudarstvennyi Pedagogicheskii Universitet, 1996.

Drozdov, Ivan. "Posledniaia Bor'ba s Gortsami na Zapadnom Kavkaze." *Kavkazskii Sbornik* 2 (1877): 387–457.

Dumanova, D. Kh., and A. I. Pershits. "Narodnye Traditsii Kabardinstev i Balkartsev v Gody Sovetskoi Vlasti." In *RES PUBLICA: Al'manakh Sotsial'no-Politicheskikh i*

Pravovykh Issledovanii, edited by A. Kh. Borov, 2:23–35. Nal'chik: Institut Gumanitarnykh Issledovanii Pravitel'stva Kabardino-Balkarskoi Respubliki, 2001.

Dzamikhov, Kabolat. "Istoricheskii Opyt Politiko-pravovoi reglamentatsii Russko-Adygskikh Otnoshenii: Analiz Dokumentov XVI–XVIII vv." In *RES PUBLICA: Al'manakh Sotsial'no-Politicheskikh i Pravovykh Issledovanii*, edited by A. Kh. Borov, 2:5–22. Nal'chik: Institut Gumanitarnykh Issledovanii Pravitel'stva Kabardino-Balkarskoi Respubliki, 2001.

———. *Adygi v Politike Rossii na Kavkaze (1550-e—1770-x gg.)*. Nalchik: "El'-Fa," 2001.

Dzhakhiev, G. A. "Severnyi Kavkaz v Geopolitike Velikikh Derzhav vo Vtoroi Polovine XIII–Pervoi Treti XIX vv.: Istoriia i Sovremennost.'" In *Severnyi Kavkaz: Geopolitika, Istoriia, Kul'tura: Materialy Vserossiiskoi Nauchnoi Koferentsii (Stavropol,' 11–14 Sentiabria 2001 g.)*, edited by V. A. Shapovalov, 1:114–118. Moscow-Stavropol: Rossiiskaia Akademiia Nauk, 2001.

Dzidzoev, Valerii. *Natsional'nye Otnosheniia na Kavkaze.*Vladikavkaz: SOGU, 1998.

Dzidzoev, Valerii, and M. P. Mokhnacheva, eds. *Narody Tsentral'nogo Kavkaza v 40-x—nachale 60-x Godov XIX Veka: Sbornik Dokumental'nykh Materialov v Dvukh Tomakh.* 2 vols. Moscow: Pomatur, 2005.

Eliseev, Aleksandr. *Po Belu Svetu: Ocherki i Kartiny iz Puteshestvii po Trem Chastiam Starogo Sveta.* 3 vols. St. Petersburg: Soikin, 1896.

Epifantsev, Andrei. "Velikaia Cherkesiia: Vpered v Proshloe ili Nazad v Budushchee?" *Agenstvo Politicheskoi Novosti*, January 13, 2009. http://www.apn.ru/publications/article21218.htm.

Esadze, Semyon. *Pokorenie Zapadnogo Kavkaza i Okonchanie Kavkazskoi Voiny.* Moscow: Gosudarstvennaia Publichnaia Istoricheskaia Biblioteka Rossii, 2004.

Fadeev, Rostislav. *Kavkazskaia Voina.* Moscow: Algoritm, 2005.

Fedorov, V. A., ed. *Zapiski A. P. Ermolova.* Moscow: Vysshaia Shkola, 1991.

Filipson, Grigorii. "Vospominaniia Grigoriia Ivanovicha Filipsona." *Russkii Arkhiv* 6 (1883): 241–273.

Fonvill', A. *Poslednii God Voiny Cherkesii za Nezavisimost' 1863–1864 gg.* Edited by Kh. G. Karmokov. Nal'chik: Izdanie zhurnala Adygi, 1991.

Gadzhiev, V. G., Kh. Kh. Ramazanov, and A. D. Daniialov, eds. *Dvizhenie Gortsev Severo-Vostochnogo Kavkaza v 20–50 gg. XIX Veka.* Makhachkala: Dagestanskoe Knizhnoe Izdatel'stvo, 1959.

Gardanov, Valentin. *Adygi, Balkartsy i Karachaevsty v Izvestiiakh Evropeiskikh Avtorov XIII–XIX vv.* Nal'chik: El'brus, 1974.

Gardanov, Valentin, and G. Kh. Mambetov. "Vedenie." In *Zapiski o Cherkesii*, edited by Khan-Girey, 3–8. Nal'chik: Elbrus, 1978.

Gordin, Yakov. *Kavkaz: Zemlia i Krov': Rossiia v Kavkazskoi Voine XIX Veka.* St. Petersburg: Zvezda, 2000.

———, ed. *Kavkazskaia Voina: Istoki i Nachalo, 1770–1820 Gody.* St. Petersburg: Zvezda, 2002.

———. "O Roli Kostromskoi Ssylki v Formirovanii Lichnosti 'Prokonsula Kavkaza.'" In *General A. P. Ermolov i Rossiisko-Kavkazskie Otnosheniia v XIX–Nachale XX Veka*, edited by Yakov Gordin, 3–13. St. Petersburg: Zvezda, 2009.

"K." "Obzor Sobytii na Kavkaze v 1846 Godu." *Kavkazskii Sbornik* 16 (1895): 279–351.

Kabuzan, Vladimir. *Naselenie Severnogo Kavkaza v XIX–XX Vekakh.* St. Petersburg: BLITs, 1996.

Kalmykov, Zhiliabi. *Ustanovlenie Russkoi Administratsii v Kabarde i Balkarii (Konets XVIII–Nachalo XX Veka).* Nalchik: Elbrus, 1995.

Kapaeva, Asia. "Cherkesskaia Obshchesvennost' Obzhalovalos' Rukovodstvu NTV na Iskazhenii Istorii Cherkesov Kosova." *Kavkazskii Uzel,* November 29, 2001. http://www.kavkaz-uzel.ru/articles/196671/.

Kardanov, Chalimat. *Agrarnoe Dvizhenie v Kabarde i Balkarii (Konets XIX–Nachalo XX v.).* Nalchik: Kabardino-Balkarskoe Knizhnoe Izdatel'stvo, 1963.

Kasumov, A. Kh, and Kh. A. Kasumov. *Genotsid Adygov: Iz Istorii Bor'by Adygov za Nezavisimost' v XIX Veke.* Nal'chik: Logos, 1992.

Kazenin, Konstantin. *"Tikhie Konflikty" na Severnom Kavkaze: Adygeia, Kabardino-Balkariia, Karachaevo-Cherkesiia.* Moscow: Regnum, 2009.

Kazharov, A. G. "Etnoterritorial'nyi Aspekt Stanovleniia Kabardino-Balkarskoi Avtonomii." In *RES PUBLICA: Al'manakh Sotsial'no-Politicheskikh i Pravovykh Issledovanii,* edited by A. Kh. Borov, 1:7–36. Nal'chik: Institut Gumanitarnykh Issledovanii Pravitel'stva Kabardino-Balkarskoi Respubliki, 2001.

Kazharov, Valerii. *Traditsionnye Obshchestvennye Instituty Kabardintsev i Ikh Krizis v Kontse XVIII–Pervoi Polovine XIX Veka.* Nal'chik: El'-Fa, 1994.

Khadzhibiekov, R., and T. Poliakova. *Etnopoliticheskaia Situatsiia v Adygee.* Moscow: Rossiiskaia Akademiia Nauk, 1994.

Khanakhu, Ruslan. *Traditsionnaia Kul'tura Severnogo Kavkaza: Vyzovy Vremeni (Sotsial'no-filosofskii analiz).* Rostov na Donu: Adygeiskii Respublikanskii Institut Gumanitarnykh Issledovanii, 2001.

Khan-Girey, ed. *Zapiski o Cherkesii.* Nal'chik: El'brus, 1978.

———."Besl'nii Abat, Chast' I." In *Cherkesskie Predaniia. Izbrannye Proizvedeniia.* Nal'chik: El'brus, 1989. http://www.circassianlibrary.org/lib/00018/text_1_5_1 .html.

Khatazhukov, Valerii. "Zaiavlenie Kabardino-Balkarskogo Pravozashchitnogo Tsentra v Sviazi s Ubiistvom Egora Sidorova i sobytiiami na Manezhnoi Ploshchadi." *Za Prava Cheloveka,* December 15, 2010. http://zaprava.ru/201012152620/ zayavleniya-i-obrascheniya/zayavlenie-kabardino-balkarskogo-balkarskogo -pravozashhitnogo-czentra-v-svyazi-s-ubijstvom-egora-sviridova-i-sobytiyami -na-manezhnoj-ploshhadi [a censored site].

Kokiev, Georgii, ed. *Krest'ianskaia Reforma v Kabarde: Dokumenty po Istorii Osvobozhdeniia Zavisimykh Soslovii v Kabarde v 1867 Godu.* Nalchik: Kabardinskoe Gosudarstvennoe Izdatel'stvo, 1947.

———. "Pereselenie Kabardinskikh Kholopov v Mozdok v XVIII v." In *Istoriia Kabardino-Balkarii v Trudakh G. A. Kokieva,* edited by G. Kh. Mambetov, 224–231. Nal'chik: El'-Fa, 2005.

———. "Raspad Kabardy na Bol'shuiu I Maluiu I Ustanovivshiesia Otnosheniia s Sosednimi Narodami." In *Istoriia Kabardino-Balkarii v Trudakh G. A. Kokieva,* edited by G. Kh. Mambetov, 198–206. Nal'chik: El'-Fa, 2005.

"Komissiia po Protivodeistviiu Popytkam Falsifikatsii Istorii v Ushcherb Interesam Rossii." *Prezident Rossii.* http://state.kremlin.ru/commission/21/news.

Koshelev, A., ed. *Polnoe Sobranie Russkikh Letopisei.* 17 vols. Moscow: Yazyki Russkoi Kul'tury, 2000.

Kovalev, Boris. *Natsistskaia Okkupatsiia i Kollaboratsionizm v Rossii 1941–1944.* Moscow: Tranzitkniga.

Kudashev, Vladimir. *Istoricheskie Svedeniia o Kabardinskom Narode.* Kiev: Tipo-Litografiia "S. V. Kul'zhenko," 1913.

Kumykov, Tugan, ed. *Arkhivnye Materialy o Kavkazskoi Voine i Vyselenii Cherkesov (Adygov) v Turtsiiu.* 2 vols. Nal'chik: El'-Fa, 2003.

———. *Ekonomicheskoe i Kul'turnoe Razvitie Kabardy i Balkarii v XIX v.* Nal'chik: Kabardino-Balkarskoe Knizhnoe Izdatel'stvo, 1965.

———. *Obshchestvennaia Mysl' i Prosveshchenie Adygov i Balkaro-Karachaevtsev v XIX-Nachalo XX v.* Nal'chik: Elbrus, 2002.

———. *Vyselenie Adygov v Turtsiiu: Posledstvie Kavkazskoi Voiny.* Nal'chik: El'brus, 1994.

Kushkhabiev, Anzor. *Cherkesy v Sirii.* Nal'chik: Vozrozhdenie, 1993.

Lapin, Vladimir. "K Obrazu A. P. Ermolova v Istoricheskoi Literature i v Kollektivnom Istoricheskom Soznanii." In *General A. P. Ermolov i Rossiisko-Kavkazskie Otnosheniia v XIX–Nachale XX Veka,* edited by Yakov Gordin, 14–36. St. Petersburg: Zvezda, 2009.

Lapinskii, Teofil. *Gortsy Kavkaza i ikh Osvoboditel'naia Bor'ba Protiv Rossii.* Translated by V. A. Kardanov, Nal'chik: El'-Fa, 1995.

Liausheva, S. A. *Evoliutsiia Religioznykh Verovanii Adygov: Istoriia i Sovremennost'.* Rostov na Donu: Izdatel'stvo SKNTs VSh, 2001.

Maksimov, Evgenii. "Kabardintsy: Statistiko-Ekonomicheskii Ocherk." In *Terskii Sbornik,* edited by P. Stefanovskii, 2.2:139–187. Vladikavkaz: Tipografiia Terskogo Oblastnogo Pravleniia, 1892.

Malakhova, Galina. *Stanovlenie i Razvitie Rossiiskogo Gosudarstvennogo Upravleniia na Severnom Kavkaze, v Kontse XVIII–XIX vv.* Rostov na Donu, 2001.

Mal'bakhov, Boris. *Kabarda v Period ot Petra I do Ermolova.* Nal'chik: Kniga, 1998.

Malyshev, Aleksei. "Izgnanniki." In *Tak Eto Bylo: Natsional'nye Repressii v SSSR 1919–1952 Gody,* edited by Svetlana Alieva, 1:274–291. Moscow: Insan, 1993.

Mambetov, G. Kh., ed. *Istoriia Kabardino-Balkarii v Trudakh G. A. Kokieva.* Nal'chik: El'-Fa, 2005.

Mambetov, Z. G. "Agrarnaia Politika Sovetskoi Vlasti v Kabardino-Balkarii: Analiz Prichin Krest'ianskikh Vystuplenii v 20–30e gody." In *RES PUBLICA: Al'manakh Sotsial'no-Politicheskikh i Pravovykh Issledovanii,* edited by A. Kh. Borov, 1:37–47. Nal'chik: Institut Gumanitarnykh Issledovanii Pravitel'stva Kabardino-Balkarskoi Respubliki, 2001.

Maslov, E. P., ed. *Severnyi Kavkaz.* Moscow: Akademiia Nauk SSSR, Institut Geografii, 1957.

Namitokova, R. Iu., ed. *Kosovskie Adygi v Adygee: Problemy Adaptatsii Repatriantov i Ustoichivoe Razvitie Regiona.* Maikop: Adygeiskii Gosudarstvennyi Universitet, 2008.

Narochnitskii. A. L., ed. *Istoriia Narodov Severnogo Kavkaza (Konets XVIII v.–1917 g.)*. Moscow: Nauka, 1988.

Nemzera, A. S., ed. *Memuary Dekabristov*. Moscow: Pravda, 1988.

Nevskaia, Valentina. "Karachay v XIX Veke." *As-Alan* 1, no. 6 (2002): 130–475.

Ol'shevskii, Milentii. "Kavkaz i Pokorenie Vostchnoi ego Chasti," *Russkaia Starina* 27, no. 2 (1880): 289–318.

———. *Kavkaz c 1841 po 1866 god.* St. Petersburg: Zvezda, 2003.

Pchelintseva, N. D, and L. V. Samarina, *Sovremennaia Etnopoliticheskaia i Etnokul'turnaia Situatsiia v Respublike Adygeia*. Moscow: Rossiiskaia Akademiia Nauk, 1993

Pershits, A. I., ed. *Abaziny: Istoriko-Etnografacheskii Ocherk*. Cherkessk: Stavropol'skoe Knizhnoe Izdatel'stvo, 1989.

Polovinkina, T. V. *Cherkesiia—Bol' Moia: Istoricheskii Ocherk (Drevneishee vremia—nachalo XX v)*. Maikop: RIPO (Adygeia), 1999.

Potto, Vasilii. *Kavkazskaya Voina v 5i Tomakh.* 5 vols. Stavropol: Kavkazskii Krai, 1993–1994.

Riazantsev, S. V. *Sovremennyi Demografacheskii i Migratsionnyi Portret Severnogo Kavkaza*. Stavropol: Servisshkola, 2003.

Romaskevich, A. A., and S. A. Volin, eds. *Sbornik Materialov Otnosiashchikhsia k Istorii Zolotoi Ordy.* 2 vols. Moscow/Leningrad: Izdatel'stvo Akademii Nauk SSSR, 1941.

Shamanov, I. M., ed. *Karachaevtsy: Vyselenie i Vozvrashchenie (1943–1957). Materialy i Dokumenty*. Cherkessk: Respublikanskaia Komissiia po Reabilitatsii Karachaevskogo Naroda, 1993.

Shcherbina, Fyodor. *Istoriia Kubanskago Kazach'iago Voiska.* 2 vols. Ekaterinodar: Pechatnik, 1913.

Shcherbina, Fyodor, and Evgenii Felitsyn. *Kubanskoe Kazachestvo i ego Atamany*. Moscow: Veche, 2007.

Shukhov, Zamir. "Rezoliutsiia Foruma Cherkesskoi (Adygskoi) Molodezhi." *Justice for North Caucasus Groups Message Boards*, September 12, 2009. www.justicefornorth caucasus.com/jfnc_message_boards/russian.php?title=Резолюция-форума -черкесской-(адыгской)-молодежи&entry_id=1252947053&comments=comments.

Smirnova, Ia. S. *Karachaevo-Cherkesiia: Etnopoliticheskaia i Etnokul'turnaia Situatsiia*. Moscow: Rossiiskaia Akademiia Nauk, 1993.

Solov'ev, Sergei. *Istoriia Rossii s Drevneishikh Vremen.* 24 vols. St. Petersburg: Obshchestvennaia Pol'za, 1879.

Stal', K. F. "Etnografacheskii Ocherk Adygskogo Naroda." *Kavkazskii Sbornik* 21 (1900): 53–173.

Ter-Sarkisyants, A. E. *Sovremennaia Etnopoliticheskaia Situatsiia v Krasnodarskom Krae Rossiiskoi Federatsii*. Moscow: Rossiiskaia Akademiia Nauk, 1992.

Tornau, Fedor. *Vospominaniia Kavkazskogo Ofitsera*. Moscow: Airo-XX, 2000.

Tuganov, Rashid Umarovich. *Izmail-Bei*. Nal'chik: El'brus, 1972.

———. *Tragicheskie Posledvstviia Kavkazskoi Voiny dlia Adygov. Vtoraia Polovina XIX–Nachalo XX Veka: Sbornik Dokumentov*. Nal'chik: El'-Fa, 2000.

Varle, E. V. *Krymskaia Voina.* 2 vols. Moscow/Leningrad: Izdatel'stvo Akademiia Nauk SSSR, 1950.

Veniukov, Mikhail. *Iz Vospominanii M. I. Veniukova. Kniga Pervaia.* Amsterdam, 1895.
———. "K Istorii Zaseleniia Zapadnogo Kavkaza." *Russkaia Starina* 22, no. 6 (1878): 249–251.
Yarlykapov, Akhmet. "Sovremennye Islamskie Dvizheniia na Severnom Kavkaze: Obshchie Tendentsii i Razlichii." In *Islamskoe Vozrozhdenie v Sovremennoi Kabardino-Balkarii: Perspektivy i Posledstviia,* edited by Irina Babich and Akhmet Iarlykapov, 122–143. Moscow, 2003.

SOURCES IN TURKISH

Aslanbek, Mahmut. *Karaçay ve Malkar Türklerinin Faciasi.* Ankara: Çankaya Matbaası, 1952.
Aydemir, Izzet. *Goç.* Ankara: Gelişim Matbaasi, 1988.
Berzeg, Sefer E. *Gurbetteki Kavkasya'dan Belgeler.* Ankara: S. E. Berzeg, 1985.
Dündar, Fuat. *Ittihat ve Terakki'nin Müslümları İskân Politikası.* Istanbul: İletişim, 2001.
Habiçoğlu, Bedri. *Kafkasyadan Anadoluya Göçler.* Istanbul: Nart Yayıncılık, 1993.
Ipek, Nedem. *Rumeli'den Anadolu'ya Türk Göçleri (1877–1890).* Ankara: Türk Tarih Kurumu Basımevi, 1994.
Kuşba, E. "Türkiyedeki Çerkes Varlığı ve Çerkeslerin Yakın Tarihi." *Arıkbaşı Net.* http://arikbasi.wordpress.com/2009/04/20/turkiyedeki-cerkes-varligi-ve-cerkeslerin-yakin-tarihi/.
Saydam, Abdullah. *Kırım ve Kavkas Göçleri (1856/1876).* Ankara: Türk Tarih Kurumu Basımevi, 1997.
———. "Kavkaz Muhacileri." In *Sürgün: Büyük Çerkes Sürgünü 147 Yıl,* edited by Muhittin Ünal, 9–45. Ankara: Kafdav, 2011.
Şimşir, Bilâl N. *Rumeli'den Türk Göçleri. Belgeler, Cilt I: Doksanüç Muhacereti 1877–1878.* 2 vols. Ankara: Türk Kültürünü Araştırma Enstitütüsü, 1968.
Tunçay, Mete, Cemil Koçak, Hikmet Özdemir, Korkut Boratav, Selahattin Hilav, Murat Katoğlu, and Ayla Ödekan. *Türkiye Tarihi 4: Çağdaş Türkiye 1908–1980.* Istanbul: Cem Yayınevi, 1989.

SOURCES IN FRENCH

Atrocités Russes: Documents Soumís a la Conference de Constantinople. Constantinople, 1877.
Toumarkine, Alexandre. *Les Migrations des Populations Musulmanes Balkaniques en Anatolie (1876–1913).* Istanbul: Isis, 1995.

INDEX

Abazas, 3, 38, 57, 66, 77, 132, 142, 147, 150, 152, 153
Abdullah, king of Jordan, 124, 125
Abkhaz-Georgian War of 1992, 159
Abkhazia, 62, 110, 150, 159, 167, 169; Abkhazians, 151, 159, 164, 167
Abramov, Ya., 136
Abuke, Ishak, 14
Abzakhs, 4, 31, 44, 62, 66, 67, 70–73, 75, 78, 79, 80, 82, 83, 84, 86, 87, 103, 114, 132
Acre, Palestine, 114. *See also* Palestine
Adagum Zafes of 1848, 59
Adil-Girey, Sultan, 138
adyge habze (code of behavior), 6, 47, 99, 100, 143, 175
Adyge Hase (organization), 150, 151, 153, 154, 161, 164, 165, 169, 170
Adygeia, 132, 153–155, 157, 158, 164, 166, 173; Adygeis, 143, 151, 164
Akhmed Pasha, 108
Alexander I, tsar of Russia, 8, 10, 24, 31, 38
Alexander II, tsar of Russia, 63, 69, 70, 73, 74, 75, 78, 79, 88, 95, 96, 131, 132, 136, 138, 139, 140
Alexander III, tsar of Russia, 139
Amin, Muhammad, 59, 62, 64, 67, 70, 157
Amman, Jordan, 111, 112, 123, 124, 125. *See also* Jordan
Anapa, Russia, 3, 57, 62, 74, 77, 86
Ankara, Turkey, 127, 128, 129, 174. *See also* Turkey, Republic of
Arab-Israeli War: of 1948, 120, 121, 122, 125; of 1967, 121–123
Arab Spring, 121, 159
Arakcheev, Alexei, 11, 14
Armenians, 107, 118, 128, 132, 150, 151
Atakhukin, Kazi, 138
Atazhukin, Adil-Girey, 9, 14
Atazhukin, Izmail-Bey, 9–11, 13–17, 18
Atkin, Muriel, 7, 12
Aydemir, Izzat, 114

Ba'ath Party of Syria, 121, 159, 170
Baddeley, John, 12, 18–21
Baderkhan, Fasikh, 166

Balkars, 134, 139, 141, 142, 144, 145, 146, 147, 150, 156, 157
Barclay de Tolly, Michael Andreas, 16
Barrett, Thomas, 36, 38
Baryatinsky, Alexander, 54, 65, 66, 67, 68, 69, 70, 71, 73, 83
Battle of Bziuk (1796), 35, 37, 52
Bedouins, 113, 114, 115, 117, 123, 124
Beituganov, Safar, 29
Bekovich-Cherkassky, Fyodor, 31, 44
Bell, George, 50
Bell, James, 50, 51–52, 53
Beria, Lavrenty, 146
Berzhe, Adolf, 35, 65, 77, 89, 91, 96, 132, 182n25
Besleneys, 4, 6, 30, 66, 71, 72, 160
Bjedukhs, 4, 33, 35, 41, 62, 65–66, 71, 79, 123, 134
Black Hawks, 157
Black Sea Cossacks, 32, 36–37, 42, 44
Bliev, Mark, 166
Bolsover, G. S., 50
Brezhnev, Leonid, 147, 152
Bulgakov, Sergei, 10, 13–18
Bulgaria, 99, 103, 104–109
Bursak, Fyodor, 35–38

Catherine II, tsarina of Russia, 8, 33, 35, 36
Caucasus Cultural Association (Turkey) 129
Chechnya, 4, 21, 26, 56, 59, 64, 66, 99, 110, 146, 150, 153; Chechens, 22, 26, 32, 54, 61, 110, 114, 132, 138, 140, 141, 146, 158
Chepega, Zakhary, 35
Cherchenays, 4, 71
Cherkes, 3, 56, 142, 164
Cherkesov, Aslan, 171–173, 177
Cherkessk (Batalpashinsk), Russia, 152, 153, 160, 163, 164
Chernyshev, Alexander, 58
Circassian Benevolent Association (United States), 122
Circassian Benevolent Society (Syria), 121
Circassian Charity Organization (Jordan), 126

ABOUT THE AUTHOR

WALTER RICHMOND is the director of Russian Studies at Occidental College, Los Angeles. He has been writing about the North Caucasus since 2001. His first book, *The Northwest Caucasus: Past, Present, Future* (Routledge, 2008), is the first comprehensive history of the peoples of the Northwest Caucasus. He has also written on Stalin's deportation of the North Caucasus peoples and current conflicts in the region.

www.ingramcontent.com/pod-product-compliance
Lightning Source LLC
Chambersburg PA
CBHW021346290326
41932CB00043B/195